By the same author

By the same author

BOOKS:
Let There Be a World
Awakened China
    (published in paperback under the title
    China: The Country Americans Are Not Allowed To Know
    and in Britain under the title *The Wall Has Two Sides*)
A Curtain of Ignorance
Vietnam! Vietnam!

FILMS:
China!
Inside North Vietnam
Cuba Va

THE ENEMY

What Every American Should
Know About Imperialism

THE ENEMY

What Every American Should Know About Imperialism

by Felix Greene

RANDOM HOUSE, NEW YORK

Acknowledgment is gratefully extended to the following for permission to reprint excerpts from their works:

The *Guardian:* "From the Other Side of the Tracks," by Julius Lester, in the November 2, 1968 issue.

The Sunday Times and Norman Lewis for an article in the February 1, 1970 issue.

Time, The Weekly Newsmagazine: for excerpts from the February 2, 1970 issue. Copyright © 1970 by Time Inc.

The New York Times: for excerpts from the April 24, 1969 issue. Copyright © 1969 by The New York Times Company.

The Times, London: for extracts from an article by Victoria Brittain in the March 13, 1970 issue.

All rights reserved under International and Pan-American Copyright Conventions. Published in the United States by Random House, Inc., New York. Originally published in Great Britain by Jonathan Cape Limited, London.

ISBN: 0-394-46279-3

Library of Congress Catalog Card Number: 67-12745

Manufactured in the United States of America by
H. Wolff Book Manufacturing Co., Inc.

Designed by Paula Wiener

2 4 6 8 9 7 5 3

FIRST AMERICAN EDITION

Acknowledgments

It would be impossible for me to list all those who have helped me with this book. Some do not know me and are unaware of how much their books and articles have added to my general understanding of imperialism. Among those who have helped me personally I wish particularly to thank Mr. Richard Krooth, who is himself writing a book about imperialism—a far more fundamental and original work than my own. I am grateful to him for the discussions and correspondence we have had and for his generosity in allowing me to read his manuscript and to make use of information it contained. Mr. John Kelly, Dr. Hershel Meyer and Mr. Adolph Sliver have also given me valuable assistance. They are all busy men but they were ready to put aside time not only to read the manuscript as it progressed but to discuss the many political questions the book raises.

I wish also to express my gratitude to the *Monthly Review* of New York, a journal, alas, far more influential abroad than it is in its own country. It would have been impossible to have kept count of the number of times I referred to its current and past issues while preparing this book. One need not agree with all its conclusions (I do not) to appreciate the very high standard of interpretation of events which it provides and the extraordinary clarity with which it deals with even the most complex problems. Mr. Harry Magdoff, one of the editors of the *Monthly Review,* deserves the thanks of all of us who are trying to understand the subject we are dealing with for his meticulously researched book *The Age of Imperialism.* As with the *Monthly Review* I found Mr. Magdoff's book an invaluable source of information and insight.

Whatever usefulness this book may have is largely due to these friends known and unknown who have helped me write it.

F. G.

To Elena, without whose affectionate
persistence this book would never have
been begun, and without whose help and
insight it would never have been completed

"Know the enemy and know yourself; a hundred battles, a hundred victories."

(Sun Wu Tzu, military scientist of ancient China, quoted by Mao Tse-Tung)

A Personal Preface

This book is about imperialism—what it is and how it works, and why, if it goes on, it will eventually destroy us. This book is also about the revolutionary consciousness that is rising throughout the world, a consciousness that repudiates the basic assumptions of imperialism and is directly challenging its power. This world-wide struggle between imperialism in its many forms and those who are determined to overthrow it, is the single greatest issue of our era; every lesser struggle is linked to it. The battle is engaged and will grow in intensity and whether we like it or not, or even know it or not, we are all participants.

Though the United States is by no means the only imperialist country, a good deal of this book is about that country, for the United States today provides the main strength and sustaining force of imperialism everywhere. Without her imperialism as a system could not long survive. But America herself is moving towards crisis. Americans increasingly feel trapped within a system which they know intuitively is leading their country to disaster both at home and abroad.

I started writing this book primarily for myself. I wanted to find answers, if I could, to certain questions which appeared to me important. I wanted to clarify for myself, for example, why violence had always been so integral a part of our Western civilization, and why it was that our supposedly advanced, enlightened, Christian nations have inflicted such enormous human suffering wherever we went in the world. "Imperialism"—yes. But the word by itself conveys very little. What are the central characteristics of imperialism? How did it start? How does it operate? What gives it such strength and tenacity? Where lie its weaknesses?

Writing this book has been a very important experience for me. Twice in my life I have been deeply shaken, personally and in my political thinking. The first time was when I went to China in 1957. As a writer and journalist I thought I was fairly well informed about the world, that I had a reasonably good idea of what was going on in China. I found when I arrived there that I had merely accepted the prevailing Western views of China and the supposed horrors of its communist rule. I have been to China five or six times since then but I shall never forget the experience of my first visit, when I was confronted with China as it really was. I was appalled both at the extent of my ignorance and to realize how tight, how cramped, how *Western*-bound my thinking had been. I remember how this experience of China immediately widened and expanded my view of human potentialities. That was the first of my momentous political experiences.

The second came with the writing of this book. As with China I assumed I knew about imperialism. After all I had written and lectured about it, and heaven knows I had denounced it often enough. I had been, at one time or another, to almost every underdeveloped country in the world and I thought I understood the operation of the imperialist system and what it does to people. But it was only while doing the reading and detailed research for this book that the full implications of imperialism struck home. Only then did I begin to grasp the true depth of its cruelty and cunning and the measureless suffering it inflicted in the past and still continues to inflict today. As my researches went on, many facts that before had appeared random and unconnected became linked together. History began to make a new kind of sense. Just as when one looks at a slide through a microscope everything at first is a little blurred and then, by turning a knob, the vague shadows and blobs spring into focus, so the writing of this book made the essential meaning of imperialism sharp and clear. Imperialism not as an abstraction but as a system, an organization that directly impinges on and degrades the lives of hundreds of millions of people. And it became clear to me, as it has of course to so many others, that imperialism means far more than the exploitation of poor countries by the rich. It involves a whole social system based on exploitation and violence, a whole way of thinking about other people. The ghettos of America, racial injustices, the glaring inequalities that exist in every Western country, the dehumanization of our industrial society, are as much products of imperialism as apartheid in South Africa or the wanton slaughter of villagers in Vietnam.

As this book attacks the very basis of our Western social order, there will be those (I know from experience) who will make it their business to scrutinize every fact and argument in it in the hope of discrediting it. I cannot, of course, promise that this book is completely free of error, though the facts I present have been checked and re-checked carefully. It is obvious, too, that this is by no means a definitive study of imperialism. That would take volumes. This book represents *some notes* on the nature of imperialism. The best I can hope is that it will encourage others to make their own study so that we can all know more completely the enemy we are.

This book, then, is the result of my explorations. In it I have attempted to trace as clearly and untechnically as I can the nature of the imperialist system and the rising world struggle against it—a bitter, life-and-death conflict which is now only in its opening phase. Much in this book, of course, has been said before, and it will be said again and again in many different ways by many different people before this enormous conflict is finally resolved.

FELIX GREENE
Paris, 1969
London, March 1970

Foreword

This book is about contemporary imperialism, and contemporary imperialism is global in character. It becomes less and less accurate to speak of "American imperialism," "British imperialism," "Japanese imperialism," and so on, as if they were separate entities. Though there exist deep rivalries between them, these national imperialisms nevertheless represent interlocking and mutually-supporting structures, bound by a common acceptance of capitalist ideology.

Readers will notice, however, that we have used aspects of imperialism as they relate to the United States for the greater part of our analysis. This was done largely for reasons of convenience and simplification; and, of course, because the United States is the most powerful partner in this global system. But unless the global character of imperialism is borne in mind this emphasis on *American* capitalism and *American* imperialism could be misleading.

It will appear to some after reading what I shall say in this book that I have grossly distorted the American image; that I have extracted from the total spectrum of life in that country only those facets which are the most deplorable and have ignored the rest.

I have lived too long in the United States and know it too intimately not to realize that almost every generalization about that country can be countered by another. It is a land of extremes and opposites. I do not minimize at all the richness, the variety, the humor, the liveliness, the sheer vitality that is contained within the American society. I am conscious too (for I have worked with them) of the large numbers of Americans who are as appalled as any foreigner can be by the social ills that are dragging the country down; and of the millions who are ashamed, despairingly ashamed, of their country's policies in Vietnam and elsewhere. Many Americans, young and old, have risked a great deal (their careers, and some their very lives) in opposing these policies. There are, indeed, very powerful forces at work that are attempting to change the direction of American society. There are forces too that believe that the social flaws are now so deeply embedded that they cannot be remedied without a total overthrow of the social structure as it now stands so that a wholly new start can be made. All this I know.

If I have chosen not to draw what might be considered a more "balanced" picture, it is because I feel that such "balanced" accounts give altogether too optimistic an assessment of America's future as an imperialist nation. I believe the United States is heading for disaster; it is approaching either a sophisticated form of fascism or still another form of social disintegration. There *are* other sides to American life—but one does not feel compelled when a ship is sinking to draw attention to how good the food is in its restaurant.

*   *

There will be those who wonder why, as I have so fiercely criticized the capitalist system, I have not written equally strongly about the failures of socialist countries to live up to their initial promise. It is, of course, manifestly easy to point to failures and mistakes, and even to the return to capitalist-like features, in some socialist countries. Much could be written about this; it is an issue of the most profound importance and it cannot be dealt with briefly in passing. What is more, it falls outside the immediate purpose of this book, which is to examine the nature of imperialism.

We should, however, remind ourselves that in terms of human history each of the socialist regimes is still in its infancy; each began in an impoverished and technically backward country; each had to fight for survival against the fiercest onslaughts of capitalist countries. We must not fall into the error of comparing the physical conditions in these socialist countries with those of the Western nations which have had several centuries in which to develop their system and consolidate their wealth. Only those with no understanding of historical processes would expect a revolutionary transformation of society, involving hundreds of millions of people, to proceed without errors, failures, splits and conflicts. What is, I believe, unquestionable is that the socialist systems have displayed a stupendous vitality and rate of growth and an astounding development of their social and human resources. Even those countries that show the least developed form of socialism have succeeded in lifting from the mass of their people—and for the first time in history—the age-old fear of hunger and the fear of becoming socially superfluous, and have provided all of their people with health services, with clothing, shelter and education. What is also unquestionable is that the influence and strength of the socialist countries is steadily rising in the world, while that of the capitalist countries is steadily declining. It would be a mistake to suppose that the setbacks and the bureaucratic restrictions we see today in some socialist countries are necessarily a permanent feature of socialism. Even the least successful socialist country carries within it the seeds of untold possibilities for the future, while the perspective open to the capitalist countries of the West can only be defined in terms of further human degradation and conflict.

For those in capitalist countries to point for their reassurance to the failures and mistakes of the socialist countries is at best an exercise in self-delusion.

*   *

Words, Meanings and Jargon

It was just one year after the publication of the complete *Das Kapital* that Böhm-Barwerk thought he had finished it off with his book *Karl Marx and the Close of his System*. Ever since, hundreds, probably thousands, of writers have been busily engaged in assuring their readers that Marx's economic analysis was "out of date," "inapplicable to modern conditions," "sterile," and so on. Meanwhile, these concepts, so disdained in Western academic circles, have formed the guidelines for revolutions that have altered the course of history, and to this day continue to move hundreds of millions to action.

With the denigration of Marx of course came an aversion to his terminology. Marxist words are now usually dismissed as "jargon," and once they are downgraded in this way, why pay attention to them? The words "exploitation," "contradiction," "expropriation," for example, do not even appear in Gilpen's *Dictionary of Economic Terms,* published in 1965.

When writing this book I had a choice: I could either use these words that are now written off or I could attempt to find euphemisms which would be more "acceptable." To find alternatives for words that describe something precisely and simply is difficult. One *could* describe a car's carburetor as "the apparatus that controls the vaporization of oil and its mixture with air to cause an explosive mixture," but the one word carburetor is certainly simpler. It is not, of course, the words themselves these men object to, but *what they stand for;* to suppress the words helps to obscure the reality. One social scientist thought that the word "exploitation" should not be used because Marx had used it; he suggested that the words "reciprocity imbalance" should be used instead as being "less charged." Another writer substitutes "socio-economic status" for the much simpler (but presumably more "charged") word "class."

I elected to use the simpler words, such as "capitalism," "imperialism," "class," "bourgeois," "exploitation," "contradiction" and the other words that today are more often than not dismissed as jargon. I do so because they are more direct, more scientific as well as more challenging. I believe that, as I have used them, their meaning is clear. It is all too easy to emasculate concepts by emasculating the words that describe them.

* *

The great American historian Charles A. Beard once wrote:

It may be appropriate to remind those who may be inclined to treat Marx as a mere revolutionary or hot partisan that he was more than that. He was a doctor of philosophy from a German university, possessing the hallmark of the scholar. He was a student of Greek and Latin learning. He read, besides German, his native tongue, Greek, Latin, French, English, Italian, and Russian. He was widely read in contemporary history and economic thought. Hence, however much one may dislike Marx's personal views, one cannot deny to him wide and deep knowledge—and a fearless and sacrificial life. He not only interpreted history, as everyone does who writes any history, but he helped to make history. Possibly he may have known something.[2]

NOTES

1. I am indebted to Mr. Robin Blackburn's admirable essay "A Brief Guide to Bourgeois Ideology" in *Student Power* (London: Penguin, 1969), for this and other facts I have mentioned in this note and in the body of this book.
2. *American Historical Review*, October 1935.

Contents

The Face of Capitalism

Section One: How It Began

Section Two: The Anatomy of Imperialism

Section Three: Imperialism's Home Base

Section Four: The Great Hang-Ups

Section Five: Revolution

The Face of
Capitalism

The Face of Capitalism

No one in the United States believes more firmly than I
do in the system of private business, private property
and private profit . . . It was this Administration which
saved the system of private profit and free enterprise
after it had been dragged to the brink of ruin.

PRESIDENT FRANKLIN D. ROOSEVELT

Whatever else capitalism has done or failed to do, it has
sold the mass of the people on a total, passionate, committed belief in its values.

ALAN BRIEN in a report from America
in the *Sunday Times,* April 6, 1969

The capitalist system is extolled by the great majority of
Americans and by most citizens of Western countries. It is
the system that President Kennedy pledged America would
defend "regardless of the cost, and regardless of the peril." It
is the system which millions of young men in successive
wars have sacrificed their lives to preserve—because they
were led to believe that it is only *this* system and no other
that can preserve their freedom. "Freedom" for most Americans means freedom to do what they please without inter-

ference from the state—and they have shown by their actions that they believe this freedom is worth dying for. Capitalism, in the minds of most Americans, is synonymous with democracy; outside of capitalism, they believe, all the civil rights that men have fought for—freedom of religion, freedom of thought and speech, freedom of assembly, freedom of the press, freedom from arbitrary arrest—would be endangered.

These liberties are precious, but they have only been achieved, and then only partially, through great struggle over a long period. They were, however, liberties fought for by the bourgeoisie for the bourgeoisie against feudalism. When capitalism became established, their extension to the workers was resisted. So for the workers their freedoms were not achieved *by* capitalism but *in spite* of it. Each new development of individual liberty has *always* been won against the most bitter opposition of those in control of the capitalist societies. Today capitalism, far from defending these hard-won rights of the people, represents their greatest threat.

If capitalism was all that its defenders claim it to be, we would expect to find in the land where this system has reached the highest level of development a society whose citizens would reflect in their behavior the nobility and wisdom that must arise from a humane and rational ordering of affairs. We would not expect a perfect society, or a society of perfect individuals, for humans even under the best of conditions are not angels. We would find greedy, passionate and bigoted people there as we find them everywhere. But in a social order extolled so highly by its citizens for the freedoms and democracy it provides, we can legitimately expect to see public philosophies and an overall quality of life that would encourage the rest of mankind to follow in the same path.

The land of America itself provided a marvelous crucible for the development of such a society. In no other country could you find landscape of such infinite variety and grandeur; no land could offer more to a people setting out to build a new society. "We have it in our power," cried Tom Paine, "to begin the world over again." Here, if anywhere, was the perfect setting for this new experiment—an unspoiled land far from the wasteful rivalries and superstitions of the Old World; and below the ground almost limitless resources quite untapped. Here, in this vast new continent, capitalism was given a chance under the best possible conditions to show what kind of society it could build.

And show us it has.

*   *

Let us examine just a few aspects of American society.

America the Beautiful

Capitalism came to an unspoiled continent and has ravished it mercilessly.

Some examples:

- Almost all soil erosion is caused by man, by deforestation, by over-grazing, and by other farming methods that bring large yields for a short period, but do lasting damage to the ecology. It takes nature between 300 and 1,000 years to create one inch of topsoil—the living earth without which plant life is impossible.[1] So ruthlessly have the American people deforested the prairies and so greedily have they sought to get the maximum returns from the soil that one-half of all the topsoil in America has been lost forever.
  As early as 1939, the Chief of the U.S. Soil Conservation Service was warning Congress:

  In the short life of this country, we have essentially destroyed 282 million acres of crop and rangeland . . . About 100 million acres of cropland, much of it representing the best cropland we have, is finished in this country. We cannot restore it. . . . We are losing *every day* as the

result of erosion the equivalent of two hundred 40-acre farms. . . .
It is gone, gone forever.[2]

- One example of the wastage of this irreplaceable life-giving soil flows right by the doorstep of Congress. It has been estimated that the Potomac River carries out to sea 5½ million tons of topsoil every year.
- Originally there were two million acres of virgin redwood trees along the Pacific Coast. Some of these giant trees were 4,000 years old, the oldest living things on earth. One and seven-tenths million acres have been felled for commercial use and the lumber companies are still hard at it. Governor Reagan of California is a staunch supporter of "free enterprise." When citizens organized a campaign to save the last redwoods he was at a loss to understand what the fuss was about. "Redwood trees?" he is reported to have said, "Why, if you've seen one you have seen them all." *
- Seven-eighths of all virgin timber in the United States has been cut down by private commercial lumber companies. Some attempts have been made to reforest the denuded areas but nothing on a nearly adequate scale. Lumber companies plunder the woodlands for their own profit without any regard for what they might be doing to the intricate balance of nature or their effect on the wild animal, bird and insect life, the local climate, or the water shed; and least of all what damage they do to the beauty of the landscape.
- Professor J. W. Watson of Edinburgh University reported to the British Association for the Advancement of Science on September 7, 1970, that the United States had killed off 85 per cent of its wildlife and 80 per cent of its forests.
- The newsprint for a single edition of *The New York Times* Sunday edition uses the equivalent of the net annual growth of 6,000 acres of trees.

---

* Some time later Mr. Spiro Agnew, when during his campaign for the Vice Presidency he was chided for not going to see for himself the conditions in the cities, made use of the same formula: "If you've seen one ghetto, you've seen 'em all."

• On average, 10 million acres of forest are destroyed by
fire every year—yet the money allocated for fire protection
and control is ridiculously inadequate.[3]

While hundreds of thousands of acres of former forest
stand scarred and bulldozed as if they have been hit by high
explosives, and the rains wash away the humus and topsoil
that the roots of the trees had formerly held together, the
water of the United States is being polluted on an unprecedented scale. Almost every river and lake of any size in the
United States is now polluted with sewage, industrial waste
and acid drainage from mining operations. Every day, according to a 1968 report, New York City dumps 200 million gallons of raw sewage into the Hudson River. The
National Academy of Sciences warns that if water pollution continues at the present rate, by 1980 there will be
enough waterborne waste to consume all the oxygen in all
22 river systems of the U.S. When that happens fish will not
survive in these rivers. The first critical warning is what happened to Lake Erie. This large, wonderfully productive in-
land sea is now almost without fish life due to the huge
quantities of sewage dumped into it from Detroit and other
cities.

Time of February 2, 1970, devoted its main feature story
to a description of how the Americans are destroying their
environment. Here in these statements quoted from the survey is some of the startling information they conveyed to the
readers:

• Modern technology is already pressuring nature with tens
of thousands of synthetic substances, many of which almost
totally resist decay—thus poisoning man's fellow creatures,
to say nothing of himself. The burden includes smog fumes,
aluminum cans that do not rust, inorganic plastics that may
last for decades, floating oil that can change the thermal
reflectivity of oceans, and radioactive wastes whose toxicity
lingers for literally hundreds of years . . . The winds that

ventilate the earth are only six miles high; toxic garbage can kill the tiny organisms that normally clean rivers.

• Although the U.S. contains only 5.7 per cent of the world's population, it consumes 40 per cent of the world's production of natural resources.

• The result of massive production is massive filth. Every year Americans junk seven million cars, 100 million tires, 20 million tons of paper, 28 billion bottles and 48 billion cans.

• Every year U.S. plants discard 165 million tons of solid waste and gush 172 million tons of smoke and fumes into the air.*

• The Apollo X astronauts could see Los Angeles as a cancerous smudge from 25 thousand miles in outer space.

• Trouble may well loom for Los Angeles, which sits in a smoggy bowl that often contains only 300 feet of air. Almost every other day, the city's public schools forbid children to exercise lest they breathe too deeply.
[Dr. Jerome D. Frank of Johns Hopkins University found that the chances of a man dying between the ages of fifty and seventy from respiratory disease are twice as great if he lives in a polluted area than if he is fortunate enough to find one where the air is still clean.] 4

• Every year, Greater Los Angeles' growth consumes 70 square miles of open land. Not only is prime farm land taken out of production, but it is also developed in an inefficient way; the term "slurb" was coined in California to describe sleazy, sprawling subdivisions.

• The United States produces almost 50 per cent of the world's industrial pollution.

The American people are at last awakening to the damage that they are doing to their environment but, as *Time* says in its report, they have a record of acting for their own benefit only after the damage is done.

The need to correct this is obvious.

---

* The tonnage of aerial garbage that is allowed to be disposed of every year in the atmosphere of the United States is about 40 million tons *more* than the country's annual production of steel.

But the cost?

Even if there were a *will* to do something about it, where is the money, the fabulous sums of money, that would be needed to clean the rivers and air and to undo the damage that has been done to the land and forests? We have taken only three examples of the despoliation of America: soil erosion, deforestation, and pollution. Just taking these, how much would it cost each year to begin to heal the wounds caused by generations of avarice and irresponsibility?

Some damage—the loss of the topsoil, for instance—can never be undone. But as for the others a start can be made. Estimates of the annual cost involved have been compiled. Here are some:

For reforestation	$124 million
To save the redwoods	80 "
Soil conservation	300 "
Water pollution	10,000 "
Air pollution	1,500 "
	$12,004 million[5]

A lot of money—yes. But the United States spends more than this in just twenty weeks fighting the Vietnamese!

The problem is not one of cost, but of priorities.

To a nation that is prepared to spend over $4½ million every hour, year after year, in a stubborn and savage attempt to lay waste a small Asian country, the *financial* cost of these programs does not present a problem.

We have quoted one report from *Time*.

Once before, in 1968, this magazine printed an essay on this subject:

What ever happened to America the Beautiful? While quite a bit of it is still visible, the recurring question reflects rising and spreading frustration over the nation's increasingly dirty air, filthy streets and malodorous rivers—the relentless degradation of a once virgin continent.[6]

*   *

Medicine

Americans are totally convinced that in the medical sciences they are supreme (they take it for granted, it would not occur to them to question it.) There, they feel, capitalist society has proven itself. But even in this field the facts are not quite what they think they are, not by a long way.

"If you take a people's average longevity, for example," writes Dr. Jerome Davis, "it does not merely reflect a few geniuses' medical competence, but the social values of those in power—values which determine to what degree human health and hygiene are accepted as public responsibilities. It may therefore be particularly significant to deny the unjustified notion of most Americans that, at least, medically, ours is the most advanced country. Statistics of average longevity disprove this. A full twenty countries have a higher average life expectancy than the United States." [7]

Other facts regarding their national health may come as a surprise to Americans. After twenty-five years of unparalleled "prosperity":

- Half of all U.S. children under fifteen have never visited a dentist.
- Eleven million children between the ages of 15 and 17 have eye disorders that need attention.
- Two million children in America have untreated hearing defects.
- Nearly three million children have untreated speech disorders.
- Untreated emotional disturbances affect some 4,600,000 children.
- Two million children have untreated orthopedic problems. [8]

There are other desperately revealing statistics: five million alcoholics; the U.S. ranks eighteenth among the nations in infant mortality; and—perhaps most telling of all—more hospital beds are used for the treatment of the mentally ill than for all physical diseases, accidents and illnesses put together.*

In no other country is the fear of the medical cost of ill health so terrifying as in the United States. There is no general public health insurance as exists in so many places. For the very poor and the aged there are now some medical aid schemes (only passed by Congress after repeated postponements due to the violent opposition of the medical profession). But for those in neither of these categories private insurance is the only safeguard, and medical insurance is exorbitantly expensive. To go to a hospital without insurance on the other hand may be to see one's life's savings dissipated within a few weeks. The cost of a bed in most hospitals in the United States is $50 a day or more. All medicine, even aspirin, is extra. It is expected that before long some hospitals will be charging $100 a day. (A friend of mine, a brick mason, was not permitted to leave the T.B. sanatorium where he had been for a year until he had signed away the ownership of his house in payment for his bill. Another personal friend, injured badly in a road accident, found that the ambulance crew who came to pick her up would not even lift her off the highway—though her shoulder was badly shattered and she was obviously in shock—until she had signed—with infinite agony—the forms thrust

---

* The Vietnam war has added its medical problems too, particularly in the rate of venereal disease. According to *The Observer* of March 23, 1969, a report published by the World Health Organisation shows that the situation is rapidly becoming more acute than ever before in conditions of war. In one unit of U.S. troops it is estimated that about *700 out of every 1,000* men are infected every year. Even more worrying is that gonorrhea has developed resistance to a whole range of antibiotics. The more highly paid prostitutes who associate with the armed forces dose themselves with inadequate amounts of penicillin. They thus provide weak ammunition against the bacteria and only succeed in "becoming living culture media for the selection and breeding of the more resistant organisms."

"We have made a brothel of Saigon," said Senator Fulbright. He seems to have been right. Another blessing bestowed by the missionaries of capitalism.

before her which ensured the ambulance people that they would be paid).

Such is the state of medicine and the medical services available to the citizens of the most advanced capitalist country in the world.

* *

The Sunday Telegraph, London, February 1, 1970 printed a report by David Adamson on medicine in the United States:

The American medical-industrial complex is riding high these days, some would say dangerously high. Last year £26,250 million [$63 billion] went into its collective pocket—roughly two-and-a-half times what was spent on the Vietnam war.

Boom days, and with them one would expect a healthier nation and vast improvements in the standard of care. Yet the facts are that Americans are not particularly healthy . . . and the patients are probably the most dissatisfied in the Western world . . .

Most but not all of the blame for this situation can be placed on the doctors. The richer they become, the less inclined they are to work long or inconvenient hours . . .

Corruption has been another by-product. In California, MEDICAL (the local variant of MEDICAID) is said to have been milked of between $6 million and $8 million as a result of "illegal and unethical activities." In Kentucky, one of the poorer states, a chemist who once would have considered himself lucky if he did ten thousand dollars worth of business in a year was suddenly discovered to be receiving $300 thousand from MEDICAID alone.

* *

Corruption in High Places

An aspect of American society that, needless to say, doesn't get much mention in all the ringing speeches about the need for law and order is the lawlessness and corruption within the Government itself. "Crime," said Justice Brandeis, "is contagious. If the Government becomes a lawbreaker, it breeds contempt for law."

I will not attempt, in this short mention of the Government as lawbreaker, to deal with the many large acts of lawlessness committed by the Government of the United States—such as the undeclared Vietnam War (condemned by every responsible body of lawyers in the U.S. as an illegal war under the laws of the country) or the illegal refusal to implement the laws regarding equality of treatment for the Negro minority. Rather, I will draw attention briefly to another aspect of government lawlessness—the corruption with which the entire process of legislation and governmental administration is riddled.

> While Americans continue to denounce corruption, they also continue to practice it. It must be obvious that such features of American life as the "fix," the "shakedown," "protection," the "pay-off" and the "rackets" go deeper than the nature of politics itself.[9]

Political corruption has for so long and so continuously been a feature of the national scene of the United States that to call a man "a politician" to his face is to insult him. When a particularly flagrant abuse of public responsibility (as for example, in the Senator Dodd case) is brought to public attention by private individuals in a way that forces the Congress to act, it does so with great circumspection, knowing only too well that a single false move would bring a whole mountain of skeletons rattling out of Congressional cupboards. When these instances do occur it is not the *fact* of corruption that surprises the general public, but that for once it was at least partially made public.

Senator Dodd was accused by some of his own staff of having used for his own purposes large funds that had been collected from his supporters for his election and other political expenses.

After a dramatic hearing his Senate colleagues merely "reprimanded" Senator Dodd for his unethical conduct. At the time of writing this, the Senator, unabashedly, has announced his intention of seeking another term of office, and retains his position as chairman of the Senate Juvenile Delinquency Subcommittee!

Another example of public exposure with more effective results was that of J. Parnell Thomas, who was Chairman of the House Un-American Activities Committee. He was exposed by the columnist Drew Pearson, brought to trial and convicted of having placed some of his relatives on the public payroll and having them "kick back" to his personal bank account. He was sent to the Federal Correctional Institution at Danbury, Connecticut where he was put to work cleaning out the chicken run. A beautifully ironic twist to this story is that while in prison for swindling the public he came face to face with one or two of those whom his Committee had sent to prison. Their un-American activity was not the swindling of the public but a refusal to disclose the names of their friends who were members of the Communist Party. Thomas was paroled after only eight months in prison, and one of President Truman's last acts as President was to grant Thomas a full pardon. Politicians in the United States take care of their own.[10]

When Congress appropriates large funds that move into public circulation there invariably arises the sick, sweet smell of corruption. It doesn't matter what the money is voted for—where there is money there will be those who want to get hold of it. The multi-million-a-year "Anti-Poverty Program," for example, initiated by a frightened Congress after the city riots, proved a bonanza. From one end of the United States to the other, politicians could now give thousands of cushy jobs to their friends—"to administer" the program. A large national project of this kind required, of course, big-time men; annual salaries of $30 thousand were not uncommon. In some cities more money

was squandered for "administration" than was spent on the
program itself. For some, even the big salary was not big
enough. With one million of New York's poor on relief, considerable sums were allocated for the program there. But
the poor didn't get it all.

> Multiple investigations of the city's $122 million-a-year anti-
> poverty program are disclosing chronic corruption and ad-
> ministrative chaos that have already cheated New York's
> poor of uncounted millions of dollars.
> "It's so bad that it will take ten years to find out what's
> really going on inside the Human Resources Administration,"
> said an assistant district attorney who has spent the last four
> months studying the superagency.[11]

"Administrative chaos" . . . "ten years to find out
what's going on". . . . These phrases to Americans have a
very familiar ring. Ten years is a long time, and by then who
will care?

The "uncounted millions" perhaps sound worse than they
really proved to be. The accountants finally decided that a
mere $2.7 million had been stolen by officials from the
Neighborhood Youth Corps.[12] This, however, is just one
program in one city—multiply the $2.7 million by ten or
twenty and the amount of money siphoned off is not exactly
chicken feed.

The United States is a big country and does everything,
even its corruption, on a grand scale. In Britain not long
ago, the public was shocked to learn that three Scotland
Yard detectives were alleged to have "shaken down" a sus-
pected criminal on a promise to have the charges against
him reduced. The amounts they were said to have extorted
were a few hundred pounds. The British were right to be
shocked. But it must have made the big-time boys in the
United States laugh. A public fuss about a few hundred
pounds! It is estimated that at least $25 billion a year is ex-
torted from the public by criminals and police in the United
States.

The Senate of the United States (so American school-children are told) is an august body of men who ponder long and hard on how best their nation can be governed. The Senate, perhaps more than any other body, with the possible exception of the Supreme Court, sets the moral tone of the nation. Senators are further removed than the members of the House of Representatives from the untidy political bustle, the cruder forms of lobbying by special interests. There are, for one thing, fewer of them, and they don't have to worry so constantly about their next election.

But how representative of the people are the Senators? Twenty per cent of the present Senate are millionaires; it is therefore sensible to surmise that they are likely to represent and understand better those of their own class than they would represent and understand those living in the ghettos. But in one aspect they represent the national code of ethics, or non-ethics, well enough. From *The New York Times,* an editorial (reprinted in the *International Herald Tribune,* October 25–26, 1969):

> The United States Senate is a body of men . . . who entrust their tax reform program to a member who regularly makes far more money on *tax-free* oil royalties than he gets in salary —and five times as much on oil royalties altogether.
>
> Since 1964 Sen. Russell Long of Louisiana has enjoyed a total, tax free income of over $300 thousand by virtue of a depletion allowance for oil industry . . .
>
> . . . there is good reason why a member should not be allowed to serve on committees which are overwhelmingly concerned with matters bearing directly on his main source of income.
>
> Yet there is no restraint on such needless conflict. Sen. Eastland of Mississippi, who has received more than $100 thousand a year for three consecutive years in agricultural subsidies, sits on the Agriculture Committee and regularly votes for such subsidies . . .
>
> And these cases . . . are typical rather than unique.

A high percentage of Mr. Nixon's cabinet are millionaire businessmen—and *these* men are meant to understand the problems of poverty, of the ghettos and of injustices to the Negro population! Mr. Nixon chose as his Deputy Secretary of Defense, Mr. David Packard, a millionaire 300 times over, a great deal of this huge fortune having been made by selling his company's electronic wares to the very Pentagon he now helps to administer. There was some low-key murmuring at the time of his appointment about "conflict of interest," but some formula was devised to overcome that little difficulty. Through his own holdings in his company have been "put in trust" while he is helping to run the military affairs of the nation, his company will continue to sell its products to the Pentagon. His salary is a mere pittance for him, but it is unlikely that Mr. Packard will suffer too great a deprivation while at the Pentagon. To reassure those who might have been anxious over how he would make out, Mr. Packard announced when he took over, "I do not intend to live on $30 thousand a year." So now we can all sleep easier.

* *

Crime and Violence

As Attorney General, I can tell you that street crime is exploding with unpredictable viciousness. Street crime and the fear of street crime is changing the fabric of our society. The fear of crime is forcing our citizens to change their traditional living patterns, to stay off the streets at night, to shy away from helping strangers, to be distrustful and insecure in their own neighborhoods.

U.S. ATTORNEY GENERAL JOHN N. MITCHELL
Herald Tribune, March 10, 1969

In 1967 the editors of *U. S. News & World Report* were already warning Americans that crime in the United States was rising seven times as fast as the population increase. Since then it has risen even faster than they predicted.[13]

Crime has always been endemic in the U.S. It is, as one

writer put it, "as American as apple pie." However, there is a general impression abroad that the really high watermark of American lawlessness was during prohibition, the days of Al Capone and John Dillinger and the Chicago gangsters. That is not so. Bank robberies have more than doubled since 1932! [14]

London authorities today are worried about the rise in armed robberies in that city. If the police in Washington, D.C. had London's crime rate to cope with they would throw their caps in the air and cheer. The number of armed robberies in London in 1968 was the highest ever recorded, namely 278. Washington, D.C. had 3,400. On a *per capita* basis this puts Washington in the lead by 1760 per cent. In the one month of January, 1969, Washington had more armed robberies than London (with a population three times as large) had in all of 1968.[15] The number of murders in Washington in 1969 was 50 per cent higher than in 1968.[16] The number of murders in Washington alone in 1968 was 50 per cent higher than the murders committed in the entire United Kingdom.

The police are dangerous too. Seventeen citizens, thirteen of them black, were killed by police in Washington, D.C. in a period of twenty months but no policeman was indicted for homicide.[17] One of the seventeen, a Negro, was shot for jay walking.

> Whatever the full story, it is impossible to imagine a policeman killing a white man simply for crossing the street against a red light . . . A long history of police complaisance in the ghetto toward drug sellers and prostitutes combined with a readiness to humiliate and harass the self respecting black who tries to insist on his rights has built an explosive bitterness everywhere. Even the decent policeman, doing no more this his duty, may be the prisoner and victim of this past.[18]

In dealing with the problem of crime, and drawing attention to how serious the situation in the capital had become, President Nixon in his State of the Union Message, delivered to a joint session of Congress on January 22, 1970, said, "I doubt if there are many members of this Congress who live more than a few blocks from here who would dare leave their cars in the Capitol garage and walk home at night." What an admission!

What he failed to mention, as Colin Cross pointed out in *The Observer* a few days later, was that:

Near the Capitol are some of the worst slums in America, populated by blacks who speak a dialect which is almost a separate language from standard English. This winter, part of the capital of the richest nation is being treated as a starvation area. It is difficult to see how the problem of street crime can be eliminated until such black communities are brought back into the American mainstream.[19]

Washington is not, of course, the only city with a runaway crime rate. Violent crime in New York City, for instance, increased by 35 per cent in 1968,[20] that is in *one year*, and all the other major cities followed much the same pattern. In some cities the statistics are worse. In several cities bus conductors have been subjected to so many holdups that they now refuse to carry change or issue scrip to passengers who don't have the exact fare. The exact fare is deposited in a non removable steel box.

It is a curious commentary on American life that a high rate of crime has been accepted by the public almost as a normal phenomenon. According to an article from Washington by Henry Brandon:

Washingtonians have become accustomed to living with crime almost in the way that Londoners learned to live with the blitz. You carry only sufficient money to keep the hold-up man satisfied enough to let you go unharmed, you assume hopefully, after you have handed it over. You acquire a burglar alarm or a watch dog; you don't stay out late; you avoid walking in unfrequented streets; you leave the lights on when you leave your house; you acquire your own gun . . .[21]

Alan Brien, another British reporter, presented this account of what it was like living in the States:

> The train I took out to New Haven had two bullet holes in its carriage windows. In the course of two hours, I saw two boys hurl stones at the driver and another attempt to roll a log on to the track. On the same train, making its return journey through Harlem, a sniper on a roof shot and killed the guard . . .[22]

One wonders whether in any other city in the world crime is so prevalent that the official tourist guidebook must devote a whole section to warning the visitor (as *The New York City Handbook* does) to walk only "where it is well lighted and where there are people—doormen, kids at candy stores, men in bars. (Do not rely much on the fact that cars are passing.)" This book also gives advice on how to deal with burglars and how to double lock and protect doors and windows. Perhaps this advice is necessary in a city that has 15 thousand burglaries a month, and almost a thousand murders a year. (With less than 200 murders a year in the whole country Britain is not in the same league. London in 1968 had fifty-eight murders, giving New York the lead by a cool 1,728 per cent.)

It has been estimated that no fewer than 750 thousand Americans have been killed since 1900 by gunshot wounds. Today, because of the increased lawlessness of the society, most Americans have bought weapons, thereby only increasing the likelihood of expanding it still further. The Government, after Senator Kennedy was assassinated, wished to put some legal restraints on the purchase of private firearms. "The Attorney General," reported *The International Herald Tribune* on September 11, 1968, "predicting that 20 thousand Americans will die this year from gunshots, asked senators to adopt strict gun control laws." The senators refused. The gun lobby is powerful. It has the backing of strong right-wing organizations which invariably cite the Second

Amendment to the American Constitution, which gives all citizens the right to bear arms. Arms can be bought cheaply and easily. *The London Observer* reported from the U.S. that "The lowest estimate of privately owned weapons in the country is 90 million—the highest, by California's Stanford Institute, is 200 million." [23]

America is fast becoming a society of frightened people. That is, a people who have lost their basic confidence in the ordinary decency and kindness of those around them. Only *fearful* people would arm themselves on such a scale. Perhaps, you say, their apprehension is exaggerated, unjustified by the conditions of their society. If so, what a commentary on a social order that induces such fear! The statistics show that every year Americans stand a one-in-fifty chance of being victims of some crime. At what point does a fear become a justified fear? At what point does it become ordinary prudence, and not paranoia, for a girl to carry a revolver in her bag?

What aggravates the situation is that there exist organizations in the United States which make it their business to frighten people. The "Minutemen" is one such organization which deliberately sets out to terrify They are the self-styled defenders of American "freedom." They act secretly, they arm themselves secretly, they threaten anonymously. They consider themselves the watchdogs of all that is best in America. Not long after she had spoken at an anti-Vietnam war rally, a friend of mine received the following letter. It was printed on one side of a folded sheet; on the facing page were the crossed-hairs of a rifle sight:

TRAITORS BEWARE
See the old man at the corner where you buy your papers? He may have a silencer-equipped pistol under his coat. That extra fountain pen in the pocket of the insurance salesman who calls on you might be a cyanide gas gun. What about your milk man? Arsenic works slow but sure. Your auto mechanic may stay up nights studying booby traps. These

patriots are not going to let you take their freedom away
from them. They have learned the silent knife, the strangler's
cord, the target rifle that hits sparrows at 200 yards. Traitors
beware. Even now the cross-hairs are on the back of your
necks.

MINUTEMEN

Of such stuff is fascism being made.

Those who run this capitalist Eden are using the popular
alarm about the rise of crime to justify their preparations
against political protest, in other words their preparations
for mass repression. The blurring together of crime and political opposition is a trick by means of which the U.S.
leaders have confused the public, and this has enabled them
to have a "pacification" program for the war at home as
well as in Vietnam.

> The army is stockpiling riot control equipment in strategically
> located depots across the country, officials said today, and is
> ready to airlift it to any city if civil disorders break out . . .
>
> Army and National Guard officials said their planning has
> been extensive as well as diverse, ranging from obtaining
> maps of subway, sewer, water and electrical systems in po-
> tential trouble spots to preparing menus for mobilized na-
> tional guardsmen.
>
> In city after city across America, the police are stockpiling
> armored vehicles, helicopters, high powered rifles.
>
> They are recruiting civilians as ready reserves. They are
> sending undercover agents into the slums.[24]

These preparations are as elaborate as America has made
for many a foreign war, but this is *a war against Americans*.
And being war it is only natural that the military are in
charge of it, with the High Command located deep in the
bowels of the Pentagon. According to one report:

> The Defense Department is rushing to completion a multi-
> million-dollar Army Operations Center in the Pentagon base-
> ment to serve as a "war room" in the event of urban riots
> this summer . . .

After describing the elaborate electronic and computer equipment which was being installed in this "war room," the elaborate alarm devices which would prevent it from being captured by unexpected attack, and the hundreds of "protected" telephone lines which will link this command post to every corner of the country, the report continues:

> The size of the Defense Department's growing commitment to such domestic crises was evidenced by the disclosure that it spent more than $9.8 million during 1968 in this category.
>
> Prior to the Washington, Baltimore and Chicago riots, Pentagon strategists were talking of coping with five concurrent disorders—a number which has since been escalated to 25 for planning purposes.[25] *

* *

The Urban Blight

We can only briefly mention in this section the creeping horror of the cities. The cities stand, as does the pillaged countryside, as an indictment of a social order that places material advantage for the individual at the very center of its philosophy. Given this basic philosophy, how can we expect things to be otherwise? Why would men with money invest in slum clearing and decent housing for the poor when their capital can earn so much more elsewhere—in building houses for the rich, for example? Wherever the accumulation of wealth and power is equated with supreme success, there you will find the sociology of grabbing.

* On August 31, 1970, in an open letter of protest to Secretary of Defense Laird, Representative Paul Findley of Illinois made a disclosure of further ominous preparations. He revealed that the Department of the Army, without public announcement, had decided to supply the National Guard with 228,000 M-16 combat rifles. The M-16 fires at the phenominal rate of 850 shots per minute—faster than a machine gun—and (in Mr. Findley's words) "can spray a large area with deadly firepower." The primary role of the National Guard over the past quarter of a century has been the controlling of crowds and quelling domestic civil disturbances. These highly lethal combat weapons are presumably for use against *Americans*.

The cities are the outward projection, the material crystallization of this inner philosophy. Over one quarter of the living units in the United States in 1960 were substandard, dilapidated or lacking adequate plumbing facilities. More than one million New Yorkers live in slums.

> Perhaps (as one official remarked) we need fewer statistics and instead a few good old-fashioned walking tours: walks through the slums, up the stinking stairways into the crowded, shabby rooms; walks through the run-down commercial areas, taking care to glance above the first floor store fronts at the dusty windows of the deserted upper floors; walks through the oil-soaked, dreary factory lofts built before the assembly line was ever heard of. The filth, the misery and danger are all there—easy to see and, once seen, impossible to forget.[26]

The enormity of the system's failure to provide decent housing for the people is staggering—and for those who see the United States in terms of an "affluent" society, difficult to believe. The 1960 Census of Housing, for example, shows that there were nearly 9 million housing units that lacked private toilets and running water. More than half of America's non-white population today lives in substandard housing. Nor is this a characteristic only of the larger cities. For example, in 1950 in Robbins, Illinois, a town of only 4,766 population, 85.6 per cent of all dwelling units were dilapidated, lacking running water, toilet or bath. And even in a city such as Cambridge, Massachusetts, the seat of Harvard, the nation's oldest and most famous university, 57 per cent of the housing in 1958 was substandard.[27]

There is a general belief that the urban squalor of American cities is merely a legacy from the bad old past and that the housing situation is now improving.

The reverse is true. In many areas (though not all) it is getting worse.

Slum clearance (as one authority put it) under present rules should be labeled properly as slum relocation or slum shifting. It is not true urban renewal. Instead of being social uplift programs as sometimes depicted, the big renewal projects in residential areas have been called land grabs aided by government subsidies . . .[28]

In other words, slum clearance projects help land speculators to become richer; and this has nothing to do with solving the nation's housing problem.

It is a very noticeable phenomenon that as capitalist society develops to its limit it is less and less able to meet the most rudimentary social needs of the people, and this is particularly obvious to anyone visiting the cities of the United States even from the less advanced capitalist countries of Europe. Despite the huge sums of money allocated to them, public services are visibly breaking down. *The New York Times* complained that the average letter today takes longer to travel from New York to Washington than it did a hundred years ago. One need only walk through the poorer sections of any American city to see that garbage collection is inadequate and that some of the streets seem hardly ever to be cleaned. There are cities in America today where there is no public transportation at all—no buses, no trams, nothing—leaving those who cannot afford cars (and there are still many), children and old people to manage as best they can.

* *

The Grapes of Wrath—1970 Vintage

The squalor of the cities has its counterpart in the country too.

California, if it were a separate country, would be the sixth wealthiest nation, and its *per capita* income would be the highest in the world. Yet within California can be found working conditions recalling nineteenth-century Britain before the first agricultural union was formed in 1872. It is largely Mexicans and Mexican-Americans who pick the fruit, pull the lettuce, and gather the tomatoes that grow in the hot central valleys of the state. Two-and-a-quarter million Mexican-Americans live in California; another 90 thousand cross the border every day on passes to search for work. It is only a few years since the Mexican-American agricultural workers began to organize to improve working conditions. They are led by a remarkable Mexican-American, Cesar Chavez, who himself started as a grape picker when he was ten years old.

In a feature article by Norman Lewis in *The Sunday Times* of London on February 1, 1970, the working and living conditions of these agricultural workers is spelled out in meticulous and shocking detail. Under the heading "Slave Laborers in the Vineyard" this report presented to British readers what Californians have been aware of all their lives and have done almost nothing about:

> Poverty in the richest state in the richest land is more abject than anything to be seen in, say, Northern Europe. A grape picker works 82 days in a year, and the average migrant's income is . . . less than half the amount a U.S. family requires to live above the poverty line. . . . Until recently some workers were kept behind barbed wire . . .
>
> U.S. citizens of Mexican origin are a very much depressed minority. . . . Eighty per cent of them are housed in slums. . . . Their children average two years less at school than the children of Negroes and four years less than the children of whites, and they are still punished for speaking Spanish within earshot of their teachers. . . . Later they are likely to find that, whatever their scholastic achievements, only menial employment will be offered them . . .
>
> The picture of exploitation on the Victorian model is completed by the presence of child labor. When I was in Delano, last November, the local paper, the *Fresno Bee,* reported the case of Theresa Arellano, a girl of eight, who worked a 70-

hour week on a grape ranch. . . . by my own experience the
spectacle of young children at work in conditions which are
arduous and even dangerous for an adult is commonplace indeed . . . When the Guimarra Vineyards—largest of the
growers—was tried and convicted on nearly forty violations
of child labor and health laws, it was fined a total of $1,000
by the Kern County Superior Court—and the fine was suspended . . .

Of all the jobs that automatically fall to the Mexican,
whether migrant or U.S. citizen, the most unpleasant is the
grape picker's. Grape harvesting is done under a raging sun
from which the low vines themselves offer little shade. The
skin's surface is soon coated with a sludge of grape juice
mixed with sweat and dust, which attracts so many winged
insects that at worst the pickers appear to be working in a
snowstorm. Chavez, from bitter experience of this work, described it to me. "It's degrading. Dehumanizing. After an
hour or two everybody gets in such a mess you can't tell a
man from a woman." It is rare in the fields for proper drink-
ing water to be available, or any form of latrine provided.
More seriously, in recent years growers have taken to the use
of toxic sprays that have caused innumerable cases of severe
illness and some deaths. Workers are housed in compounds
on company property which members of Chavez's organization are frequently prevented from inspecting, and are said, at
worst, to resemble concentration camps.

Tests carried out on 774 people showed that only 121
had no symptoms of pesticide poisoning. The report in *The
Sunday Times,* referring to another investigation, states
that

Of nearly 800 workers interviewed, practically all showed
signs of poisoning, and 163 reported *five or more* of the following symptoms: vomiting, abnormal fatigue, abnormal per-
spiration, difficulty in breathing, loss of fingernails, loss of
hair, itching in the ears, nose bleeds, swollen hands and feet,
and diarrhoea.

The first field worker I spoke to in Delano was a cook in

one of the immigrant camps . . . I noticed the man's hands looked like a leper's at the stage just before the fingers drop off.

He had been caught in the fields, the report explains, when a plane had sprayed the vineyard, but the spray wasn't vaporizing properly and it fell in drops. But the workers are not even allowed to know what kind of poisons they are being sprayed with, because the courts made orders forbidding the agricultural commissioner from revealing the composition of some of these pesticides.

The grape pickers, under Chavez's leadership, finally went on strike against their unspeakable working conditions. That strike is now in its fifth year.* It hasn't harmed the vineyard companies much, as they can ship in other Mexicans from across the border to do the picking. A nationwide appeal to Americans to boycott the purchase of California grapes might have been more successful if the Government had not helped the large grape companies by having the army increase its grape purchases by 50 per cent.

At the root of these evils is the single staggering fact that the Government of the United States has never recognized the right of agricultural workers to form a union. To quote the introduction to Cesar Chavez's statement to the House of Representatives last October:

Farm labourers are excluded from minimum wage legislation and from unemployment insurance . . . They are denied the collective bargaining rights guaranteed to non-farm workers, and are effectively cut off from every benefit of a negotiated contract. So the vast majority of Californian farm workers have no contract, get no overtime, and may not even know their rate of pay . . . They are often victims of deception and graft. They get no time off with pay, no health or pension plans, no regular rest periods. . . . Workers may be laid

---

* Since this was written the grape growers have at last capitulated and the strike is ended. The extent to which the condition of the pickers will be significantly improved remains to be seen.

off at any time and for any reason, as for objecting to being assaulted by an owner . . .

Mr. Ronald Reagan, the Governor of California, called the grape pickers' strike "immoral" and an "attempted blackmail of free society."

We are not describing England during the industrial revolution; nor the struggle of the Tolpuddle Martyrs. These are the conditions permitted today by the people of the richest state of the richest country in the world.

* *

"Black is Beautiful"

The unlovely cities of America, which have seen so many lives frustrated and so many children stunted in body and mind, have in recent years been the scene of rioting on a mass scale. There have been riots before, of course. Toward the end of the last century, as increasing numbers of Negroes migrated to northern cities, race riots were frequent. In those days it was northern whites who initiated anti-Negro riots. (Lynchings—the hanging of individual Negroes—had also become commonplace. About 100 lynchings occurred every year throughout the 1880's and 1890's. In 1892 there were 161 such lynchings.) After the turn of the century northern whites resorted to mass violence. Anti-Negro riots broke out in New York in 1900; in Springfield, Ohio in 1904; in Greensburg, Indiana in 1906; in Springfield, Illinois in 1908. In July, 1917 a particularly brutal anti-Negro riot broke out in East St. Louis, caused by the fear that Negro advances in economic status were threatening the livelihood of the white workers:

> The area became a "bloody half mile" for three or four hours; street cars were stopped, and Negroes, without regard to age or sex, were pulled off and stoned, clubbed and kicked, and mob leaders calmly shot and killed Negroes who were lying in blood in the street . . .

Other rioters set fire to Negro homes, and by midnight the Negro section was in flames and Negroes were fleeing the city. There were forty-eight dead, hundreds injured and more than 300 buildings destroyed.[29]

The list of major riots by whites against Negroes could go on. In 1919 alone there were lynchings and mob violence against Negroes in Washington, D.C., Omaha, Charleston, Longview, Texas, Chicago and Knoxville.

By the 1960's the Negro population had had enough. They were ready to rebel—and rebel they did.

Nothing, even in the most violent of these earlier riots initiated by the whites, can remotely compare in scale to the huge outbreaks that began with the disorder in Watts, in 1965, where thirty-four people were killed, nearly 4,000 people were arrested and $25 million in damage was inflicted. This was merely the prelude to the major rebellions that followed in 1966 and 1967 in 128 U.S. cities.

Later in this book we will examine the underlying politics of the racial issue. Here, our purpose is to underline the fact that racial discrimination is not a recent phenomenon and that it is one of the most ugly and sordid of all the features of capitalist America.

If crime is "as American as apple pie," then racism is still more so. The first slaves from Africa arrived in August, 1619, over 150 years before the Declaration of Independence, by which time there were 500 thousand slaves in a total population of 3 million. Every Black has a longer ancestry on American soil than all but a few "white" Americans, yet this whole line of Negro descent, from generation to generation, knew nothing but servitude. And servitude is still the way of life for the majority of Blacks alive today. The *form* of the slavery has changed—but it is anybody's guess whether the condition of the Black today, in a rat-infested Harlem or Chicago slum, is better or worse than that of the tobacco slaves of Virginia in the seventeenth century.

And American racism cannot be mentioned without reference to its "final solution" of the Indian question:

> Reciprocity for the friendliness and assistance with which the settlers had at first been received by the Indians depended on moral values. Fair play, justice and abhorrence of cruelty, were needed as ingredients of easy coexistence with the Indians. But . . . the Indians merely excited the white man's greed. All of their lands were coveted for their own value as well as for the gold that might be stored in them . . . first things come first. And when it came to choosing between the survival of the Indians and satisfying one's acquisitiveness, hardly a dilemma was involved. What "needed" to be done to the Indians may have been regrettable, but this could hardly reverse the basic priorities, and thus it merely became a dirty part of a sound and desirable job. So the Indians were exterminated *en masse,* deliberately and methodically, and they became the unhaunting price of the American Civilization.[30]

By 1880, only a shattered handful of the tribes who had roamed the American lands before the advent of "civilization" were alive.

White America was racist from her first beginnings and remains so to this day.

In regard to the attitude of whites to the Negroes, the President's National Advisory Commission on Civil Disorders put the reality bluntly enough:

> . . . certain fundamental matters are clear. Of these the most fundamental is the racial attitude and behavior of white Americans toward black Americans. Race prejudice has shaped our history decisively in the past; it now threatens to do so again. White racism is essentially responsible for the explosive mixture which has been accumulating in our cities . . . At the base of this mixture are three of the most bitter fruits of white racial attitudes . . .[31]

The Commission then lists these three "bitter fruits." The *first* is the pervasive discrimination that excludes great numbers of Blacks from the benefits of economic progress and their confinement in segregated housing and schools. The *second* is the massive and growing concentration of impoverished Blacks in the major cities while the white community flees to the suburbs. The third and "most bitter fruit" is the existence of the black ghettos.

> The ghettos too often mean men and women without jobs, families without men, and schools where children are processed instead of educated, until they return to the street—to crime, to narcotics, to dependency on welfare, and to bitterness and resentment against society in general and white society in particular.[32]

Unable to secure justice in any other way, the black community and others took to the streets. It was generally assumed at the time that the giant riots of 1967, in which great areas of some cities were destroyed, were the work of a small minority of "extremists," not at all representative of the black population as a whole. But the National Advisory Commission found a very different story. The Commission's findings, as reported by *The Washington Post,* showed that:

> About 18 per cent—instead of the commonly believed 1 or 2 per cent—of Negro residents in major 1967 riot areas participated in the disorders.
> The rioters, "far from being primarily the riffraff and outside agitators," were representative of the young adult Negro males in the urban ghetto. They were not newly arrived immigrants from the South, they were not unemployed, and they were not predominantly teenagers.[33]

What the United States is reaping today is the result of 300 years of racial prejudice, a prejudice which may today be somewhat more concealed, but which underneath is smoldering as virulently as ever. And if you don't believe it—ask any Black.

The United States chatters endlessly about the virtues of her democracy. But the brutal truth is that *white America is racist,* and by no twists and turns of semantics, by no evasions whatever, can a racist nation claim to be a democracy.

* *

The Manipulators

An extraordinary feature of the political economy of the United States (and to a lesser degree of all capitalist countries) is the extent to which it has become a psychological economy. We will see in a later chapter how, in order to keep the economy functioning, huge amounts of money and human effort are channelled into the military sector, regardless of whether there is an objective military need for it or not. We will see how to keep its system going, capitalism devised a variety of techniques which stimulated sales abroad often at great damage to other peoples. But there is another built-in compulsion that in a more immediate and personal way warps the lives of people—the pressures that are applied to them *to buy.* It doesn't really matter what they buy as long as they keep on buying, even if they buy commodities that they do not need, with money that they do not have.*

To keep people buying, you need first to make them dissatisfied with what they have. Today in the United States between $15 billion and $20 billion are spent every year on advertising, and advertising is nothing more than a technique to keep people in a state of perpetual dissatisfaction with what they possess and in a permanent state of itchy acquisitiveness. Advertising, with its insistence on buying, dominates the climate of the United States, pervades every facet of life, and has the widest possible social consequences.

It is something of a mystery why Americans, who by and

---

* Today private debt in the United States has reached the point where, on an average, every family has mortgaged more than fifteen months of its future earnings for goods already purchased.

large are hard-headed and not easily taken in by boasters and charlatans, are so ready to believe these hucksters of the advertising fraternity. They would not dream of believing Mr. Smith if he carried a placard on his back announcing that he was the most honest fellow in the world. They would immediately conclude he was a fraud. Yet when the manufacturer of an article shouts from every billboard and every magazine that his product is the best in the world, they take him seriously and they even believe him. They must believe him or advertising would have disappeared long ago.

I have in front of me as I write an American magazine, and on the inside cover there is a picture of a man with a look of sheer ecstasy in his eyes, as if he had just won a million dollars. But in this world of advertising make-believe you don't need a million dollars to reach such heights of bliss; you only need one dollar for a deodorant that promises to give you "social security in thirty seconds." Opposite is an advertisement for a suit called "The Diplomat," with a photograph of a man looking like exactly what he really is: a man from a modelling agency trying to look like a diplomat. And on another page is an exceedingly pretty girl who, it is made obviously clear, has captured her man not because of her charm, but because she uses the kind of perfume that "gets men."

Below this four-color facade, behind the blatant fraudulence, we cannot fail to sense the pressure of vital economic imperatives. Manufacturers do not spend $15 billion or more a year to advertise their wares unless they are the victims of one of the iron laws of capitalism—the need always to sell their products in ever increasing volume so they can maintain an acceptable return on their invested capital. In the world of "free enterprise" there is no standing still, no rest. There is no possibility of reaching a stage of quiet balance in which year after year that which is needed is produced, and that which is produced is sold. *Expand or go under* is the law of this economic jungle.

So the pressure on the consumer must be applied—$15 billion-a-year pressure.

A man's relationships (whether they are with people, ideas, or possessions) are healthy to the extent to which they are based on reality and not on pretense. But the subtlety and pervasiveness of advertising have created a social climate in which it is almost impossible to have a real relationship with anything, and most of all with one's possessions. It is astonishingly difficult today to know whether one really needs a particular article or has been made to feel one needs it. Advertising is essentially based on fraudulence. It promises us that we may escape from our tensions, our loneliness, our lack of inner peace—by buying things.

If even for a short while a significant number of people were to ignore these blandishments and establish a real relationship with their possessions, knowing clearly what they needed and what they didn't need, an economic calamity would result. If enough people decided that their still usable car, though "old-fashioned" by advertising agency standards, would do them for another year or two; if enough women decided that the washing machine worked perfectly well, even if it lacked "the super streamlined" look of next year's model; if enough men, instead of wanting to look like a diplomat, continued to use the still good suits they already had—the United States would head straight for a depression of the first magnitude.

The reality is that people can get along quite well with their old possessions if they are left alone. They can get along with them much better than they can get along with themselves. It is with their own lives that most Americans feel the deepest discontent. Life, they feel, is somehow slipping by . . . and it could be much more vivid and wonderful than it is, if only they were different. The advertising people, of course, have done their best to make people feel unhappy with their lot by holding up a magic world of make-believe in which everyone is gloriously happy all the time.

They are good psychologists, these advertising men, and they know it is less painful for us to think that the cause of our unhappiness is "out there" instead of "in here." It is much less painful to say, "Oh, if only I had a new washing machine" (or a new hat, or a new set of golf clubs, or a new wife) than it is to say "Oh, if only I were different!" And this all-too-human tendency to project our dissatisfaction has been exploited by them. Because the new car, the new hat, the new set of golf clubs after the first few days lose their novelty and cannot in the very nature of things provide an answer to our discontents, these discontents only grow more painful and we look more eagerly than ever to see what we can do to assuage them. And thus this spiral continues, to the great satisfaction of those whose job it is to make us buy . . . and buy . . . and buy . . .

> The American system (wrote Ronald Segal) is a hymn to personal indulgence. 'Pamper yourself, pamper him, pamper her,' is the chant of the advertisements. They address not the community, far less the nation; they address the individual American, and in particular the individual American woman. 'Buy,' they cry. 'Buy as a wife. Buy as a mother. Buy as a woman. But buy.' . . . What are they to buy? In the business recession of the late 1950's, President Eisenhower was asked just that question. His reply was, 'Anything.' [34]

If you think that the very, very rich must be beyond the reach of such huckstering, you are mistaken. There are those ingenious enough to dream up ideas that the rich could not possibly think up on their own. According to *The New York Times* you can buy on Fifth Avenue a simple sleeveless jacket in chinchilla for $7,950 or a sable evening wrap for a mere $4,000. And elsewhere we read of red silk roses imported from France at $250 a dozen; a diamond necklace at $125 thousand and clotheshangers (yes— clotheshangers—the things you and I buy at Woolworth's for 25 cents) in chinchilla for $175 each. There's someone who sells wall-to-wall carpeting in mink at $600 a square yard and (for bathrooms that need a little sprucing up) there are gold-plated faucets for the washbasin at $475 a pair.

The great American "democracy" has room for all—the very rich, the very poor, both separated from what Americans call the "mainstream" of the not so very rich and the not so very poor. Many New Yorkers (including a million on relief) know in intimate detail what the meaning of squalor is, the sheer ugliness of deprivation in a land that could provide so much. And they know it too in Chicago, where 600 Negro babies die each year from starvation, rat bites and exposure.[35] The rich are a million miles removed from that dimension of squalor. What they experience is the less lethal yet more soul-degrading squalor of the rich.

* *

A Drugged Society

For some years the nation has been uneasily aware that a growing number of school children were smoking marijuana—pot for short—and that a smaller number were going on from pot to glue-sniffing, LSD, DMT, STP, and that an even smaller number of young people were experimenting with morphine, cocaine, heroin and other "hard drugs." It was all vaguely worrying, but American parents reassured each other that only a few (and not their children, of course) were using the hard stuff and that marijuana was non-addictive and was probably less harmful than a scotch and soda.

But as an increasing number of middle-class parents found that their own children were taking the harder drugs, at first surreptitiously, then more openly and finally with the desperation of the really hooked, the nation finally had to face the stark and terrible reality that a sizable proportion of the children of America were addicts. It was recognized that the teen-age heroin epidemic was no longer limited to

New York, Chicago, Los Angeles and other large cities, but had become a menace in suburbia and the smaller towns as well. In *The Times* of London, March 13, 1970, Dr. Donald Louria, a New York expert, predicted that: "Within a couple of years every high school and college in the country will be inundated with heroin."

According to the same report from Washington by Victoria Britain:

> For some teachers the drug epidemic is the last straw which has demoralized them completely. . . . Many teachers are afraid of addicts and terrified of pushers. "You don't tangle with a suspected pusher—it's dangerously big business." . . . Nor can they count on parental support in facing the problem. "If you ring the parents merely on suspicion they either threaten to sue you or say they know but what can they do. . . ." One teacher reports ringing a parent who said: "I know, I do too and we relate real well when we're both high. . . ."
>
> School and police officials in New York say there may be anywhere from 5 to 100 heroin addicts in every high school in the city . . .
>
> At a recent seminar one expert forecast half the elementary school children in the country would soon be using some kind of drug. Elementary school children have been arrested as pushers too. . . .
>
> . . . Twenty per cent of pupils enrolled in the Washington schools are not in school on any given day. In some cases there is a routine reason—the child has a full-time job every evening and needs to sleep through the day once a week—but many teachers blame the drug problem for non-attendance either because a child is too "high" to make the journey or because he must, as one teacher dryly put it, "pursue other professions" to support a habit which may cost him anything from $20 to $70 a day . . .
>
> In a staggering survey (accurate because it was done by urine analysis rather than interview) it was found that 45 per cent of jail inmates in Washington are heroin addicts; their

average age is 19; their average length of addiction is eight years.

In an article from New York, in *The Observer* of February 15, 1970 it was reported that experts estimated that in New York alone there were at least 25 thousand youngsters on heroin and that by the summer of 1970 the figure will have reached 100 thousand. The city can only provide funds for the treatment of about 100 addicts. One of New York's few centers treating child addicts had to turn away a nine-year-old boy "runner" who had developed a heroin addiction which was costing him $24 a day. One center wanted to take the boy but could not do so because it was illegal to take a child that age. The authorities put him in a children's shelter. He was released after two months, immediately returned to his heroin habit, and after another two months he was dead. At least one child a day is dying in New York City through an overdose of heroin.

Ironically, one of the causes of the massive increase in heroin addiction in the United States was a short-lived attempt by President Nixon to stop marijuana from being brought across the border from Mexico. The Administration reckoned that a scarcity of the drug would virtually stop its use in the schools. Mr. Nixon underestimated the commercial ingenuity of the pushers, for the diminishing supplies of marijuana opened up the market for heroin. The pushers temporarily reduced the price of heroin and made it widely available among young people until they were properly hooked. Capitalism even in this unlovely field lives true to itself.

* *

Such is the face of America.

These, however inadequately we have outlined them, are some of the forces that mold lives, shape minds and determine the quality of life in the country where capitalism has reached its most extreme development.* Many people elsewhere believe that their countries are drifting in the same direction—what is occurring in America, they think, is an intimation of what is in store for them too. And with local variations, they are probably right.

It is clear to anyone who visits the United States today that the Americans are an unhappy people. There you will find a frenetic energy, a restless pursuit after fun and distraction, a spontaneous generosity to strangers, a touching readiness to concede that things are going dreadfully wrong but somehow will be righted, that conceals much of their deeper doubts about the future of their country. As Baran and Sweezy wrote in their study of the American economy:

> Disorientation, apathy, and often despair, besetting Americans in all walks of life, have assumed in our time the dimensions of a profound crisis. . . . A heavy sense of aimlessness, emptiness, and futility of national and individual life permeates the country's entire moral and intellectual climate, finding its gloomy expression in the appointment of high level committees entrusted with the discovery and specification of "national goals" . . . The malaise is depriving work of meaning and purpose; turning leisure into joyless, debilitating laziness; fatally impairing the educational system and the conditions for the healthy growth of the young . . .[36]

The central faith, the prevailing ideology of capitalism is the sanctity of private property and the right of the individual to do with his property as he wills. And this central faith is based on the assumption that self interest and self asser-

---

* Some writers have suggested that the desecration of the land and the social degradation we have described are the inescapable consequences of industrialization, of technological advance, and should not be ascribed to the capitalist system as such. We need only compare what is going on in some non-capitalist countries to see that this is false. For example the vast re-forestation in China where literally thousands of millions of trees have been planted since the revolution; the immense soil conservation programs in China, North Vietnam, and Cuba; the provision, in these countries, of free medical services for all; the rigorous control of drugs; the low level of crime and so on. Nor have even the most bitter enemies of these countries ever charged their leaders with corruption.

tion, within the broadest legal limits, will ultimately result in a beneficent social order.

We have attempted in this chapter to test this ideology against results in a country where capitalism has had exceptionally favorable opportunities to show the quality of life it can provide its people. I believe that even if the greatest possible allowances are made for human frailties, it has failed the test. Capitalism has failed to provide the foundations of a society capable of promoting the unity, the health and the happy development of its citizens. Capitalism stands condemned by the very nature of society in the country that most loudly extolls its virtues.

NOTES

1. Dr. Hugh H. Bennett, Chief of the U.S. Soil Conservation Service, in testimony before a Congressional Committee in 1939; quoted in an article by "Cassandra," *Monthly Review*, March 1962.
2. *Ibid.*
3. I have drawn on the article in the *Monthly Review* mentioned in 1 above for many of the facts in this passage.
4. An address by Dr. Jerome D. Frank, "Galloping Technology, a New Social Disease," quoted by Dr. Robert Hutchins in the *San Francisco Sunday Examiner and Chronicle*, 18 September 1966.
5. These estimates were compiled by Alexander L. Crosby, "The Price of Utopia," *Monthly Review*, May 1968. I have here quoted only a few of Mr. Crosby's many interesting estimates and conclusions.
6. *Time*, 10 May 1968.
7. Jerome Davis, "American Self-Appraisal," *Minority of One*, April 1968. Dr. Davis is the author of 21 volumes on international, economic and social subjects. He held professorships at the universities of Harvard, Wisconsin and Yale and was a one-time president of the American Federation of Teachers.
8. From a paper presented to a meeting of the American Academy of Pediatrics in San Francisco, in April, 1967, by Dr. Julius Richmond, Chairman of the Department of Pediatrics and Dean

of the State University of New York Upstate Medical Center College of Medicine.

9. Max Lerner, *America as a Civilization* (New York: Simon & Schuster, 1957), p. 384.

10. For a far more detailed account of the Thomas case I refer readers to Alvah Bessie, *Inquisition in Eden* (New York: Macmillan Co., 1965).

11. *The New York Times,* 13 January 1969.

12. *The International Herald Tribune,* 25–26 January 1969.

13. *U.S. News & World Report,* 21 August 1967.

14. *Associated Press,* 11 September 1968.

15. Henry Brandon, "Living Round the Crime-clock," a report from Washington, D.C. *The Sunday Times,* 26 January 1969.

16. *International Herald Tribune,* 2 January 1970.

17. *Washington Post,* 13 October 1968.

18. *I. F. Stone's Weekly,* 21 October 1968.

19. Colin Cross, "Enter the new Nixon," *The Observer,* 25 January 1970.

20. *International Herald Tribune,* 10 February 1969.

21. Henry Brandon, *The Sunday Times,* 26 January 1969.

22. Alan Brien, "New York Nightmare," *Sunday Times Weekly Review,* 6 April 1969.

23. Charles Foley and William Scobie, "The Road to Death Valley," *Observer Review,* 7 December 1969.

24. *The Minority of One,* April 1968. Quoted from an *Associated Press* dispatch from Washington, 15 February 1968.

25. *I. F. Stone's Weekly,* 7 April 1969. Quoted from Robert Walters in the *Washington Star,* 24 March 1969.

26. Edward J. Logue, "Urban Ruins—Or Urban Removal," *The New York Times Magazine,* 9 November 1958. Quoted in extracts from the book *Monopoly Capital* by Paul A. Baran and Paul M. Sweezy in *Monthly Review,* July–August 1962.

27. Cambridge Civic Association, *Civic Bulletin,* November 1958. Quoted by Baran and Sweezy, *Monthly Review,* July–August 1962.

28. Edward Highbee, *The Squeeze: Cities without Space* (New York), p. 83. Quoted by Baran and Sweezy, *Monthly Review,* July–August 1962.

29. *Report of the National Advisory Commission on Civil Disorders* (New York: Bantam Books), p. 218.

30. M. S. Arnoni, "Spaghetti and the American Civilization," *Minority of One,* March 1968.

31. Report of National Advisory Commission on Civil Disorders, p. 203.
32. Ibid., p. 204.
33. *International Herald Tribune,* 29 July 1968.
34. Ronald Segal, "America's Receding Future" (London: Weidenfeld and Nicolson, 1968), p. 53.
35. Report from Chicago by Colin McGlashan, *The Observer,* 20 April 1969.
36. Paul A. Baran and Paul M. Sweezy, *Monopoly Capital,* quoted from extracts printed in the *Monthly Review,* July–August 1962, p. 167.

SECTION ONE

How It Began

I

"God Save the King"

It was formerly the custom in British schools, even during my own childhood, to hang a large map of the world on the wall of each classroom. The dominant color was red, for this was before the Russian Revolution, and red had not yet been appropriated by the Communists. India, Canada, Australia, New Zealand, huge areas of the African continent running from Cairo to the Cape of Good Hope, Samoa, Burma, Malaya, Hong Kong, the West Indies, Ceylon—all colored red. And scattered across every ocean hundreds of islands and small outposts, obscure harbors and refuelling stations— also red. Here on these maps, for the edification of British youth, was spread the British Empire in all its majesty. One-quarter of the land surface of the world, one-fifth of the human population intimately linked with or controlled by our own tiny island. It made us feel very superior.

We took for granted that this vast medley of people, of every possible creed and color, were under us because they wanted to be. Who better could they be under? We British were just; our rule was benign. The young men we sent out to administer the empire were hardworking, they lived on a pittance, had enormous self-reliance and were incorruptible.

Were we not demonstrating to these backward peoples what good government was? Were we not leading them towards the infinite consolations of Christian civilization? Were we not teaching them, with the patience of a father toward his children, that it was part of God's plan that young men wear trousers and that the breasts of young women be covered? In our generosity we were even providing them with schools where they could learn English and could broaden their minds by reciting Shakespeare.* We built hospitals and clinics to improve their health, and agricultural colleges where they could learn how to grow their crops better. No wonder they respected us. It gave us a curious thrill, as we looked on those maps, to think that all these people scattered around the world saluted our flag and sang "God Save the King"—*our* king.

What was more, this admirable state of affairs was clearly destined to continue indefinitely because we British were more clever and more humane than the Romans and Spaniards and the others who had tried to run an empire and had made a mess of it. Besides, we were the richest people in the world, our fleet was by far the most powerful and so our empire would go on and on forever, Amen.

That, in all its fraudulent innocence, was the vision of the world entertained by our young minds and most of the British people not so many years ago.

No one of course mentioned such words as exploitation, expropriation or forced labor. No one told us that the

---

* Writing in the *New Statesman* (April 4, 1969), Sir Jock Campell gives a marvelous example of the non-education that was provided, until quite recently, in the British colonies. "I was shown over a high school in British Guiana a year or two before it became independent Guyana. The English Literature class were reading an erotic short story in Cornish dialect; for Geography the children were studying the [English] Lake District; for Agriculture, the dust bowl of the American Middle West. They were doing sums in pounds, shillings and pence (when the 'colony' used dollars and cents). And the girls' domestic economy form room was bedecked with . . . posters showing how to buy, cook, serve, and carve beef: most of the class were Hindus."

schools "we" provided were paid for by the people we ruled; that the "medical services" on which we prided ourselves often provided only one doctor for 10 thousand or more people (and in one case, Nigeria, only one for 34 thousand people); and that the increased profits resulting from improved agricultural methods benefited the plantation owner and not those who labored for him. No one told us about the conditions of work in the African diamond mines or in the cotton fields of India. No one talked about relative infant mortality rates or expectancy of life. We heard a lot about the *cost* of running the empire, and the enormous effort it took (the "white man's burden" we called it). But we never heard a word about the millions of pounds sterling (far, far more than the visible budgetry costs) that flowed back each year to British investors in the form of interest and profit; or the millions made by the bankers who financed it all, and by the insurance and shipping companies; or of the salaries and pensions paid out to Britishers from the colonial funds. No one explained to us that much of the cost of the empire was borne by the colonial people themselves. Nor that the costs that were paid for were paid by the British people as a whole through taxation, while the *benefits,* the fabulous financial benefits, were being reaped by a relatively small handful of individuals.

People who run empires have to be disingenuous, and they must not ask themselves too many questions. They need to have at their command a rhetoric of justification that will shield them from realities. They need to be serenely confident that they are doing humanity good.

But why bother with justifications when none were needed? Words and ideas only get in the way, and can be disturbing. There, on the map, was something more real than words. The British Empire—solid and permanent as Gibraltar.

* *

Those maps, of course, no longer hang in British classrooms. The old methods of empire have changed. Such control as the British ruling class still retains is more indirect, less visible. A new empire, the American Empire, has replaced the British Empire as the leading imperialist power. Exercising its power in a structurally different way, but nevertheless seeking the same ends and often with the same means, it is the American Empire which today bestrides the world. Though militarily and industrially vastly more powerful than the British Empire ever was, the new Empire is subject to greater challenge and greater uncertainty and is much less likely to last as long.

Before we examine the factors which allowed the United States to wrest the position of world supremacy from Britain, it may be useful to go back yet further and remind ourselves how it came about that a very few individuals were able to subject so many others to their will and live off their labor. For at this point we touch the very origin of empire.

History, they tell us, doesn't repeat itself. Perhaps not, but the study of history can help us to understand today more clearly.

2

"The Rise and Fall"

Empires domination of one power over another—have been a feature throughout recorded history.

China, Egypt, Greece, Rome—all exercised control over peoples outside their own formal borders. These empires of antiquity were primarily concerned with tribute or the plunder of wealth. It was for treasure that Spain sent her galleons and armed caballeros to Mexico and South America; it was plunder that made Spain the richest country in the world in the sixteenth century.

The emphasis then was on the looting of gold and silver. Our concern in this book is not with the empires of long ago but of today. A central characteristic of modern imperialism is its emphasis on a different kind of plunder— the pillage of other countries' wealth through *unequal trade* and through *investment* which draws out far more wealth than it puts in.

The people of Britain (or more precisely, a relatively small controlling group within Britain) were the first to apply these new methods of plunder on a truly global scale. They became, before long, the real professionals of empire building. The system they developed, in its magnitude, diversity and in the complexity of its operations, dwarfed all previous empires. Never before had so many people—one-quarter of the entire human race—been subjugated and put to work for the enrichment of so few.

What were the conditions that made it possible for the British to develop such a wondrously profitable system? Of course, innumerable factors contributed to the success, but we can isolate four closely related conditions that were of basic importance:

1. The new technology of the industrial revolution.
2. The availability of an abundant supply of cheap labor.
3. The accumulation of capital.
4. The development of foreign markets.

The New Technology

As the new steam-powered factories increased their production capacity, the nations of Europe soon realized that commodities could be produced faster than they could be sold in the home market. This does not mean that there was a "surplus" productive capacity in any real sense. The workers themselves needed the goods, but their wages were so low that they did not have the money with which to buy. At this early stage capitalism was already confronted by its own fundamental contradiction—the capacity to expand production faster than the market can absorb it.

The fundamental, built-in, inescapable contradiction of capitalism can (even at the cost of over-simplification) be briefly summarized as follows: The profit an employer makes is secured by selling goods at a price higher than they cost him to make. The total earnings of workers can never match the full value of what they produce or there would be no profit. What is paid out in wages is therefore *never* sufficient to purchase all that is produced. This basic contradiction is hidden by the complexities of the economic process, and the consequences of the inability of purchasing power to absorb all that is produced can be postponed by enhancing consumer demand by buying on credit—but this merely stimulates demand today at the expense of tomorrow. There are other methods of boosting consumer demand, by stage-engendered monetary expansion, governmental consumption for military spending and so on. Ultimately, however, the decisive market factor is consumption by individuals. As long as the total amount paid out in wages and salaries is less than the value of the goods manufactured (and in a capitalist system based on profit it *must* be less) available purchasing power will never be able to absorb the output of consumer goods.

British industry, first in the field, was technically the most advanced and the most efficiently managed. In almost every branch of technical innovation British engineers led the way. Others merely followed. Thus the British gained a clear start over other industrializing countries of Europe.

* *

Cheap Labor

Britain could not have advanced her industrialization so rapidly if, just when owners of factories needed it most, an abundant supply of cheap labor had not made itself available.

Britain had been an agricultural country, but with wool becoming Britain's chief export, the landowners found raising sheep more profitable than renting land to tenants. Thousands of peasant farmers were evicted from their cottages, uprooted, often with no warning, from the land that they and their fathers had used from time immemorial.

What caused even more widespread suffering were the Acts under which public or "common land" was enclosed. In accordance with age-old tradition all men were free to use these common lands for the grazing of sheep and goats; in the economy of the peasant farmers access to this land was an essential element without which they could not survive. Between 1760 and 1810 no fewer than 2,765 Enclosure Acts were passed. The human suffering they caused is beyond imagination.

Thus it happened that when the new factories that were springing up required labor, tens of thousands of homeless and hungry agricultural workers, with their wives and children, were forced into the cities in search of work, *any* work, under any conditions, that would keep them alive.

The emergence of a huge, property-less and impoverished working class was precisely what the new industrialists wished for. They could, and did, dictate their own conditions. The laboring people of Britain were subjected to treatment so inhuman that today we would have difficulty in believing it if the official records were not there for us to read. For wages that would barely keep them alive workers were herded into huge slums that had no sewerage, no adequate water supply, no beauty, no cultural amenities, no playgrounds. The company-built hovels in which they had to live were of such meanness that today it would be illegal to use them to house animals. In the cotton mills near Manchester the workers were required to work fourteen hours a day in a temperature of eighty-four degrees. They were not permitted to send out for water or to open a window. Penalties were exacted and deducted from their wages for the most trivial offenses. Some factory owners devised ingenious rules which insured the further reduction of their workers' already miserable wage. Thus from a Parliamentary Report we learn that one regulation posted in a factory warned that "Any spinner found dirty at his work will be fined one shilling." And in the same factory another regulation stated "Any spinner found washing himself will be fined one shilling." (A shilling, at that time, was approximately a day's wage.)

Children were cheaper to hire than adults, so children frequently became the wage earners while their parents remained unemployed. Pauper children, bought from the Guardians of the Poor, were cheaper still and were shipped in groups from London to the mining towns of South Wales and the northern cotton mills. Boys of nine were sent down the mines to work for fourteen hours a day hewing coal; and in the cotton mills of Lancashire girls of seven would work as "apprentices" from five in the morning until eight at night —a fifteen-hour work day.

Under what were known as the "Combination Laws" all forms of collective bargaining, all associations of workers to improve their position, were considered "conspiracies" punishable by imprisonment. If the workers rioted, they were fired on by troops. When, in sheer desperation, men began to wreck the machinery, Parliament passed an act making the damaging of machinery punishable by death.

In ways such as these did those with wealth and power achieve the continuation of the supply of cheap labor—the second of the 4 basic factors which made the development of the empire possible.

For those looking only at the statistics, Britain showed extraordinary advances during the industrial revolution. Production of cotton, of iron and coal and of every commodity was being multiplied tenfold. Profits were soaring. Wealth was pouring into Britain from all over the world. For the few it was a field day. Money, money, money . . . it was rolling in. Money for country mansions; money for huge London houses; money for carriages and servants and elegant clothes; money for weekend parties and tours around the Continent; money for plays and entertainment and fancy-dress balls; money for music and education and seaside holidays; money just for fun. This rich man's London might have been a million miles away from the dark cities where the great mass of the British people were existing in inconceivable degradation. In 1836, at a time of unprecedented "prosperity," thousands of people were literally starving.

This was the cost that successive generations of the British working class paid for Britain's industrial leadership, which made possible the "glories of empire."

* *

The Accumulation of Capital

The third major factor which made possible the new methods of global plunder was the accumulation of capital. This derives from the exploitation of the workers which we have just described.

Capital is the wealth produced by the workers but expropriated from them. To put it differently, the worker produces a given amount of value but he is paid not the full amount he has produced but only a part—the existential minimum necessary to guarantee his return to the same work tomorrow. The value he produced but did not receive, that value which was appropriated (stolen would be the better word) is the source of all capital. "Capital," said Marx, "is but yesterday's frozen or dead labor." This is true whether the capital is represented by money, machinery, factories, or anything else. Accumulated capital, arising from the exploitation of workers yesterday, perpetuates the enslavement of the living workers today.

But there is one question on which we must be clear if we are to understand the workings of capitalism. At what stage is wealth created? The capitalist convinces himself that it is *he* who has created wealth, capital, when he sells an article for more than it cost him. But in actual fact wealth is not created at the time when a commodity is sold but when it is produced. It is true that it is only when he sells an article and gets paid for it that the capitalist can lay his hands on the excess value—that portion that was not paid to the worker. But this value was already *contained in the product itself* before it was marketed. The real issue is not whether the accumulation of capital is "wrong"—for capital is an essential element of progress—but who owns it, who controls it, and for whose benefit it is to be used.

The relatively small group of capitalists who developed British industry had no doubts as to the answers. The capital belonged to them, would be controlled by them and would benefit them. This was, as they saw it, the natural law of things. It never occurred to them to question it.

* *

The Development of Foreign Markets

From the sixteenth century Britain had recognized the importance of the seas as her main trade highway, and had thereafter built a powerful fleet of merchant and war ships. The aim was trade, and particularly trade which exploited the profitability of cheap labor in the overseas territories. There was the slave trade, organized as a "business-like" operation, in which the British ships plied the "triangle" of trade. The ships transported slaves from Africa to America, carried tobacco and cotton from America to Bristol and Liverpool, and then returned with manufactured goods (including guns, whiskey and Bibles) to the African ports. There were also the products of the East which were handled by the East India Company—a powerful government organ in its own right.

Though the British took the lead in expanding their foreign markets, there was nevertheless a continuous bitter rivalry among the newly industrialized powers. The French, the Germans, the Belgians, the Dutch, as well as the British, were faced with the same problem (factories able to produce more goods than could be sold at home) and all were seeking the same solutions. The wars between France and Britain from 1792 to 1815 were essentially a struggle for markets and for sources of raw material which could be obtained at the least possible cost through the use of cheap labor.

The century from Britain's victory over France at Waterloo in 1815 to the start of World War I in 1914, the century during which Britain exercised to the highest degree her world-wide power and plundered the wealth of other nations most successfully, is often referred to as a peaceful period. *Pax Britannica* it is often called. It was a century of almost continuous strife. Only by the use of aggressive military force was Britain able to seize one after the other, her overseas possessions.

1814	British Guiana
1816	Gambia, Sikkim
1819	Singapore
1821	The Gold Coast
1826	Assam
1833	Falkland Islands
1839	Aden
1840	New Zealand
1841	Hong Kong
1842	Natal, Sind
1846	North Borneo
1849	The Punjab
1852	Burma
1853	Nagpur
1854	Baluchistan
1861	Nigeria
1868	Basutoland
1874	Fiji
1878	Cyprus
1882	Egypt
1884	Somaliland
1887	Zululand
1888	Southern Rhodesia, Sarawak
1890	Kenya, Zanzibar
1891	Northern Rhodesia, Nyasaland
1894	Uganda
1900	Transvaal, Orange Free State, Tonga
1906	Swaziland

The West Indies, India, Australia, Ceylon, Mauritius and part of North America were already colonized, and with the defeat of the French, Britain had assumed control over large areas of the North American continent. That was only the start. Here is the timetable of British penetration into almost every corner of the world during this century of "peace."

There were only fifteen years in that century when Britain was not engaged in some bloody military struggle. So much for Pax Britannica!

* *

The development of Britain's global system of exploitation would have been impossible if the small group with capital had not learned to pool their resources, to gather together, to concentrate, to centralize large reserves of money—the capital that was never rightfully theirs in the first place.

Because of the volume of her trade, London became the financial center of the world. Merchant bankers combined the role of both merchants and bankers. A network of credit agencies was established throughout the empire whose sole purpose was to encourage British investments and trade and to increase profits. Branches of London banks were set up in all colonial territories. It was *capital* that enabled the factories and ships to be built, credits to be extended to cover purchases, the necessary reserves to be built up for insurance. At certain moments the immediate availability of large sums of money enabled the British to jump ahead of others. When, for example, the British Government heard that financial control of the Suez Canal could be seized (it was then owned by the French) if 4 million pounds were found immediately, the Government turned to the bankers and the money was provided overnight.

Those making commodities and selling them abroad, the bankers making money by extending credit, the insurance companies, the shipping companies, the entrepreneurs were not of course engaging in their activities for the "glory of empire" or "to bring civilization to the backward people"— this was merely the rhetoric. They were out for themselves, they were out for *profit*. And they made it. The empire, this intricate, complex system which was using the cheap labor in Britain and the still cheaper labor in the colonies as a means of amassing wealth, seemed foolproof. Outwardly it gave every appearance of stability and strength. Yet, even as it grew, there were intimations that the system contained its own built-in contradictions which must sooner or later prove fatal.

But before we examine the reasons why Britain lost her position of supremacy, we must discuss the question often raised in justification of the system, of whether—in spite of the unspeakable miseries it brought to generations of the working people—the industrial revolution and the rise of British imperialism brought with it compensating advantages and a general advance in the conditions of mankind.

*   *

Bourgeois Democracy

After decades of prolonged and bitter struggle the working class in Britain did secure some political and social rights. Workers finally forced the industrialists and government to legalize trade unions; maximum working hours were set, the franchise was gradually extended; political parties began to be formed. Although the newly organized power of the workers brought some gains, the power structure remained essentially unaltered, as it is even today.

Bourgeois democracy is a form of class rule; it provides the appearance of democracy without its substance. It is an effective screen behind which class rule can continue. After a century and a half of "democracy," power and wealth still remain in the hands of a very small group within the British population. The great mass of workers are still being denied the wealth that they produce. Most of the "freedoms" that were won through their struggles are freedoms in form only and have no functional reality. (Anyone is "free" to start an independent newspaper—if he has a million pounds to do it with. Anyone is "free" to start his own business—if he has 20 thousand pounds in the bank.)* Within Britain's bourgeois democracy there still exist today grotesque and deep-seated inequalities—in educational opportunities, in wealth, in social status, in treatment before the law.

But what about the advances (such as the legalization of trade unions) won only after the most bitter struggle by the workers of Britain, the United States and other industrially advanced capitalist countries? These advances—and they *were* advances— must be seen for what they really are. It is one of the hideous ironies of capitalism that gains achieved by one section of the working class are paid for by another section. Capitalists, finding that the higher wages they were forced to give the workers at home to avoid revolt reduced their profits, went abroad and there, with total ruthlessness, systematically stole the land and destroyed the primitive self-sufficiency of colonial peoples, driving them (much as was done in the enclosure movement in England) into the arms of the "free labor" market. From there they could be recruited for work in the mines and the plantations at wages that barely kept them alive. In other words, the amelioration of the sufferings of the workers at home led to the increase of the sufferings of the workers in the colonies. Such is the relentless mathematics of imperialism.

Viewed within the context of a single country the British working people did, as in the United States, improve their conditions through their struggles. But if one takes not a regional view but considers the working class as a whole—

* Henry J. Kaiser once remarked somewhat ruefully, "It cost me $34 million to find out that I was too poor to get into the automobile manufacturing business."

the hundreds of millions in the poorer countries the surplus value of whose labor works its way through the world-wide apparatus of imperialism—one must see that the so-called "bourgeois democracy" has brought no improvement, no amelioration of conditions, but rather an *increase* of repression.

The Fate of the Parasite

Capital has no loyalty but to itself. It follows its own built-in rules. It will at times for tactical reasons appear to give some consideration to other factors than its own immediate purposes, but in the end it will seek its own advantage regardless of more general social consequences. Capitalists were not concerned with the appalling conditions they imposed on the working people of Britain as long as they were able to extract from them high profits; nor with the slavery, or near-slavery, they imposed on the people overseas. As the wealthier class accumulated capital, they found lending their capital abroad or investing it in overseas enterprises to be more profitable than investing in Britain herself. Especially toward the end of the century the *export of capital* (which is characteristic of imperialism) became as important to the British economy as the export of British goods.

On the eve of World War I, Britain's foreign investment represented one-quarter of Britain's total national assets. One-half of Britain's annual savings were being placed abroad. This exported capital brought in huge annual revenues in the form of interest and profits, but it also brought consequences which were detrimental to the economy as a whole. Britain in this sense had become a parasite, drawing its nourishment from the toil of millions overseas. Capital that should have been invested to keep factories in Britain up-to-date went abroad where the returns were greater. Inevitably Britain's industrial plant began to suffer and her manufacturers were less and less able to produce goods in competition with other countries.

By 1870 Britain's industrial monopoly was lost. Germany and the United States, especially, were not ready to see Britain's position of supremacy continue unchallenged. Rising later on the industrial scene, they could take advantage of more advanced technology, more modern factories, and little by little these countries began to out-produce and undersell Britain. Britain was saddled with old machinery and cheap labor scattered in distant colonies, while a growing imperialist rival, the United States, used "free" wage labor and slavery (a "colony" much more conveniently placed within her own territory) to amass sufficient capital eventually to render British factories obsolete.

On the eve of World War I Britain was still very powerful. The empire at that time consisted of fifty-five countries, 12 million square miles of territory, over 400 million people. The British navy was the most powerful in the world, and British merchant ships represented 50 per cent of the world's tonnage. The pound was the currency against which all other currencies were measured. But both the United States and Germany had out-stripped British industrial production, and Germany was challenging Britain's naval supremacy on the high seas.

In Germany Britain saw still another threat.

For several centuries Britain had realized that she would become vulnerable if ever Europe was unified under a single power. Britain had already fought three major continental wars to prevent such unification. She had fought Philip of Spain, Louis of France and Napoleon. Now, in 1914, she felt herself threatened again. Not only was Germany encroaching on Britain's commercial position overseas, but, with plans for a huge expansion of naval forces, her supremacy on the seas. Added to these fears was the possibility that if Germany were victorious in another war she might gain power over all of continental Europe.

Britain had no choice. Though in an already weakened position, Britain and her empire had to turn to meet this challenge in the first of two prolonged, destructive, costly and bloody wars. Britain was on the winning side of both, but they brought to an end her position of world supremacy.*

* *

Every empire at the height of its success has appeared indestructible and permanent. With such wealth and massive power at its disposal, such sophistication and administrative experience in its leadership, why should it ever be eclipsed? Yet within every empire there are built-in antagonisms which make its eventual decline inevitable. Today the world supremacy of the United States appears as unassailable as did that of Britain at the height of her imperial might. But America's present power and wealth cannot in any conceivable way prevent her economy from declining. For this very power and wealth, as we shall see later in this book, require the continued economic enslavement of other peoples and these peoples (and not only in the poor countries) are no longer prepared to submit.

All empires rise and fall, and the American empire will be no exception. As the decline of Britain shows us, when empires begin to crumble they may crumble fast.

---

* Just how quickly Britain's military power was supplanted can be seen by the decline of her naval forces. Until after World War I the British navy was supreme; by 1922, under the Washington Treaty, she "granted" equality of naval strength to the United States. For a short period in 1947 the British navy was down to a total active strength of one cruiser and four destroyers.

3

America's Fatal Legacy

> For this is a beautiful world, this is a wonderful America, which the founding fathers dreamed until their sons drowned it in the blood of slavery and devoured it in greed. Our children must rebuild it. Let then the dreams of the dead rebuke the blind who think that what is, will be forever and teach them that what is worth living for must live again, and that which merited death must stay dead.
>
> W. E. B. Du Bois

Across the Atlantic a new nation had emerged. Thirteen years before the French Revolution the American colonies had broken their colonial ties and had enunciated what was up till then the most revolutionary doctrine in history. The United States was the first nation to be founded openly on the right of rebellion, the right of revolution; on the proposition that a people may legitimately abolish their existing government, if necessary by force, and institute a new one. The principles propounded by the American colonists were at the time (and still are) explosive: all men are created equal; all men have a right to life, liberty and happiness; the purpose of government is to guard these rights; the people are sovereign—government is the peoples' servant and not their master. Other principles were adopted that must have struck the ruling classes of Europe as terrifyingly subversive. No aristocracy; no established church; freedom of speech; freedom to criticize the rulers; education for everyone; a society without class distinctions. The new Americans believed that men could remake their society and, more important, that a re-made society would remake men.

This was the new revolutionary message to the old world. It was not a socialist, but a bourgeois-democratic ideal, but as such it was an historic milestone. It represented the most advanced, the most humane, the most optimistic thinking of that time. Other countries since then, as they have "freed" themselves from colonial rule, have taken the principles expounded by the eighteenth-century Americans as the basis on which their new societies were to be formed. (Even Ho Chi Minh's 1945 Declaration of Vietnam Independence refers to and is based on the Declaration written in America 169 years before.)

To the hungry and oppressed masses of Europe—many of them living in the most terrible conditions of poverty and ruthlessly exploited by the new industrialists—America then represented the land of hope. Millions came across the Atlantic to start their lives anew. The words on the Statue of Liberty in New York Harbor expressed the promise that the new world held out to Europe:

. . . give me your tired, your poor, your huddled masses yearning to breathe free—the wretched refuse of your teeming shore—send these, the homeless, tempest-tossed, to me.

They came. Not the rich, but the very poorest, the most destitute. Many arrived owning nothing but the tattered clothes they wore on their backs.

The treatment they received on their arrival was often

brutal. They were cheated and exploited; they were herded into the most frightful slums, and could find work only in sweatshops where they were paid a pittance. They suffered agonies of homesickness for their homeland and for families left behind; they comforted themselves by living close to others from the same country, singing the old songs, speaking the old language. *But they did not go back.* Dreadful though their conditions in America were, they were still better than those they had known in Europe.

The American dream for many seemed real enough. Men like Jefferson, Paine, Whitman, Emerson took it seriously—they were not cynical men. They did not realize that from the start, at the very heart of the American vision, there was already a fatal flaw: a society built on the principle of human equality could not at the same time be a slave society, and that is what the United States had already become; nor could it condone the ruthless massacre of the indigenous Indian peoples; nor is human equality possible while the means of production remain in private hands. This contradiction between the ideal as expressed in the rhetoric and the reality as expressed in action was to have untold consequences, and the time would come when it would tear the whole nation apart.

The social history of the United States in the nineteenth century is the story of the growing disparity between the initial impetus, the hope and the promise, and the despoilers. As the mercantile class grew more powerful, as industry expanded and the nation became more capitalist, we see repeated in the United States many of the same features that marked the industrial revolution and the growth of imperialism in Britain. What Britain did to the "natives" in her overseas colonies, the United States was doing to her internal "colonies"—the slaves, the Indians and the immigrants. In the South the economy was firmly established on slave labor supplied originally by the British slave traders who sold their human cargoes to the cotton and tobacco growers. Meanwhile the landgrabbers moved westward, exterminating the indigenous population of Indians so as to possess their lands and the gold that perhaps lay beneath the surface. Whole Indian nations were slaughtered. The extermination was deliberate—the men, the women, the children by the tens of thousands, and then by tens of thousands more. By the time the slaughter ended, of an original population of about a million, three-quarters of a million had been killed by murder or starvation.

In the expanding cities of New York, Pittsburgh, Chicago, we see repeated the same exploitation of the workers by those who had accumulated capital as occurred in London, Manchester or Sheffield. The 12- or 14-hour working day under unspeakable conditions; the same slums; the same inhuman exploitation of children. Thousands of workers died of overwork, undernourishment and tuberculosis. As in Britain every effort was made to prevent the workers from mobilizing their collective power. Unions were illegal; strikes were forbidden and when they occurred were often forcibly ended by military action. Those attempting to organize the workers were arrested and imprisoned. Even as early as 1890 the *New York Tribune* was referring to those who were attempting to improve the workers' conditions as "communist agitators"—a phrase that was to become monotonously familiar even to the present day.

Thus was the peoples' dream prostituted. The new world, like the old, became dominated by the few with wealth. With its legacy of genocide and slavery and the appalling mistreatment of those who arrived from overseas, what possible chance did the American vision ever have of becoming a reality? It was a great dream, and the nation's poets and writers put it into words that even today evoke a nostalgia for the land that might have been—if those with power had not "drowned it in the blood of slavery and devoured it in greed."

4

The Roots of American Imperialism—I.

The Free-For-All

In the nineteenth century while the British, the French and the Dutch were grabbing colonies all across the world, the United States was busy enlarging its territory on the North American continent. In the first half of the century, at the expense of the Indians, the Mexicans, the Spanish and the British, the United States expanded, from a narrow and sparsely populated area along the Eastern Seaboard, to the Pacific. She could now stake her claim as a continental power.

Industrialization in the United States at first proceeded slowly. We saw how, in the case of Britain, it was the confluence of four circumstances that made possible industrial expansion—availability of capital, a supply of cheap labor, technology and markets. British capital was ready to invest in the United States but the cheap labor was largely *slave* labor tied to the plantations in the South. The frontier to the West was open; among the free workers in America there were relatively few who would choose to work for wages rather than seek out land that was still abundantly available and be their own master.

However, by 1820 the steady influx of immigrants from Europe had begun and an increasing number of factories were established. In addition to the immigrants from Europe hundreds of thousands of Mexicans, Chinese, and Filipinos were imported to build the railroads and to work on the huge ranchlands in the Southwest.

The up-and-coming northern industrialist wanted the slaves to be set free, not necessarily because he was against slavery as such, but because he was dependent on an ever expanding pool of propertyless and unorganized labor. Cheap labor tied to the plantations in the South was no help to him; he wanted the slaves released to expand the "free," exploitable labor market. It was this clash between the northern capitalists and the southern plantation owners in regard to labor that was one of the root causes of the Civil War. Lincoln, in calling for the end of slavery, was but echoing the demands made by the northern industrialists.

With the Civil War and government orders, large-scale production became possible and industrialization expanded rapidly—more rapidly than in any other country. Tariff measures imposed during the war gave the domestic manufacturers protection against foreign competition. The demand for war supplies, iron, steel, textiles, food, energized every enterprise in the North. Profit as always was the goal, the highest possible profit, and government contracts, speculation and land grants produced very handsome profits indeed.

And, as might be expected, an array of economists were at hand to assure the new industrialists and businessmen that they were *right,* that profit was precisely what they should be interested in, for by striving for profit they would not only enrich themselves but they would benefit everyone else as well. It was a comforting philosophy. *Me first! Every-*

one out for himself! Grab what you can! And—heh presto!
—all of society will be the better for it. Governments (so
goes this doctrine) exist only to see that nothing is allowed
to interfere with this great free-for-all.

> All systems (wrote Adam Smith in *The Wealth of Nations,*
> a book which quickly became the bible of the new business-
> men) either of preference or restraint therefore being com-
> pletely taken away, the obvious and simple system of natural
> liberty establishes itself of its own accord. Every man, as long
> as he does not violate the laws of justice, is left perfectly free
> to pursue his own interest in his own way, and to bring his
> industry and capital into competition with those of any other
> man or order of men.

But what about the "laws of justice"? Don't they provide
the necessary restraint? No!—for the beauty of the scheme
is that the businessmen themselves determine what these
laws shall be. Equality? Yes, the law must of course be equal
—so it will be equally illegal for the poor man in rags and
the rich man to sleep under the bridge. Opportunity, too,
must be equal. Everyone is equally free to start his own industry—those with a million dollars and those with fifty
cents. This was the "obvious and simple system of natural
liberty" to which America was now dedicated.

The building of the railroads presented the capitalists of
the United States with their biggest opportunity to fleece the
public. Between 1860 and 1910 railway mileage increased
from 30 thousand to 242 thousand. This impressive engineering success was accomplished with prodigious waste
and unprecedented fraud. Shameless swindles, involving
tens of millions of dollars and some of the most "respected"
men in the country, were imposed upon the public. Fabulous land grants were voted to construction companies by
bribed and manipulated politicians. Scandal followed scandal yet nothing effective was done. Worthless shares were
sold to the public in non-existing companies, while the com-

panies that did exist gained huge benefits at the public expense. By 1872 the federal government had granted private construction companies 155 million acres of land—an area half as much again as the combined areas of the New England states, New York State and Pennsylvania! To the Union Pacific Railroad the Government granted a free right of way and twenty square miles of land for each mile of railway built, plus a loan of $50 million. In this way were the people of America swindled out of their own lands to enrich the wealthy and the crooked politicians. When the Union Pacific was finally completed it was saddled with interest payments on $27 million first mortgage bonds, $27 million government bonds, $10 million land grant bonds, $10 million income bonds, and if anything was left, dividend payments on $36 million of stock. The actual cost of construction was of course only a fraction of this combined indebtedness—the balance going into the pockets of the swindlers and racketeers. Capital borrowed from Britain for railways was also not repaid—one of the cases where Britain was unable to use military measures to enforce her capitalists' "rights."

We need not pursue all the ramifications and consequences of this period of unbridled "free enterprise," but the effects of it were to leave a lasting impression. The totally unprincipled activities of those who pushed themselves forward to become the "leaders of industry" during this period and who amassed for themselves enormous private wealth, set the tone for big business that has lasted to this day. Business still bitterly resists any and every public control over its activities; still fleeces the public how and when it can; still exerts enormous influence upon Congress and the Executive; and (as we shall see in later chapters) is still able to secure fabulous benefits for itself at the public expense.

Several circumstances made possible the extraordinarily rapid expansion of American industry. First, a huge home territory, virgin, undeveloped, rich in raw materials, an area (unlike the British Empire) geographically unified, providing ready at hand the basis of a mass market. Secondly, arriving relatively late on the industrial scene, United States industry could start at a more advanced technical stage, making use not only of innovations developed in Europe, but the skilled workers who had been trained there.

There was a third reason for American industrial success. While the open frontier to the West existed there was always a shortage of skilled labor and wages were relatively high. Great attention was therefore paid, even at this early stage, to the development of labor-saving methods, which enabled the United States to increase the productivity of labor and reduce production costs.

But the success of American industry was based, at bottom, on the huge pool of unpropertied and unorganized labor that became available. "Behind every great fortune," said Balzac, "there lies a crime." Behind the great fortunes that were then being built in the United States there lay a million crimes, for these fortunes were being wrung out of the inconceivable sufferings of the slaves, the dispossessed and murdered Indians, and the hideous exploitation of the immigrants. And even those who had acquired small surpluses for investment were mercilessly swindled for the benefit of the handful who wielded economic power.

> The robber barons, as the tycoons of the post-Civil War era came to be called, descended upon the investing public much as a swarm of women might descend into a bargain basement on Saturday morning. They exploited national resources, waged economic war among themselves, entered into combinations, made private capital out of the public domain and used any and every method to achieve their ends. They made agreements with railroads for rebates; they purchased newspapers and bought editors; they killed off competing and independent businesses, and employed lawyers of skill and statesmen of repute to sustain their rights and secure their privileges . . . it is not merely rhetoric to call them robber barons . . .

. . . The general facts . . . are clear: the very rich have used existing laws, they have circumvented and violated existing laws, and they have had laws created and enforced for their direct benefit.*

So important, so central in the development of American imperialism, is the role of the financiers that it is worth examining briefly how they came to achieve such a position of extraordinary dominance.

* C. Wright Mills, *The Power Elite* (Liberty Book Club edition, Oxford University Press, 1957), pp. 95, 99.

5

The Roots of American Imperialism—II.

The Bankers' Racket

Bankers live on debt. If there is no debt, there is no money and no interest.

WRIGHT PATMAN
Chairman of the Congressional
Joint Economic Committee

The history of the bankers in the United States has been a long sordid tale of the cheating of the American people.

It began during the reign of George III, when the English Government prohibited the colonies from printing, minting or issuing money. The private bankers in Britain retained for themselves this lucrative monopoly of the money-creating power and they grew rich through their control of credit in the colonies. This was one of the reasons why the American merchants were determined to break from Britain —so that they could gain the money-creating powers for themselves.

But it wasn't easy for the American merchants to break their British ties. The British bankers and merchant capitalists still controlled the goods that the colonists needed and they had the capital, the reserves, which allowed them to extend credit to colonial buyers. This gave the British traders an advantage over their competitors—they could sell their goods without demanding immediate payment from their buyers.

The War of Independence interrupted the flow of British manufactured goods, and with it the supply of credit. Americans could not all at once produce the manufactured goods that they had until then imported from Britain. When they attempted to buy these goods elsewhere they had difficulty in financing their purchases. When the Continental Congress began issuing paper money to pay for these goods ("Continental dollars" they were called) the money proved to be nearly worthless. "Not worth a Continental" became a common saying of the day. The worthlessness of this currency was doubly ensured when the British counterfeited the "Continental" and the various states refused to make them good for the payment of debts.

The American merchants, the plantation owners and the proprietors of the workshops realized that their only defense against British trade was to increase their own ability to produce. In the larger towns small factories began to manufacture a wide variety of goods. In the South, with the help of slave labor, the plantation owners produced an ever growing volume of cotton and tobacco for sale at home and overseas. Eventually, with the growing production and sale of goods and the resulting accumulation of capital, credit could be extended to purchasers and money with value could be printed. The merchant capitalists became the principal *creditors;* purchasers, operating on credit, became the *debtors*.

Despite the increasing ability to produce, the system of exploitation of man by man continued in North America. The framing of the American Constitution, the control of the Government and the regulation of social relations were the result of a struggle between the two main sections of the capitalist class—those who owned the plantations and those who were engaged in workshop production, commerce and finance. From the beginning, the latter forces held the upper hand. They were able to develop trade and extend the money economy from the farthest reaches of the frontier back to England. American merchant capitalists exploited producers at both ends of the trade transaction, buying low in America and selling high in Britain (and vice-versa); buying low from the plantation owners and selling high in the Northern cities (and vice-versa).

Merchant capital remained the principal form of capital accumulation, as banking was still in its infancy. Before the Civil War, the states of the Union followed the so-called "free" banking rule. Almost any group that wished to do so could open a bank and issue money. The various states had their own rules permitting such banking operations and the money (called notes) issued by the banks stood on the reputation of the bank itself. These banks were usually isolated and did business within a limited area. The banks were not known outside the locality where they did business and their notes were not considered as money for trading goods in other areas. As a result, these small banks could not pool their capital and combine their economic power. But this the merchant capitalists were able to do.

The Civil War, as we have seen, hastened the development of American industry. It also accelerated the accumulation and centralization of capital. To conduct the war the government needed finance, a large portion of which was provided by the Federal Debt. As a result of the war the Federal Debt increased enormously. It shot up from $64.8 million in 1860 to $2,677.9 million in 1865. It remained over $2 billion into the early eighties.

The *debt* was that of the whole American people; the *creditors* were the merchant capitalists and other financiers who had created the necessary credits or printed the paper currencies lent to the Government. The Government then used these financial credits to purchase war goods and material from the manufacturers and food from the farmers. In other words, the financiers "purchased" the Federal Debt— a bookkeeping transaction with no cash expenditures involved—and periodically obtained from the taxpayers great amounts of monies as interest on the new government debt. In 1860 interest paid by the government to the banks was $3.2 million; in 1865, $77.4 million; in 1870, $129.2 million—all this interest for "money" that the banks had created themselves!

President Lincoln was alarmed at the power of bankers to create money for profitable lending. "Money," he said, "is the creature of law, and the creation of the original issue of money should be maintained as an exclusive monopoly of the National Government." He urged the passage of the National Bank Act of 1863, which attempted to impose Federal regulations on private banks. From then on, it is true, private banks had to receive their charters from the Federal Government, but this provided in practice little control over the banking institutions. While the Federal Government printed the currency, the bankers centralized the financial power of the country in their own hands through their control of credit and the government debt. Despite Lincoln's efforts the bankers ruled the day—*and they still do*.

While the financiers were centralizing their power, the industrialists were also merging into giant trusts. During the latter part of the century the production of steel, oil, chemicals, rubber and, later, electrical equipment, was controlled by huge cartels which were in turn closely linked to and financed by the large banking houses.

By April 1913, a *Report* of the Ways and Means Committee of the United States House of Representatives enumerated some 224 consolidations of varying degrees of magnitude, the chief ones of which can be seen in the following table.

Name of Company	No. of Plants	Capital ($000's)
U.S. Steel Corp.	800	720,000
American Cotton Oil Co.	60	19,200
American Agricultural Chemical Co.	45	21,800
American Linseed Co.	30	16,800
American Tobacco Co.	180	268,000
American Sugar Refining Co.	70	67,000
Central Leather Co.	40	52,800
International Harvester Co.	30	74,400
National Fire Proofing Co.	30	6,240
National Lead Co.	15	26,880
United Box Board Co.	28	7,200
United Shoe Machinery Co.	15	18,240
United States Rubber Co.	22	67,200
General Electric Co.	30	4,320

This was only part of the story, for in addition to these centralized capital hoards there were perhaps 500 more agreements and pools between competing manufacturers and transporters.

In sum, then, the giant trusts, corporations and pools centralized capital and control, using their consolidated might against both workers and consumers.

These large, centralized monopolies caused the bankruptcy and ruin of countless smaller businessmen and farmers. In spite of continental expansion, the outlets for investment within the territory of the United States were not commensurate with the huge concentration of capital that these giant trusts now had at their disposal and so, as happened in Europe, they looked abroad for profitable investment opportunities. The famous British economist J. A. Hobson, writing in 1902, described this drive for foreign acquisition:

It was this sudden demand for foreign markets for manufacturers and for investments which was avowedly responsible for the adoption of Imperialism as a political policy and practice by the Republican Party to which the great industrial and financial chiefs belonged, and which belonged to them. The adventurous enthusiasm of President Theodore Roosevelt and his "manifest destiny" and "mission of civilization" party must not deceive us. It was Messrs. Rockefeller, Pierpont Morgan, and their associates who needed Imperialism and who fastened it upon the shoulders of the great Republic. . . . They needed Imperialism because they desired to use the public resources of their country to find employment for their capital which otherwise would be superfluous.[1]

American imperialism launched its major military expansionist policy in 1898 with the war against Spain—a small war against a weak enemy. And (for the small group who benefitted) what enormous dividends it paid! The outright takeover of the Philippines and Puerto Rico; the virtual takeover of Cuba; a sphere of influence over all of Central America; strategic domination of the Caribbean; and the opening of all South America to United States' investments—an area which, until then, had been predominantly under British and French influence.

The war against Spain was just the beginning, but with it the United States was fully launched upon her imperialist course.

Without capital accumulation and centralization, the corporations and banks in the United States would have been unable to finance either trade or foreign investments. By 1888, U.S. banks held more deposits than the banks of their major competitor nations, namely Britain and Germany. As American capital flowed abroad, U.S. private investments rose from $100 million in 1869 to $2,500 million in 1908. Industry became increasingly centralized until by the turn of the century a small number of large, interlocking monopolies were controlling an increasing share of American production.

This same process of centralization had during this period been effecting an important change in the structure of capitalism both in America and in Europe, until by the end of the nineteenth century *monopoly had become the dominant form of capitalist organization.* Marx, in his *Das Kapital,* published in the earlier years of this period, had drawn attention to capitalism's built-in tendency towards concentration, and had suggested that this would lead to the growth of giant enterprises which, by their sheer size, would dominate a whole industry and would thereby approach the status of a *monopoly,* capable of dictating the amount of production and the price at which an article was sold.

Strictly speaking a "monopoly" means the possession of the sole right to produce and sell a particular kind of article, but the word is used by economists to refer to enterprises which are so large relative to others in the same industry that they have a dominance approaching that of a true monopoly. In the development of capitalism from its earlier form (in which the "free enterprise" and competitiveness of the individual capitalist was the main characteristic, and which reached its peak in about 1865) to its modern form of imperialism, the driving force was the incessant pressure of capitalism towards concentration—concentration of labor, raw materials, machinery and power in the factory, concentration into larger and larger units of capital to finance the growing size of the productive units and all the auxiliary services which they required.

The large enterprise had an advantage over its smaller rivals for the higher the number of units manufactured the lower is the per unit fixed cost and hence the larger manufacturer could make a wider margin of profit than the smaller, and it is by profits alone that capitalism judges success.

This process of concentration of capital accelerated during the final decades of the nineteenth century, and produced modern imperialism. In his "Imperialism—Highest Stage of Capitalism," written in 1916, Lenin described the main features of imperialism as follows:

1) the concentration of production and capital has developed to such a high stage that it has created monopolies which play a decisive role in economic life;
2) the merging of bank capital with industrial capital, and the creation, on the basis of this "finance capital," of a financial oligarchy;
3) the export of capital as distinguished from the export of commodities acquires exceptional importance;
4) the formation of international monopolist capitalist combines which share the world among themselves, and
5) the territorial division of the whole world among the biggest capitalist powers is completed.

Lenin illustrated this with statistics which are of interest today because they show that, although the process of monopoly was far less advanced in Lenin's day than it is now, its main features were already present. He gave figures published in 1911 on German industry, showing that although the large enterprises numbered less than 1 per cent of the total, they employed nearly 40 per cent of the workers, and used over 75 per cent of the steam and electric power in industry. In the U.S.A. in 1904, large-scale enterprises with an output of $1 million and over comprised about 1 per cent of the total, but employed over 25 per cent of all workers and produced 38 per cent of total production. By 1909, only 5 years later, the figures had risen to over 30 per cent of workers and 44 per cent of production. Lenin continued:

> From this it can be seen that, at a certain stage of its development, concentration itself, as it were, leads right up to monopoly; for a score or so of giant enterprises can easily arrive at an agreement, while on the other hand, the hindrance to competition, the tendency towards monopoly, arises from the very dimensions of the enterprises. This transformation of competition into monopoly is one of the most important—if not the most important—phenomena of modern capitalist economy.

Lenin then draws attention to a feature of monopoly capitalism which is important for us today, for it explains why our revolution is socialist in its aim. This feature is the *socialization* of production under monopoly capitalism. Instead of production being based on the individual peasant or artisan, producing by his own efforts a single item one at a time, capitalism could now produce large numbers of a commodity by concerting the work of many employees. In the beginning the group of wage-workers assembled by the capitalist would simply be many people doing the same work. But as capitalism developed in complexity, certain skills and specializations became necessary to cope with the increasing intricacy of the productive operation. Before, if an artisan stopped work others could take his place, but with specialization of labor it became possible for workers performing a vital operation by refusing to work, to halt the functioning of an entire factory. There was now, in other words, an inter-relatedness between many people performing different functions. It is in this sense that production was becoming a process, a *social* process.

> Competition becomes transformed into monopoly. The result is immense progress in the socialization of production.

This, as Lenin describes so well, is quite different from the old free competition between manufacturers scattered and out of touch with each other. This is why he notes that

> Capitalism in its imperialist stage leads right up to the most comprehensive socialization of production; it, so to speak, drags the capitalists, against their will and consciousness, into some sort of a new social order, a transitional one from complete free competition to complete socialization. Production becomes social, but appropriation remains private. The social means of production remain the private property of a few.

Even at the time he wrote, concentration had reached the point at which it was possible to make an estimate of all sources of raw materials (for example, the iron ore deposits) of a country and even of several countries, or of the whole world. Such estimates were made, and these sources were already being captured by gigantic monopolistic combines. They made estimates of the capacity of markets which the combines "divided" up amongst themselves by agreement.

With banking, capital and industry becoming centralized in the hands of giant monopolies, the entire American economy—and the direction of American national policies—came under the sway of a very small proportion of the American population. As great corporations bought control of other companies—often the activity of those they acquired having nothing to do with that of the parent company—the power became increasingly centralized, and, because of their sheer size, they have been even further insulated from the control of Congress or the Executive.*

Marx and Lenin were right. They saw that there is an inevitable, a built-in tendency of capital and production to centralize in ever fewer and more powerful units, and with merger following merger, this concentration of power in ever fewer hands is still continuing today.

There are approximately 200 thousand industrial corporations in the United States.[2] One hundred of them, representing 1/2,000 of all these corporations, own *half* of all the manufacturing assets in the country. In 1968 1/400 of these 200 thousand corporations earned nearly 75 per cent of the total profit earned by all the 200 thousand. The *top ten* industrial corporations (representing 1/20,000 of all industrial corporations) earned more than 22 per cent of *all* the profits earned by *all* the corporations.[3]

Put another way, for every million dollars profit earned

---

* If in Marx's day governments were only the "Executive Committees" of the bourgeoisie, today they are no more than minor departments of the giant corporations. In Britain, the state power is used by the monopolies, through "nationalization" of the railways and the coal and steel industries, to keep alive, at the expense of the public, the more inefficient sections of the economy which they need.

by the other 199,990 corporations each of the *top ten* corporations earned *$5 billion*.

Such is the face of monopoly capitalism. If this isn't concentration of industrial power—what is? *

NOTES

1. J. A. Hobson, *Imperialism, a Study* (London, 1938), pp. 77–78.
2. *Fortune Magazine*, 15 July 1966.
3. *The Fortune Directory of the 500 Largest U.S. Industrial Corporations*, 15 May 1969.

* For those wishing to see in greater detail the extent of the concentration of industrial power this table may be of interest. It was compiled from figures given in *The Fortune Directory of the 500 Largest U.S. Industrial Corporations, May 15, 1969.*

Industrial Corporations	Share of all industrial profits	Average profits per Corporation	Comparison of average profits
Top 10	22.5%	$732 million	17,535 times
Next 40	17.3%	$141 million	3,370 "
Next 450	34.6%	$ 25 million	599 "
Remaining 199,500	25.6%	$41,738	1
Total 200,000	100%	$162,625	

6

The Thieves Fall Out

We have seen how, prior to 1914, Germany's productive capacity had been growing rapidly, challenging and even exceeding in some spheres that of the older colony-owning imperialisms headed by Britain. Germany had some African colonies but—at least in her own mind—she had become an anomaly—an imperialism without an empire. Germany needed more colonies—for markets, for raw materials, for access to cheap labor. And this meant war. Not because the German people were inherently aggressive or militaristic, but because the redivision of what was already fully divided meant war and so German imperialism imposed on the German people the ideology and psychology of war.

Capitalism had developed unevenly, some capitalist countries advancing more rapidly than others. The very nature of capitalist growth and its development into imperialism implied that it would be a race in which some countries would gain a lead, but in which late starters (provided they could get into the race at all) would have the advantage of youth. They could, among other things, by making use in their newer factories of the latest technological improvements, reduce their costs. They could also, in their commercial dealings, risk more and act with greater audacity, having less to lose. The prize was an empire—cheap labor, access to raw materials, markets in which the "surplus" products of the industry of the metropolitan country could be sold, areas for highly profitable investment. Wars between those who held an empire and those who aspired to one were inevitable.

Wars for colonies and markets are not merely accidental appendages of the imperialist system which, with skill, can be avoided. They do not arise because of the machinations of "evil men", or "mistakes" in diplomacy. They are an inherent, inescapable, built-in feature of imperialism. Quite literally, *imperialism means war.*

In the 1914–1918 war, Britain and its colony-possessing allies defeated the challenge of the German "upstart" imperialism, but only at great cost.

The physical devastation caused by the First World War, in comparison with the war that was to come, was light. But the human slaughter on both the Western and Eastern fronts was appalling. With senseless stubbornness the high commands on both sides hurled the very finest of their young men into the conflict often tens of thousands being killed in a single battle in a futile attempt to gain a few yards of territory. Little did these young men know for what they were being sacrificed. What did they know of the rivalries for markets and investment opportunities? They believed— as so many others in other wars—that they were fighting for great and noble causes—for King and Country, for *Das Vaterland,* to preserve "freedom." Opposing armies on all fronts were told that God was on their side. This war, these young men were told, was "the war to end war"; it was a war for "justice," for *"lebensraum";* it was a war that would "make the world safe for democracy." From all this welter of sacrifice and death the young believed, they had to believe, a new world would emerge. Little did they know! As one extraordinary young soldier serving in another front of that same war was later to write:

> We lived many lives in those swirling campaigns, never sparing ourselves any good or evil; yet when we achieved and the new world dawned, the old men came out again and took from us our victory and re-made it in the likeness of the former life they knew. Youth could win, but had not learned to keep and was pitiably weak against age. We stammered that we had worked for a new heaven and new earth and they thanked us kindly and made their peace.[1]

Germany, the upstart, wanting to elbow her way into the imperialist club, had been defeated. That was what the old men had planned. But the war solved nothing. Germany was still an imperialism without an empire. In the very treaties which ended the war the seeds of the next war were planted.

One imperialist power was destroyed before the war's end —Tsarist Russia. The October Revolution, which had been maturing for decades and was led by a great revolutionary leader and party, was able to overthrow the Russian bourgeoisie and the first socialist state was established. One imperialist power *gained* greatly from the First World War: the U.S.A. It had adopted (for itself) the sensible strategy of letting the European imperialisms fight it out among themselves until she was sure of the outcome, when she could step in to gain the greater share of the fruits of victory.

During the 1920's, the requirements of post-war reconstruction gave the capitalist system a boost. (This rebuilding after the destruction of war is part of the "advantage" capitalism gains from war.) But the imperialist governments had not yet learned the lessons, later preached by Keynes, about the necessity for these governments, as serving the interests of the bourgeoisie, to control the capitalist economies actively, by direct intervention. The vast expansion of investment and productive potential in the 1920's and the mad rush to make money the quick and easy way burst the balloon. The Wall Street crash of 1929 and the Great Depression which followed proved that the *"laissez faire"* governmental policies of Adam Smith were no longer appropriate to the new structure of imperialism. (We should not forget that the Great Depression had its value for the really wealthy, those who were able to weather the storm. It "shook out" of the economy the weaker elements and enabled the giants to absorb their assets for a song.)

Even before the 1929 crash, a development had occurred which was significant. In the mid-1920's Britain first began its chronic deficit on its balance of payments. The *trade* deficit had existed for several decades before that, but that deficit had been met by the surplus on "invisibles"—the net income from overseas investments, from shipping, insurance, and so on. But in the mid-1920's that surplus, large though it still was, was no longer sufficient to balance Britain's books. From then on, Britain's vast stock of net overseas assets began gradually but continuously to dwindle.

The 1914–1918 war had not, as we have said, in any way solved the problem of Germany, the "imperialism without an empire." An inflation which made worthless whatever money Germans had saved, the depression, huge unemployment and misery, a rigid allied demand for reparations which could not conceivably be paid, provided German imperialism with a new opportunity to mobilize the German people behind its chauvinist and demagogic slogans, to organize fascism.

Fascism is one of the many forms which imperialism takes at different times as occasion demands. It is imperialism without the social-democratic "liberal" mask which the "satisfied" colony-owning imperialisms are able to assume. Fascism involves repression. It serves the interests of monopoly capitalism which, through demagogy, acquires a mass base. Repression *and a mass base* are both essential features of fascism. Fascism is a form appropriate only to a weak "have not" imperialism, or an imperialism in deep crisis. Its chauvinist and racist slogans are designed to mobilize the people to a maximum extent behind the policies of the State, to concentrate hatreds upon a helpless minority and to divide the workers from their fellows overseas. All this with the objective of the weakening of the power of the working class, and war.

During the thirties the tensions between the colony-owning and the colony-hungry nations intensified. War between them was brewing once again. In fact World War II could be said to have begun with the Italian invasion of Abyssinia, the German and Italian-backed establishment of the Franco regime in Spain, the Japanese invasion of China in 1937, the seizure of Austria in 1938 and the Sudetenland later that year—all these were preludes to the final inter-imperialist showdown.

But there was a new powerful factor which made the situation in the 1930's altogether different from that of 1914—the existence of the Soviet Union as a powerful and consolidated socialist state. In 1914, the imperialists had had, as it were, a "clear field" in which to stage their wars against each other with no fear of interference from a hostile "stranger." After 1918 the military and political leaders of the rival groups of imperialisms were obliged to take the existence of the Soviet Union very much into account. For years after World War I the single greatest fear that obsessed successive British governments was that "bolshevism" would spread beyond the Soviet Union. The United States is not the only country that developed a paranoiac apprehension of Russia and the possible spread of socialism—there it was merely made more public.

In the thirties, as the tension between the imperialist nations mounted, the question of the Soviet Union became dominant; it was to have an overriding influence on the diplomacy to be followed before the outbreak of major hostilities and the military strategy to be pursued once the war began.

In the Depression years of the thirties the appeal of the Soviet Union became politically dangerous to the Western countries. With millions out of work in the capitalist countries and no unemployment in the Soviet Union, socialism began to seem a viable alternative to capitalism. Germany and the allies, though rival imperialisms, were united in one objective—the weakening and, hopefully, the destruction of the Soviet Union. The supreme aim of the allies was to maneuver Hitler into a war with Russia, then, with both countries weakened, they could strike at Germany and defeat her and, if Russia was sufficiently weakened, they could then march through Germany to Moscow.

(These dreams sound strangely unrealistic today. We must remember that no Western government had grasped the immense strength that lay latent in the Soviet Union. When Hitler in 1941 turned his armies eastward and attacked the Soviet Union allied strategists gave the Russians six weeks at most. Hitler was also confident that he could secure a victory before winter. His armies were not even supplied with winter clothes.)

Germany was in a tactically weaker position than the Western allies; her problem was more complex. Germany, as a "have not" imperialism, knew that her ambitions could be fulfilled only through war. She knew she *had* to fight the allies to get what she wanted, and the allies knew it too. Germany's strategy was to avoid an active war on two fronts— to defeat the weaker adversary first, and then with access to Soviet oil and Soviet grain and the danger of a two-front war eliminated, she could then turn on the West. Hitler was, rightfully, confident that the Western allies would not engage him too heavily in the West while he was fighting their common enemy. All this was clear even before the start of the war itself. The difference in posture between Germany and the Western allies arose from the fact that the allies did not *need* war, and could afford to wait. Germany needed it and was thus forced to take the initiative.

That is why, in the mid-thirties, when it became clear that Germany was bent on war, the allies reacted calmly. "Non-intervention," and "appeasement" were the policies intended to bring Hitler to move against the Soviet Union and not against the West. Across the Atlantic Washington was watching the unfolding of this drama but did nothing. Roosevelt was pursuing the waiting strategy that Wilson had followed in the First World War. Churchill, though not yet Prime Minister, had realized that the *immediate* danger to British interests lay not in the spread of communism (that could be handled later) but in the German military challenge. In speech after speech he warned his countrymen of the German danger and begged the Government (in his words) "to get some of these brutal truths into their heads. Without an effective Eastern Front, there can be no effective defense of our interests in the West, and without Russia there can be no effective Eastern Front." In other words— make sure that Russia does the fighting! This policy was expressed later with more brutal frankness by Harry S. Truman (then still a Senator): "If we see that Germany is winning we ought to help Russia, and if Russia is winning we ought to help Germany, and in that way let them kill as many as possible." [2] But Chamberlain and his advisers were, until the eleventh hour, until it was too late indeed, unable to bring themselves to make a deal with Russian communism. Stalin, who with Churchill and Roosevelt was to become one of the "big three" in the wartime alliance against Hitler, understood the Western strategy and, six months before the war began, described its aims accurately:

> The policy of non-intervention reveals an eagerness, a desire, not to hinder the aggressors in their nefarious work; not to hinder Japan, say, from embroiling herself in a war with China, or, better still, with the Soviet Union; not to hinder

Germany, say, from enmeshing herself in European affairs, from embroiling herself in a war with the Soviet Union; to allow all the belligerents to sink deeply into the mire of war, to encourage them surreptitiously in this; to allow them to weaken and exhaust one another; and then, when they have become weak enough, to appear on the scene with fresh strength, to appear, of course, 'in the interests of peace,' and to dictate conditions to the enfeebled belligerents. Cheap and easy! [3]

No words could have expressed more precisely the basic strategy of the Western powers. Had the "democratic" imperialisms wanted to be fully prepared for a massive counterattack against the fascist thrust of 1939, they would of course have organized it, together with its political justifications, in the several preceding years. If they were "weak" in 1939, it was because they had no intention of engaging the fascist armies more than was necessary.

The period of "phoney war" was the next extension of this policy of driving Hitler eastward. In 1941, Hitler could no longer avoid doing so and his armies marched into the Soviet Union. The Anglo-American plan appeared to be proceeding perfectly. Compared with the vast armies locked in bitter and bloody combat on a front of many hundreds of miles in the east, the Anglo-U.S. engagements in the West were no more than skirmishes. Even these had the long-term purpose of preparing for the possibility of an Anglo-U.S. thrust towards both Berlin and Moscow.

Meanwhile in Asia, the Japanese advance was allowed to go virtually unchecked. Again the explanation for this lies in the main strategy of non-intervention—to wait until intervention could be decisive, this time against the weakened and over-extended rival imperialism of Japan.

Then came the Battle of Stalingrad. It was the crucial turning point. Both Germany and the Soviet Union understood its meaning, that on this battle hinged not only the outcome of the war but the future of the Soviet Union. Both countries committed immense amounts of men and supplies to this long and bloody battle. Both suffered enormous losses. In early 1943 it was clear that the Red Armies were about to inflict a military defeat on the fascist armies and would drive them back through Eastern Europe to Berlin. It was only then that a real effort was made by the Anglo-Americans to mount an invasion, to engage the fascist armies in the West and prevent the Red Army from overrunning the whole of Germany.

The Second World War was, then, both a war of imperialist attack on the socialist state, as well as an inter-imperialist war. Its *main* feature, in terms of the scale of the battlefronts and of casualties, was that of imperialist attack on socialism, but that feature cannot be disentangled from the second. The more powerful allies followed a strategy that they hoped would not only defeat the Soviet Union but would at the same time solve the problem of the inter-imperialist challenge of Germany, by forcing her, the weaker, to make the attack.

The strategy did not work.

The Western allies won the inter-imperialist war against their German rival; but they lost, once and for all, their hope of eliminating the Soviet Union as a socialist state by means of war. And of the victors, U.S. imperialism once again gained more, far more, than its imperialist allies.

NOTES

1. T. E. Lawrence, *The Seven Pillars of Wisdom* (London: Jonathan Cape, 1935).
2. *New York Times,* 24 July 1941.
3. Speech before the 18th Congress of the Communist Party of the Soviet Union, March 1939.

7

The Inheritor

When the guns and the bombing of the Second World War finally fell silent, the world woke up to the fact that while the fighting was on the United States had grabbed the loot.

The people of the United States represent 5.7 per cent of the world's population. At the end of the war this small fraction of humanity had within its borders almost half of the world's wealth.

The U.S. was:

harvesting one-third of the world's wheat
picking half the world's cotton
smelting 55 per cent of the world's steel and other basic metals
pumping 70 per cent of the world's oil
using 50 per cent of the world's rubber
generating 45 per cent of the world's electrical energy
producing 60 per cent of the world's manufactured goods
in possession of 81 per cent of the world's automobiles
flying 83 per cent of the world's civilian aircraft
enjoying 45 per cent of the world's entire annual income.*

* I am greatly indebted for many of the figures and statements on this and the following three pages to a book by Gunther Stein, *The World the Dollar Built* (Dennis Dobson Ltd., 1952).

In other words, the United States, a country that came late onto the industrial scene, had in the course of a few years acquired as much wealth and productive capacity as all the other 94 per cent of mankind had acquired throughout the centuries.

What is more, she had acquired this fabulous share of man's total wealth with relatively little human loss due to war, and no physical destruction.

The two world wars that brought ruin to other countries were a windfall to the United States. Britain, Germany, France, Japan, Italy, China, the Soviet Union—all had lost millions of their finest men, their industrial plants were devastated, millions of their people had been made homeless, their national reserves were greatly depleted or altogether exhausted. In a world of unprecedented tragedy and destruction, the United States alone among the great powers stood unscathed.

The First World War cost America 130 thousand dead, the Second, 296 thousand dead. America's allies lost over 5 million lives in the First World War, and another 40 million in the second, including some 15 million civilians who had died in air-raids, land warfare or were victims of the concentration camps and gas chambers. Put in another way, the U.S. suffered only 2.6 per cent of the combined allied losses in the first war and (even excluding unnumbered Chinese losses) only 0.6 per cent of their combined losses in the second. America's allies sacrificed sixty times as large a proportion of their people in these two wars as did the United States. American losses *in these two wars together* were approximately two-thirds of her losses during the Civil War when her population was only 30 million. America's loss of life in World War II was approximately the same as the number of her citizens who are today killed by ordinary accidents in the same period of time.

The people of the United States during the Second World War never had it so good. They may have found the coffee, meat and gas rationing a little irksome, but the average American was eating about twice as much during the war as the average non-American was eating in time of peace. The average national income in terms of goods at the end of the war was 57 per cent higher than it had been in the last pre-war years. Corporation profits (after making allowance for the depreciation of the dollar) were two and one-half times higher than they were just before the war. During the war, which shattered the industrial plant of all her leading competitors, the productive capacity of American industry had almost doubled.

Britain—her main capitalist competitor—had, during World War II, incurred over $70 billion in debts; incurred a net private capital loss of over $8 billion; used up $750 million of her gold reserves; had had to sell $6 billion of her overseas investments; had lost $3.5 billion in shipping losses; and was faced with the need of rebuilding almost one-fifth of her housing.

Germany, America's second capitalist rival, was totally prostrated, bankrupt, with much of her industrial capacity destroyed. The Soviet Union, her main *non*-capitalist competitor, had lost 30 million citizens and had the most productive industrial areas of her country levelled by the fascist German invaders. President Kennedy described the destruction suffered by the Soviet Union as equivalent in America to the total destruction of everything that lay between the Atlantic and Chicago.

A myth is prevalent in America. "Ah yes," so it goes, "it is true our casualties and physical destruction were much less than those of our allies, but we *paid* for it all, didn't we?"

The facts show otherwise.

The cost of World War I to the United States was $26 billion—about one-eighth of the total allied cost. The second war cost the United States $330 billion—about one-third of the total allied cost. The second war cost the average American $2,430, very little more than it cost the poorer average British citizen, who paid $2,350 and not so much more than it cost the much poorer citizen in the Soviet Union, who paid $2,160. These figures do not include the enormous sums that fell on the British and Soviet citizens for reconstruction after the war was over.

* *

The Second World War ended a quarter of a century ago. What is the relative position of the United States today?

- The United States produces 70 per cent of the world's machinery, controls 73 per cent of the world's oil, 68 per cent of the world's electronics, 62 per cent of the world's chemicals.
- The U.S. produces almost twice as many goods as its largest industrial competitor, the Soviet Union. It produces one-third of the total production of the entire world. One truck out of three is American-made; Americans own three out of every five of the world's automobiles; half the passenger miles flown every year are flown by U.S. airlines. One-third of the world's highways are in the United States.
- America *increases* her production every two years by as much as the total annual production in Great Britain.
- The total national income of India's 400 million people is less than the annual *increase* of the national income of the U.S.
- If you take the profit earned by the ten largest non-American corporations, the total profit of these companies would be about equivalent to the profit earned by a *single* American company (General Motors).
- The United States has girdled the globe with a military network of unprecedented power; her navy in total tonnage is greater than that of all the other navies of the world combined; she has three and one-half million of her young men in the military services; her air force and striking capacity are capable of bringing total and irreparable destruction to the entire human race.

The United States has become the new world colossus, the inheritor of inconceivable wealth and power. But power for what ends? And where does the wealth go? Who controls this immense and complicated system? Is it, in fact, controllable? And is the United States using its new and extraordinary position of influence to ameliorate the poverty and injustices of the world, or are we seeing only the latest of the long line of imperialisms out only for themselves?

8

"But We Are *Not* Imperialists!"

To be called imperialist even now touches a very sensitive American nerve.

> Nobody (wrote Professor Magnus Enzensberger) is shocked any more by the ancient and indispensable four-letter words. At the same time, a new crop of words has been banished, by common consent, from polite society: words like *exploitation* and *imperialism*. They have acquired a touch of obscenity. Political scientists have taken the paraphrases and circumlocutions which sound like the neurotic euphemisms of the Victorians. Some sociologists have gone so far as to deny the very existence of a ruling class.

The traditional self-image, the picture that most Americans have of their country, is wholly opposite. The Vietnam war has somewhat disfigured that image but a surprising number of Americans still cling to the notion that their country is *the* anti-imperialist country, the nation which was *born* fighting imperialism, which (with a few lamentable lapses) has always stood for the weak against the strong.

"Show us," (they say) "just show us on a map, where this so-called American empire is!"

So, before we go further we had better make a few things clear.

Colonialism is Not the Only Form of Imperialism

There are many forms of imperialism. The *substance* of imperialism, we must repeat, is economic exploitation of other peoples buttressed by military and political domination. Colonialism is only *one method* by which such exploitation is achieved. Britain herself learned that it wasn't always necessary to set up formal colonial rule (that is, direct sovereignty) to reap the benefits.

It was often cheaper and politically less troublesome not to. There were countries in South America—never part of the British Empire—over which Britain exercised enormous influence through finance and commerce. Today the U.S. exercises this influence. Britain devised a whole series of methods for dominating nominally independent countries— she used words like "mandated territories," "trusteeships," "protectorates," and so on. These were not *colonies,* but they were certainly part of the British imperial system. China was never a formal colony, but for over a century she was in the grip of a merciless consortium of Western powers that controlled her currency, managed her customs, decided what industries she should be allowed, and how large an army she should have. What was this if not a form of joint imperialism?

Thus colonialism is but one of many methods by which an imperialist country can conduct its pillage of other nations. The imperialist countries were forced to abandon their method on account of the growing political consciousness of the people under colonial domination. The United States employs more indirect methods; the structural *form* of her imperialism is not colonialism, but imperialism it still is.

Imperialism and Its Concomitants

The basic impetus of imperialism is to make the maximum profits, to expand, to dominate. Imperialism is this but it is more than this. Imperialism of necessity involves the defense of the social order out of which it developed. Of necessity it must accept a series of assumptions about people and their relationship to each other. It involves concepts of what governments are for, and what commerce is for and what money is for. It grows out of a very specific set of class relationships and can only continue while these exist.

We have seen how at the very heart of capitalism (the "free enterprise system") there lies the assumption that it is normal, natural and right for individuals of one class to reap the wealth at the expense of those who actually produce the wealth. If it is in the very nature of things for one group of men to exploit others within their own country, then it is clearly normal, natural and right for this class to search for ways in which it can enrich itself by exploiting people abroad as well. This is a very natural progression and there is nothing mysterious about it.

Not only did the U.S. wrest from Britain her role as the world's top-dog naval and commercial power, but it inevitably assumed the same attitudes on which the British Empire was based. An empire can only be administered by a people who feel supremely certain that they are right, benevolent and just. "We make mistakes, of course," they will say, "but then, who doesn't? Our intentions are good, that's what matters. We mean well, for at heart we are a generous people. It is regrettable that it is occasionally necessary to use harsh methods—napalm, for example, and in extreme cases genocide—and that it is quite often necessary to prop up dictatorial governments of which we disapprove. We do this only to save the world from a far worse fate, from communism, which would mean the end of all human progress, all individual freedom."

Americans were made to feel that the very survival of civilization in some way depends on *them*. "The cause of all mankind," declared John F. Kennedy, "is the cause of America . . . we are responsible for the maintenance of freedom all around the world."

This sense of *rightness,* this identification of her own interests with the interests of the world, is explained and justified with all kinds of mystical talk about the nation's "destiny," that it was in some way *ordained* that the United States should become the richest and strongest in the world, and that Americans *deserve* this role because of their quite exceptional qualities. And by a process well known to psychology, their own unrecognized hostilities and aggressive desires are projected upon others. *"We* aggressive? *We* cruel? *We* exploitative?" The very notion appears ludicrous —or did until Vietnam.

It is quite extraordinary how the American self-image (described by former Under-Secretary of State George W. Ball as "our humane political heritage and aspirations") can magic history away. As the noted American historian Henry Steele Commager wrote in *The New York Times Magazine:*

> When we speak of Communist slavery, we might remember that we retained legal slavery long after other civilized nations had abandoned it . . . we appear to forget that so far we are the only nation that has used the atomic bomb in anger . . .
>
> . . . It was the West—not Communist countries—that invented imperialism and colonialism . . . We should remember that in the eyes of the 19th century world it was the United States that was pre-eminently an expansionist and aggressive nation. In the first half of the century, this new nation—with an ideology as pernicious in the eyes of legitimist governments as Communism is in our eyes—expanded from the Mississippi

to the Pacific. We bought Louisiana, forced Spain out of West Florida and maneuvered her out of East Florida. We ousted the British from the Pacific Northwest. Thus in half a century, we trebled our territory at the expense of France, Spain, Mexico and Britain. In the same period, our Presidents announced the Monroe Doctrine and the Polk Doctrine, proclaiming in effect American hegemony in the Western Hemisphere. If China today should put on a show of this kind, we might truly be alarmed. . . .[1]

Empires can be administered only by those who have convinced themselves that they are indeed a superior people, which means all empires are racist. They can be run only on the basis of military superiority and elitism, and with a professional benevolence which is only another form of violence.

And Americans never have entertained many doubts as to their role. How many of them questioned the God-given right of America to take over Hawaii, or Puerto Rico? Did they ever ask the natives about it? How many Americans had qualms when their armed forces intervened (before World War II) in the Philippines, Mexico, Cuba, Puerto Rico, Nicaragua, Panama, Haiti, Colombia, Peru, the Dominican Republic, Costa Rica, Honduras, China and in about every country in the Caribbean? They suffered no qualms at all—they *cheered!* And since the war, what about U.S. military intervention in China, Guatemala, Cuba, Korea, Indonesia, Laos, Bolivia, the Congo, the Middle East, Venezuela? What about the invasion of the Dominican Republic as recently as 1965, with 23 thousand troops to suppress a nationalist rebellion of four thousand? How many Americans ever stopped to wonder what the hell their armies were doing in these places and what right they had to be there? Yes, a few. For some a twinge of shame . . .

But then came the war in Vietnam . . . and Vietnam changed everything.

This war is the turning point. From now on America's imperial future can only recede. For Vietnam represents more than a crushing military defeat at the hands of a tiny Asian country; it defines the moment when for the first time Americans began to understand the nature of their own country and the reality behind the rhetoric. With Vietnam there began to stir in the consciousness of the American people a profound and incalculable doubt.

* *

We began this chapter by saying that to be called imperialist touches a very sensitive American nerve. In spite of the stirrings of doubt brought on by the war in Vietnam—doubts which have mounted month by month—the word "imperialist" is still resented by many Americans.

But American susceptibilities were not always so sensitive. Long before the Chinese communists were around to throw this epithet in their faces, some fine, upstanding, 100 per cent Americans were using it themselves.

An early booster of American imperialism was Senator J. Beveridge of Indiana. Speaking on April 27, 1898, he said:

American factories are making more than the American people can use. American soil is producing more than they can consume. Fate has written our policy for us; the trade of the world must and shall be ours. And we shall get it as our mother, England, has told us how. We will establish trading posts throughout the world as distributing posts for American products. We will cover the ocean with our merchant marine. We will build a navy to the measure of our greatness. Great colonies, governing themselves, flying our flag and trading with us, will grow about our posts of trade. Our institutions will follow our trade on the wings of our commerce. And American law, American order, American civilization, and the American flag will plant themselves on shores hitherto bloody and benighted, by those agencies of God henceforth made beautiful and bright.

The Republican newspaper the *Argonaut* of San Francisco, in January, 1899, was a little less high-flown about the methods to be used:

> In pursuance of our imperialist plans, it would be well to hire some of the insurgent lieutenants to betray Aguinaldo and other chieftans into our clutches . . . the rack, the thumbscrew, the trial by fire, the trial by molten lead, boiling insurgents alive . . . these are some of the methods that would impress the Malay mind.

And Leo D. Welch, treasurer of Standard Oil Company (N. J.) on November 12, 1946, said:

> Our foreign policy will be more concerned with the safety and stability of our foreign investments than ever before. The proper respect for our capital abroad is just as important as respect for our political principles, and as much care and skill must be demonstrated in obtaining the one as the other.

Perhaps it needs a military man to speak in terms that we can all understand. Here is Major General Smedly D. Butler of the United States Marine Corps:

> There isn't a trick in the racketeering bag that the military gang is blind to . . .
>
> It may seem odd for me, a military man, to adopt such a comparison. Truthfulness compels me to do so. I spent thirty-three years and four months in active military service . . . And during that period I spent most of my time being a high-class muscle man for Big Business, for Wall Street and for the bankers. In short I was a racketeer, a gangster for capitalism.
>
> I suspected I was just a part of a racket at the time. Now I am sure of it. Like all members of the military profession I never had an original thought until I left the service. My mental faculties remained in suspended animation while I obeyed the orders of the higher-ups. This is typical with everyone in the military service.
>
> Thus I helped make Mexico and especially Tampico safe for American oil interests in 1914. I helped make Haiti and

Cuba a decent place for the National City Bank boys to col-
lect revenues in. I helped in the raping of half a dozen Central American republics for the benefit of Wall Street. The
record of racketeering is long. I helped purify Nicaragua for
the international banking house of Brown Brothers in 1902–
12. I brought light to the Dominican Republic for the American sugar interests in 1916. In China in 1927 I helped see to
it that the Standard Oil went its way unmolested.

During those years, I had as the boys in the back room
would say, a swell racket. I was rewarded with honors,
medals and promotion. Looking back on it, I feel I might have
given Al Capone a few hints. The best *he* could do was to
operate his racket in three city districts. I operated on three
continents.[2]

So much for the blunt words of a soldier.

For contrast, here are the words of a politician—a marvelous example of double-talk, double-think and obfuscation. Speaking on January 25, 1950, Secretary of the Navy
Francis P. Matthews had this to say about America's destiny:

To have peace we should be willing, and declare our intention, to pay any price, even the price of instituting a war, to
compel cooperation for peace . . . [this] peace-seeking policy, though it cast us in a character new to true democracy—
an initiator of a war of aggression—would earn for us a proud
and popular title—we would become *the first aggressors for
peace!*

But, it may be asked what about Vietnam? We're not
getting much out of *that!*

There are many reasons for U.S. involvement in Vietnam, and the basic ones are the retention and expansion of
U.S. power in Asia and the containment of China. But another reason, too often minimized, is the old imperialist urge
to grab what is grabbable if it is of economic advantage, and
not to let go even after the cost of holding on has become

exorbitant. President Eisenhower made his meaning clear enough when, on August 4, 1953, he justified the help that the U.S. was giving to France for the war in Vietnam:

> We are voting for the cheapest way that we can to prevent the occurrence of something that would be of a most terrible significance to the United States of America, our security, our power and ability to get certain things we need from the riches of IndoChinese territory and from Southeast Asia.

Secretary of State Dulles echoed Eisenhower's words when he spoke on March 29, 1954:

> It is rich in many raw materials such as tin, oil, rubber and iron ore . . . This area has great strategic value . . . It has major naval and air bases.

U.S. News & World Report on April 4, 1954, ran an article under the title: "Why U.S. Risks War for Indochina: It's the Key to Control of All Asia."

> One of the world's richest areas is open to the winner of Indo-China. That's behind the growing U.S. concern . . . tin, rubber, rice, key strategic raw materials are what the war is really about. The U.S. sees it as a place to hold—at any cost.

In 1965, Henry Cabot Lodge (formerly U.S. Ambassador to South Vietnam and head of the U.S. delegation at the Paris talks in 1969) spoke in Cambridge, Mass. According to the Boston *Sunday Globe* (February 28, 1965) this is what he said:

> Geographically, Vietnam stands at the hub of a vast area of the world—Southeast Asia—an area with a vast population of 249 million persons . . . He who holds or has influence in Vietnam can affect the future of the Philippines and Formosa to the East, Thailand and Burma with their huge rice surpluses to the West, and Malaysia and Indonesia with their rubber, ore and tin to the South . . . Vietnam thus does not exist in a geographical vacuum—from it large store-houses of wealth and population can be influenced and undermined.

* *

These *economic* reasons for the war in Vietnam are primarily the justifications, the pretexts, used to convince the American public of the war's necessity. The true reason, as we have already suggested, was *political*—to assure control over Asia and the containment of China. Never did the U.S. Government expect the price of this war to soar so high. But to retreat now would be to abandon the very policies which led her to engage in the war in the first place, and, far from strengthening her position in Asia, withdrawal would greatly weaken it.

United States actions in Vietnam, whether politically or economically motivated, are the actions of imperialism; and in each of the declarations we have quoted one can hear the authentic note of imperialism, the ultimate "arrogance of power."

* *

We have quoted one general. As the military play such an intimate and decisive part in implementing the policies of imperialism, we should perhaps allow another general— no other than the former Commandant of the United States Marine Corps—to have the last word. Speaking in 1966 in Los Angeles about U.S. actions in the underdeveloped countries, General David M. Shoup had this to say (the speech was printed in the Congressional Record on February 20, 1967):

> I believe that if we had and would keep our dirty, bloody, dollar-crooked fingers out of the business of these nations so full of depressed, exploited people, they will arrive at a solution of their own. That they design and want. That they fight and work for. And if unfortunately their revolution must be of the violent type because the 'haves' refused to share with the 'have-nots' by any peaceful method, at least what they get will be their own, and not the American style, which they

don't want and above all don't want crammed down their throats by Americans.

* *

It is time now to look at the compulsions that gave rise to this new world empire, to examine its structure and to see how it operates.

NOTES

1. *New York Times Magazine*, March 12, 1967.
2. From an article in *Common Sense*, November 1935.

SECTION TWO

The Anatomy of Imperialism

Imperialism is Not a "Conspiracy"

When I speak of imperialism in this book, I refer to it as a single structure, though composed of separate and often hostile national entities. From a constant repetition of "imperialism does this" or "imperialism does that," readers may get the impression that I have a conception of imperialism as some kind of conspiracy, with its leaders plotting each new reactionary move behind locked doors.

This is not the picture I have of imperialism. While there are of course discussions of detailed tactics, imperialism, like its predecessors in exploitative society, has no need of a conspiracy. The identity of the class interests of its leading elements is enough to ensure its main cohesion as a political force. The entire apparatus and structure of the society is the product of class domination. All its deepest assumptions and conditioning enable that dominant class to take its privileges and power for granted. Exploitative society has been a "going concern" for thousands of years, and its rulers constitute an organism rather than an organization.

Those of us who stand for the overthrow of this society have no such built-in unity. We *need* a "conspiracy," in the sense that we are on the offensive and must develop specific organizations of attack to achieve our aims.

I

The Built-In Imperatives

The United States at the end of the war may have been the richest and strongest country in the world, but several complex and interrelated problems demanded urgent solution if her system of "free enterprise" and imperial power were to survive. There was never any question that it was *only within this system* that America visualized her future. That there exist other ways of ordering a country's political-economic life which might more readily meet a people's human needs, was and is to most Americans unthinkable. It was never discussed. It *could* not be discussed, for to suggest alternatives was considered heretical, subversive and all but criminally unpatriotic.

To save her "free enterprise" system, America after the war was faced with five immediate imperatives:

1. There was a real danger that the United States might be left as an isolated island of capitalism in a world "gone socialist." Her capitalist system, now expanded into a global empire, could not survive as an island in a non-capitalist world. Both her capitalist allies and enemies were virtually bankrupt or on the brink of collapse. Unless help was given to them quickly, to enemies and friends alike, America

would herself face a massive economic depression and the peoples of these countries might well seek a solution in some form of socialist economy. Thus:

- *Survival Imperative No. 1:*
  To keep the existing capitalist world capitalist.

2. With the profits made during the war, huge amounts of capital were accumulating in the hands of U.S. corporations. Capital cannot remain idle and will always go to where it makes the largest profits. Thus:

- *Survival Imperative No. 2:*
  To find ways to invest surplus capital abroad where the largest profits could be made.

3. With the wartime expansion of her productive capacity (which almost doubled during World War II) and with the rapidity with which American industry reconverted its factories to civilian production, there was a growing *unused* industrial capacity. Factories and steel mills were standing idle or partly idle; men were being laid off and there was danger of large-scale unemployment. Thus:

- *Survival Imperative No. 3:*
  To find markets overseas for American goods.

4. To meet world competition it was necessary to obtain the prodigious amounts of raw materials that her industries required at the lowest possible cost. To purchase these raw materials in the open market—as other non-imperialist capitalist countries do—would not give the United States the advantage of foreign cheap labor nor the super profits that can be derived from the ownership or control of the sources of raw materials; nor would it give the U.S. the ability to deny access to these materials to competitor nations. Thus:

- *Survival Imperative No. 4:*
  To secure control over the sources of raw materials.

5. Access to the sources of raw materials and control

over them could only be made secure by having the capacity physically to control those countries that supply them. Thus:

- *Survival Imperative No. 5:*
  The establishment of a global network of unchallengeable military power.

These, then, were the immediate necessities. But on top of these there was a further, more profound fear that haunted Americans.

Britain in her days of empire was able to invest and dominate world-wide. The United States was faced with a divided world. For purposes of exploitation and investment *the socialist world was closed to her.* With the success of the communist revolution in China, one-third of the world's population had wrenched itself free and was now outside the capitalist sphere of influence. To this area—behind the KEEP OUT notices—the United States could not send her surplus capital to earn inflated profits. The socialist world, with its rapid industrial advance, would not for long need to buy U.S. commodities, and though the socialist countries would no doubt have been prepared to sell raw materials to the United States it would certainly not be at the low prices that can only come with the exploitation of "native" labor. Never before had a country been so powerful as the United States, but the world in which she could exercise this power had shrunk.

The spectre that haunted America after World War II— and haunts her still—is that it will shrink still more.

We can now examine the steps that she took to ensure the survival of her system.

2

The New Missionaries

Napoleon knew how to make use of the religious:

> The religious missions may be very useful to me in Asia, Africa and America, as I shall make them reconnoitre all the lands they visit. The sanctity of their dress will not only protect them but serve to conceal their political and commercial investigations.

Napoleon was not the only one, though he spoke more candidly than most. Spain, Belgium, Britain, the United States—all have made good use of the godly-minded. Wherever imperial penetration took place you will find that the forerunners were the religious missionaries. To China alone, the United States sent several thousand missionaries.[1] Many of them were unquestionably well-intentioned, dedicated, devout and self-sacrificing. They converted some Chinese to Christianity, though remarkably few considering their prodigious efforts. They set up schools, clinics, hospitals, food distribution centers—and most of them were totally, blindly, unaware that they were helping to make China safe for Standard Oil!

The great tidal wave of missionary effort has receded. It

is no longer the fashion to claim that Christianity has exclusive possession of the truth—even Catholics in non-Christian
countries speak with care on this point. What is more, the
deeds of the Christian nations, particularly in the past fifty
years, have hardly been such as to encourage others to em-
brace the faith. Nothing, perhaps, can so quickly erode the
credibility of Christianity as the sight of the Christian nations all praying to the same God, each asking him to help
them tear the other to bloody shreds. The words of Mark
Twain's "Prayer of War" ring bitter:

> Help us to drown the thunder of the guns with the shrieks of
> their wounded writhing in pain; help us to lay waste their
> humble homes with a hurricane of fire . . . We ask it in the
> spirit of love, of Him who is the Source of Love . . . Amen.

The apostles of Christianity are no longer as welcome as
they once were in the non-Christian areas of this world. But
another form of missionary effort has taken their place, and
a far more effective one for the purposes of contemporary
imperialism. They are the *welfare* missionaries, financed not
by missionary societies and church collections, but by all the
American taxpayers through the foreign aid program.

Most liberals of the United States, not yet ready to face
the fact that their country is running the biggest imperialist
venture in history, still believe that America's "responsibilities of power" can be exercised in a *humane* way. The late
Robert Kennedy expressed this attitude in a speech to the
Senate in May, 1966: "A revolution is coming—a revolution which will be peaceful if we are wise enough; compas-
sionate if we care enough; successful if we are fortunate
enough—but a revolution which is coming whether we will
it or not. We can affect its character, we cannot alter its
inevitability."

Liberals refuse to see themselves as supporters of imperialism. They, like the missionaries, are well-intentioned.
They believe that from the wealth of the United States, if

only it is handled well, the poor nations will reap some benefit. They fail altogether to see that it is precisely the appropriation and seizure of the labor and wealth of the poorer countries that provides the United States with *its* wealth and that keeps the poor countries poor. Liberals are against exploitation, they are against the shipment of arms to the underdeveloped countries, they deplore the fact that America buys raw materials from the poor countries cheap and sells her products to them dear. Liberals are all for foreign aid programs, for the Peace Corps, for "Food for Peace." They believe the U.S. should spend more money on academic research into the causes of poverty and should bring back for training in the United States still more educators, doctors and agricultural experts.

The United States has spread itself over the whole of the non-socialist world. There is no village so remote that you might not find there some new-style missionary from the United States. In addition to the one million armed troops stationed abroad there are today approximately two million more Americans sent out from home—teachers, technicians, scholars, businessmen, C.I.A. agents, Peace Corps volunteers and volunteers from scores of private agencies, construction engineers, doctors, entomologists, geologists, archeologists and heaven knows who else. They constitute a huge army of agents "spreading good will for the United States," doing "good to the poor," "preserving peace," and doing their bit, whether they know it or not, to keep the capitalist world intact.*

There is also a *reverse* flow—much smaller in number but very significant in function. Just as Britain (when *she* was keeping an empire together) would bring back to Eng-

---

* The length to which these efforts go is sometimes surprising. I remember on one journey to Bali—whose people are among the most artistic and musical in the world—I came across a young man from Massachusetts who had been sent to Bali under a State Department cultural program. He had never been out of the United States before. His mission? To teach the Balinese how to community sing—New England fashion!

land the sons and daughters of the colonial elites to be educated in Britain and be impressed by things British, so many thousands of carefully selected students and scholars are brought to the United States every year from overseas. Between 1961 and 1964 there were no fewer than 12,957 from Latin America alone whose travel and education was largely paid for by the U.S. Government.

Welfare liberals are every bit as well-intentioned as the religious missionaries, but they are also just as blind. What they cannot or are unwilling to understand is that this social service effort ("welfare imperialism" it has been called) does not help the poor in the underdeveloped countries, is not intended to help them, is not programed to help them. More important yet is the liberal failure to understand that just as formerly "Christianity," disseminated by altruistic missionaries, provided the opening wedge for the colonial powers, so today the U.S. through its AID programs creates the local conditions and attitudes and paves the way for economic and military penetration.

Vietnam provides an excellent example of this; for after the defeat of the French the United States at first moved in, not with its military forces, but with a vast army of social workers. As John McDermott wrote in *The Nation* (July 25, 1966):

> The Americans had influenced the choice of Diem in the first place. They gave technical and dollar support to a revamping of the entire Vietnamese educational system from elementary schools through the university and technical institute level. This included both teacher training and the rewriting of textbooks. They gave technical assistance in revising the banking and currency system and in framing the general economic and monetary policy. The United States Operations Mission (USOM—the AID Mission) undertook planning and dollar support for the reconstruction and development of the entire Vietnamese transportation and communications network—railroads, canals, highways, civil aviation, coastal transport,

radio and television, and the telephone system. They assisted in planning and executing the various agricultural programs, including crop diversification, land reclamation, land reform, agricultural extension and mass peasant regroupment (the Refugee Resettlement, Land Development, Agroville and later Strategic Hamlet Programs). Finally, they exerted extremely strong influence over the nation's two largest economic activities (exclusive of farming), military operations and the import business.

This article is a useful reminder. Across the years of bloody fighting we have all but forgotten that the U.S. intervention in Vietnam after the French were defeated and pulled out, began *ostensibly* as a *welfare* program. American liberals would support most of the projects listed in this article. What, after all, is wrong with overhauling the educational system and giving technical training? What harm could there be in making the banking system more efficient, or helping the Vietnamese to build better roads and canals? And what more effective way is there to destroy a nation's independence than by overwhelming it with a prodigious "aid" program of this kind? We now know what happened. AID disrupted (and corrupted) the urban culture of Vietnam; it Americanized the Vietnamese elite, enabled U.S. corporations to establish bridgeheads within the country and finally brought the entire South Vietnamese economy under complete U.S. control. This immense "welfare" program failed to create a unified and viable South Vietnam partly because it was never intended to (for its essential purpose was ulterior—it was planned in the interests of the United States and not the Vietnamese) and partly because it left the large mass of the people, the peasants, as poor as they were before. Between 1954 and 1961 U.S. (non-military) aid to South Vietnam amounted to $1,544 million —a prodigious sum for a small country. Though 90 per cent of the population are peasants, only 3 per cent of U.S. aid went into rural projects. The peasants, excluded from the rising consumer economy of the cities and appalled by the corruption that came with it, became increasingly hostile to the American presence and finally came into open conflict not only with the Americans but with their own Americanized urban elite.

When we hear of innocent-sounding U.S. aid programs in other parts of the world we'd better remember the Vietnam example and realize that imperialism still has its missionaries, though today they no longer wear, as they did in Napoleon's time, the "dress of sanctity."

NOTES

1. In 1875 there were 400 missionaries in China; in 1905, 2,000; by 1925 the number had risen to 8,000.

3

The Great "Foreign Aid"
Fraud

Between the end of World War II and 1968 the United States extended to other countries in the form of loans, grants, military and technical assistance etc., the prodigious sum of $115 billion.

Ask any two Americans what they think of this expenditure and you will probably find that one of them will splutter with rage at this waste of good American money given away to a bunch of "foreign bastards who are too lazy to work" to build up their own country. The other may tell you, with pride in his voice, that this is just another example of the generosity of the American people who are always ready to share their wealth to help the hungry and destitute people of the world.

Both are wrong. Quite clearly neither has understood what foreign aid is really about. It is neither a mindless give-away program, nor an act of generosity. Far from the United States being soft-headed, the foreign aid policies were shrewdly calculated. They were planned with one primary objective—*to serve American economic, political and military interests,* and to save America's "free enterprise" system for the relatively few who benefit from it.

Before we examine what the various foreign aid programs were intended to accomplish, it might be well to dispose of the carefully disseminated and widely held notion that with its foreign assistance the U.S. is playing a global lady bountiful—handing out billions of dollars worth of food, medicine, money to the needy of the world. It would be comforting if this were true.

If it *were* true, one would expect to see the major share of aid funds go to the underdeveloped countries—where, after all, more than 70 per cent of the people of the non-communist world are located. But the major share doesn't go to them. Between July, 1945 and June, 1967 the largest share, 39 per cent, went to the richer, capitalist countries; only 30 per cent went to the underdeveloped countries. The other 31 per cent went to the countries on the periphery of the communist states which the U.S. considers have special military significance—Greece, Turkey, South Vietnam, Taiwan, Thailand, etc.

Let us consider some further facts:

- President Kennedy revealed that over 80 per cent of the foreign aid program was spent on U.S. products.[1] (In other words the aid doesn't leave the U.S. at all but is paid directly to exporters, a marvelous subsidy for the U.S. corporations—paid for by the American taxpayers!)
- The Marshall Plan was the first major "foreign aid" project. Of the $50 billion in aid expenditures between the end of the Marshall Plan and 1963, 90 per cent was spent on "military" aid—either directly on military equipment ($30 billion) or on support for the budgets of those countries on the periphery of the communist countries to enable them to undertake a greater military effort than they could otherwise afford.[2]
- From mid-1949 through June, 1966 the United States Government exported (sold or gave away) $4 billion more *in armaments* than she spent on all the grants and loans and other aid programs since the middle of 1948, including the

Marshall Plan (and this doesn't include the huge private sales negotiated by armament manufacturers).[3]

- Only *"one-half of one per cent of all foreign aid funds has been spent on technical assistance in the fields of training, health, education and welfare."* [4] As U.S. aid has been distributed to about ninety countries the small proportion of aid funds used for these purposes clearly doesn't amount to more than a token gesture.

* *

Keeping the Capitalist World Intact

The Marshall Plan, proposed by the then Secretary of State George C. Marshall in the summer of 1947, was, as we have mentioned, the first large-scale program of foreign aid. Some such relief program had become urgently necessary for the United States. Europe, the United States said, was in a "state of collapse." This was not true. Europe would not have "collapsed," though it is probable that the nations of Europe would have found a socialist solution to their post-war problems. It was capitalism in Europe that was in danger. The economic situation in the United States itself was moving towards a depression. By October, 1946, the deputy director of the Office for International Trade at the Department of Commerce was warning the country that within two or three years American industry would have "pretty well supplied" the domestic demand. The only way fully to utilize the wartime-increased industrial capacity was, he said, to "plan a decided expansion in overseas business."

But where was the overseas demand to come from? With all the major capitalist countries of the world impoverished by the war they could not, unaided, provide the demand for American goods. The Great Depression of the thirties for most of us today is just an historical event of the past; twenty-five years ago it was still a vivid memory. That depression had cost the United States over $300 billion (almost as much as the entire cost of World War II), and it nearly wrecked the free enterprise system. The next depression, Leon H. Keyserling, the vice-chairman of the President's Council of Economic Advisers, warned Congress, "might cost $800 billion." [5]

"The United States," Chester Bowles told a Congressional subcommittee, "is heading for some sort of recession which can be eased by quick approval of the Marshall Plan."

"WHY U.S. OFFERS AID TO EUROPE—Loans, Gifts as one Way to Check Depression," was the headline in *United States News* on July 4, 1947. And in the same journal on February 20, 1948:

> *U.S. News,* February 20, 1948
> If world buying power is exhausted, world markets for U.S. goods would disappear. The real idea behind the program, thus, is that the United States, to prevent a depression at home, must put up the dollars that it will take to prevent a collapse abroad. The real argument for the support of the Marshall Plan is the bolstering of the American system for future years.

So the Marshall Plan was launched—$30 billion it cost in all—to save America from an $800 billion depression and to keep the capitalist countries of the world safely capitalist.

Aid as an Aid to Exports

Once launched, the Marshall Plan and all the other plans and programs that followed it—a huge, untidy, uncontrollable, incalculable medley of loans and gifts and grants— became a bonanza for the big corporations. Little did the taxpayers of America realize that when they voted for "foreign aid" (to help, as they thought, the poor and destitute!) they were providing a marvelous gravy train for a few huge corporations. No wonder that powerful business interests joined the pressure groups that insisted on the foreign aid legislation! The oil interests alone, through the Marshall Plan, were paid over $900 million of the taxpayers' money. Every big corporation scrambled for its share of the loot.

Marshall Plan aid, essentially intended to keep the postwar economies of the West Europe countries within the capitalist world, was also intended to dominate their economy. Every transaction was arranged to provide not only immediate profits, huge profits, for specific U.S. banks, finance corporations, investment trusts and industries, but to make the European nations dependent on the United States. This dependency was not only economic. By inventing the danger of attack by the Soviet Union, the United States was able to establish a permanent military presence in Europe and a dependence on U.S. military equipment under the pretext of providing "protection." As we shall see later, leaders in the United States afterwards admitted that the "danger" of Soviet attack was "largely the creation of Western imagination."

Marshall Aid provided also a glorious opportunity for dumping surplus commodities. Between 60 per cent and 80 per cent of all the United States exports of corn, peanuts, copper products, oilseeds, wheat and flour, cotton and tobacco during the first nine months of 1949 went to Marshall Aid. These commodities were not necessarily sent because Europe needed them but because American corporations had to get rid of them. Reports of Congressional inquiries held at the time indicate the tremendous pressures that were exerted by American corporations to have their products bought by the government for shipment abroad. In 1948 alone 443,109,078 pounds of dried and evaporated prunes, raisins, apricots, and other fruit, plus 10,801,424 pounds of honey were bought by the government for shipment just to Germany. But even this did not satisfy the orchard interests, whose representatives came to Washington early in 1949 and threatened to chop down 28 per cent of their trees if the Marshall Plan authorities did not buy still more of their products.[6]

Commodities sent to Europe under the Marshall Plan were not given away to the poor and needy by the governments receiving them but were sold to the public through regular trading channels. The dumping of huge quantities of surplus supplies created severe sales problems for the European governments. According to a report in the *Journal of Commerce* of New York, forty per cent of the Marshall Plan goods received in Italy during the first fifteen months of the program remained unsold at the end of that period.[7]

The United States used the immense leverage that Marshall Aid gave them to prevent European countries from selling certain items to each other. France, which had a bumper wheat harvest in 1950, was not permitted to sell more than 80 thousand tons of her wheat to Germany until Germany had imported from the United States her full quota of American wheat. A report in *The New York Times* of March 11, 1949, describes how a thousand perfectly good new tractors were rusting outside Italian factories. Why? Because the United States was financing the import of 25 thousand American tractors and was able to prevent Italy from exporting hers.

> It is not enough in Europe today (says this report) to be willing to buy tractors from producers who are willing to sell . . .
> United States tractor exporters with the help of ECA (Marshall Plan) missions are successfully persuading the French and other Western governments not to switch from United States to Italian.

This was fine for American tractor makers; but ruinous for the Italian workers; not so good, either, for the American taxpayer who financed the deal.

The Marshall Plan was just the beginning, the first thrust. For the large corporations U.S. government handouts of the taxpayers' money under the guise of "aid" turned into a life-line.

On November 18, 1964, Charles B. Baker, administrative vice president of the United States Steel Corporation, spelled out the help that foreign aid had been to the steel industry.

. . . it is largely due to the operation of our foreign aid program that the steel industry has managed to escape the full effects of the forces at work in the world market-place. We estimate that AID (Agency for International Development) procurement in the U.S. steel mill products currently accounts for some 30 per cent of the value of our steel exports, and for an even higher per cent of the tonnage shipped—perhaps as much as 40 per cent.[8]

Here are some figures which show the extent to which the taxpayers of America, through the foreign aid program, have helped to maintain the high profits of U.S. business.

U.S. Exports Financed by the Foreign Aid Program in 1965*

Fertilizer	30.4%	of total exports
Railroad transportation equipment	29.5%	" " "
Non-ferrous metals	11.5%	" " "
Iron and steel mill products	24.4%	" " "
Rubber and rubber products	9.6%	" " "
Agricultural exports, overall	30%	" " "
Wheat	68%	" " "
Dairy products	57%	" " "
Cotton	32%	" " "

* *Harvard Business Review*, January–February, 1968, p. 71.

There are further beneficial side effects that these figures do not show. For example, if the foreign aid-sponsored agricultural products were ever to be sold on the open market, the world price for these commodities would drop very significantly and reduce the prices received for the seventy per cent of the agricultural exports sold commercially. In other words, AID shipments keep up the world prices artificially, which of course benefits U.S. exporters.

The *long-term benefits* of the foreign aid program to U.S. business were clearly described by President Kennedy:

> Too little attention has been paid to the part which an early exposure to American goods, American skills, and American ways of doing things can play in forming the tastes and desires of new, emerging nations—or to the fact that, even when our aid ends, the desire and need for our products continue, and trade relations last far beyond the termination of our assistance.
>
> (*New York Times,* 18 September 1963.)

As an example of what Kennedy meant we might take the Indian railroads. Indian railroads formerly relied on British equipment. Back in the fifties the U.S. under the AID program sent American locomotives to India. Replacement orders for this equipment are still being received. In other words original equipment provided under AID results in continuing orders for the U.S. manufacturers on a commercial non-aid basis. The United States through AID has been able to penetrate markets formerly dominated by other countries. In 1938, Pakistan and India (they were one country then) imported only six per cent from the United States, the bulk of imports coming then from Britain. Today between 30 per cent and 40 per cent of the imports of these countries come from the United States. Turkey, which formerly bought only eleven per cent of its imports from the U.S., now imports 27 per cent. It was largely through the foreign aid program that these countries' import patterns were altered.

Earlier in this chapter we quoted President Kennedy as saying that over 80 per cent of the foreign "aid" funds are spent on U.S. products; in other words aid represents a subsidy for U.S. exporters. Loan contracts under aid have always stipulated that all equipment needed to complete a project must be purchased in the United States. Until recently aid funds could be used locally for labor and locally obtained materials.

In 1968 Washington added an "additionality" clause to all aid contracts that gave U.S. exporters an even better deal. This clause required that recipients of "aid" must spend the *entire amount* in the United States. That is, while this clause is in operation they must spend an amount on American goods equal to that part of the loan that they spend on local labor and materials.

But even this does not exhaust the ingenuity of the U.S. fiscal planners. A *New York Times* report of February 6, 1969, tells us that the extra goods purchased under the "additionality clause," ". . . must come from a list of United States products that are doing badly in international commerce. Generally, the reason the products are doing badly is that they are more expensive than similar Japanese or European items." The *Times* goes on to say that in the case of Bolivia, ". . . as a prerequisite for receiving a $4.5 million budget-support loan, the United States was urging the state-owned businesses here to buy American ore carts costing three times as much as a similar Belgian product and to buy American oil-well casing, costing 60 per cent more than Argentine pipe."

A final quotation from this *New York Times* report will show what this kind of "aid" implies: ". . . for the purposes of balance of payments, the United States is really getting two dollars back for every one lent—one immediately with the purchase of American goods and another when the loan is repaid."

Who, one must ask, is "aiding" whom?

"We should take pride," says former Under Secretary of State George W. Ball, "in the American businessmen who, with vigor and a spirit of adventure, are investing their capital in foreign lands." [9]

This—and Mr. Ball must know it—is sheer nonsense.

"Adventure" implies risk, but thanks to "foreign aid" the risk that the U.S. businessman is taking in investing abroad is reduced to a minimum. In negotiating the foreign aid program the United States always bears in mind the necessity of opening up private investment possibilities and normally aid is given only on condition that such private investment is protected. Furthermore, special funds have been set up under aid programs to guarantee U.S. businessmen against the loss of their capital investment, profit and interest. AID makes it almost certain that U.S. businessmen *won't lose.*

The extent to which the United States Government assists American businessmen to move into new markets (even when these markets are in countries at war) can be seen from the following report from *Nations' Business* for February, 1968:

> The American businessman moving into the Viet Nam market is protected 100 per cent by the federal government against expropriation, inconvertibility of currency and war risk. He is protected up to 75 per cent of his debt capital on extended risk, including commercial risk and 50 per cent of his equity investment . . .
>
> If he decides to make a prior survey of his business chances in Viet Nam and subsequently finds the market not worth the candle, AID pays half of his expenses. This includes costs of businessmen incurred in sending representatives abroad, their hotel, food and incidental expenses.
>
> The Rand Corporation has gone into the prospects of getting profits out of Viet Nam and says: "Many of the new industrial investment projects launched within the past five years experienced rates of return on the order of 20 to 40 per cent; a capital recovery in two or three years has not been unusual."

These are random examples of the way in which AID is used to help businessmen capture and exploit new markets with the minimum of risk. What "adventure" there is in this does not come from any financial hazard but from the excitement of seeing just how much money can be grabbed.

Aid as a Weapon for Blackmail

The billions of dollars worth of "aid," the loans, the grants, the military assistance, give the United States an unparalleled power of *coercion*. The United States is not reluctant to use this blackmail power.

- In 1963 the Argentine Government was considering cancelling her contracts with U.S. oil companies. W. Averell Harriman, on behalf of the United States Government, warned the Argentine Government that such a cancellation would "sharply impair her prospects for future American help." (*New York Times,* 11 November 1963)
- In November 1966, a dispute arose between the Algerian Government and the U.S. oil companies in that country. Two hundred thousand tons of wheat destined for relief in Algiers was held up until the negotiations were concluded to the satisfaction of the American oil companies. (*New York Times,* 15 November 1966)
- The winter of 1966 saw India in the grip of a terrible famine. Hundreds of thousands, perhaps millions, were starving. At about this time several American oil companies were negotiating to establish fertilizer plants in India. The Indian Government wished to keep the distribution and the selling of the fertilizer in its own hands. This did not at all suit the oil companies. The United States used this opportunity to "persuade India out of its socialist inefficiency," feeling that India should be "shocked out of it by superior events and pressures." While the profits of the U.S. companies might seem "inordinate to Indians" they would be small compared to the value of the know-how that the oil companies could provide. While countless Indians were starving, food shipments were ordered to be held up to force the Indian Government to capitulate to the demands of the oil companies. (From a report in the *Christian Science Monitor,* 20 December 1966)
- Bolivia is heavily dependent on its export of tin. The conditions of the tin miners have been and are appalling. After

a decade of strikes and popular uprisings—several of which were crushed by the army with extreme ferocity—the National Revolutionary Movement (MNR) and the miners in 1952 overthrew the military nationalists and in October of that year the main tin mines were nationalized. This caused great consternation in Washington. The U.S. immediately blocked exports of Bolivian tin and suspended all foreign aid. The Bolivian leaders were eventually forced by sheer economic necessity to accept the U.S. Government's terms for resuming tin exports. The Bolivian Government had also to agree to pay compensation for the expropriated mines as the price for resumed U.S. aid. The U.S. resumed aid, partly because there was no viable alternative government in sight, partly so that it could exert influence on the government. In this it was successful. Under pressure from U.S. the Bolivian Government passed a revised "mining code" highly favorable to private investments and giving more favorable economic terms for U.S. tin importers. Through using aid as a political lever the U.S. Government was able to

    (I) exercise direct control over a wide range of government functions

    (II) exert pressures which helped divide, and eventually shatter, the MNR.[10]

There is another stranglehold that the United States can apply through its aid programs that should be briefly mentioned—the control of local economies by the accumulation of local currencies.

As was already noted, most of the surplus agricultural products shipped to the underdeveloped countries by the United States under the "aid" programs are sold within each receiving country through the normal trade channels. The income from these sales *belongs to the United States Government*. Some of this local currency is used for internal purposes, to pay for American embassies and other local expenses. The rest is loaned to the government and others in the receiving country, and interest is paid on these loans.

These accumulations of local currencies held by the United States are growing all the time as sales of American aid-sponsored products continues. At the end of India's Third Five-Year Plan it was estimated that United States holdings of rupees would total 800–900 crores ($1.6–1.8 billion) or the equivalent to *one-fifth of the total Indian money supply*. This estimate, startling though it is, was too conservative. By January, 1964, more than two years before the end of the Third Five-Year Plan, U.S. holdings of Indian rupees had exceeded 1100 crores ($2.3 billion).

These huge sums of local currencies held by the United States Government in countries receiving aid are an extremely powerful lever with which the United States can exert influence over the policy decisions of these other countries.

These then, in simplified but essentially accurate form, are examples of how the U.S. uses its "aid" programs as *weapons of coercion*.

Aid and the Military

The amount of money used through the various aid programs for economic development is reduced to insignificance when compared to the prodigious amounts poured out for "military aid." As we have already noted, 90 per cent of all foreign aid expenditures between the end of the Marshall Plan and 1963 went into one form or another of "military assistance."

Military aid is used, among other things, to coerce foreign countries to grant bases on their territory for the U.S. army, navy, or air force.

For example, Spain for a long time resisted the establishment of American military bases on her soil. However, her agreement to allow American bases coincided with Export-Import loans amounting to $500 million in a ten year period.

When a new five-year agreement was arranged in September 1963, further bank loans of $100 million, nearly three-quarters of which were in the form of grants, both military and economic, were granted.[11]

We shall be referring again to the greatest threat to America's position in the underdeveloped countries—the growing resistance of the poor and exploited populations who are kept in feudal conditions of oppression by the local elites. It is in the economic interest of the American corporations who have investments in these countries to maintain this social structure. It is to keep these elites in power that the United States has, through its assistance programs, provided them with the necessary military equipment, the finance, and training. But the feudal conditions, the unequal distribution of land, the vast disparity between the great wealth of the few and the appalling poverty of the many, are creating ever growing tensions and ever louder demands for social justice. This, in turn, means that still further "military aid" must be provided for the governments who are struggling to maintain the *status quo*. The time will come, however, when the people in these countries (as they did in Cuba) will throw out the local dictators who have oppressed them and the foreign corporations that have exploited them.

It is, of course, a cardinal purpose of the American foreign aid program to postpone that day for as long as possible.

Robert S. McNamara, when Secretary of Defense, gave to a Congressional committee a remarkably candid description of what he considered the main threats to the existing regimes: the Tricontinental Congress and the efforts of Latin American communist parties to create broad popular "anti-imperialist fronts," while continuing "to penetrate student and other intellectual groups, to control organized labor, and to organize the peasants."

The need to counter these threats by appropriate means is the basis upon which the fiscal year 1968 military assistance programs for Latin American countries are predicated. More specifically, the primary objective in Latin America is to aid, where necessary, in the continental development of indigenous military and paramilitary forces capable of providing in conjunction with police and other security forces, the needed domestic security.[12]

In other words, to help in the suppression of the local population.

Mr. McNamara informed Congress that one of the most valuable aspects of the military assistance program was the training of foreign military personnel:

Probably the greatest return on our military assistance investment comes from the training of selected officers and key specialists at our military schools in the United States and overseas. These students are hand-picked by their countries to become instructors when they return home. They are the coming leaders, the men who will have the know-how and impart it to their forces. I need not dwell upon the value of having in positions of leadership men who have first-hand knowledge of how Americans do things and how they think. It is beyond price to us to make friends of such men.[13]

How "beyond price" this can be is shown by the example of Peru. The U.S. had supplied Peru, between 1945 and 1960, with $83 million of military assistance (for "hemisphere defense"). On July 19, 1962 the constitutional government of Peru was overthrown by a military *coup*. It was a U.S. Sherman tank that (at 3 A.M.) broke down the gates of the Pizarro Palace, and the officer who led the assault and arrested seventy-two-year-old President Prado was Colonel Gonzalo Briceno, a graduate of the U.S. Ranger School at Fort Benning, Georgia. The following year the U.S. military assistance program to Peru was almost doubled.

Another example, from Brazil.

On April 2, 1964, an illegal rightist *putsch* ousted the

constitutionally elected regime of Joao Goulart. Goulart was a bourgeois democrat. He was not a strong or effective leader. He attempted to institute some mild reforms and was reported to be considering nationalizing some of the U.S.-owned enterprises in Brazil. His overthrow was greeted with rejoicing in Washington. Twelve hours after the new provisional government took office, headed by an army general, President Johnson sent his "warmest wishes." The next day, Secretary of State Rusk (and with a straight face) told the American people that this totally illegal military *coup* was a "move to ensure the continuity of constitutional government."

It was left to the chairman of the House Foreign Affairs Committee to draw the conclusion (and that is why we include it here) that it was the *foreign aid* program of the United States that made this great democratic *coup* possible:

> Every critic of foreign aid is confronted with the fact that the armed forces of Brazil threw out the Goulart government and that U.S. military aid was a major factor in giving these forces an indoctrination in the principles of democracy and a pro-U.S. orientation. Many of these officers were trained in the United States under the AID program. They knew that democracy was better than communism.[14]

(What is important to understand in this instance is that there was never the remotest likelihood of a *communist* takeover in Brazil. It was not communism that was endangering the U.S. position there but the rise of bourgeois democracy. A bourgeois revolution would create social conditions that would eventually inhibit the U.S. from exercising control of the country's economy through a small organized elite. The United States will use the leverage of "aid" and whatever other coercive power it has at its disposal to prevent the emergence of a large middle class in the underdeveloped countries just as it would, and has, to suppress a socialist revolution. Both represent "threats" to United States economic interests.)

Before we leave the question of foreign military assistance there is another aspect of this that must be mentioned, namely, its effect on future U.S. *sales* of armaments to countries abroad. We find again how "aid" comes to the help of private arms manufacturers. Not only do they supply the weapons given away under the AID program, but this stimulates the subsequent demand for weapons. Mr. Eugene Black, former president of the World Bank, described what a windfall this can be for the manufacturer of military equipment:

> Over the years, a considerable portion of our [foreign aid] assistance has been in military hardware. This has naturally helped to orient national defense establishments toward American equipment, and the influence on exports has now become apparent. . . . U.S. military sales abroad amounted to less than half a billion dollars in 1960. Yet a recent official forecast predicts defense industry exports of $5.4 billion yearly by 1967. It forecasts a minimum market of $10 billion by 1971 and considers a potential market of $15 billion a reasonable expectation.[15]

The Defense Department in Washington has a special department to help manufacturers sell their armaments abroad. The sales arranged by this office between 1950 and 1967 amounted to the fantastic sum of $46.3 billion! [16] This does *not* include the sale of armaments arranged directly by the private manufacturers themselves. "Assisting" foreign countries can be a very paying proposition!

Aid as Insurance Against Revolution

We have already mentioned earlier in this chapter how military aid is being used to counter (in Mr. McNamara's words) "anti-imperialist fronts" in Latin America especially. Non-military aid is being used for this purpose also.

As an example we can look to the actions of the United States in Cuba.

The significance of the Cuban Revolution was not lost on the ruling circles in the United States. Here a small country had successfully overthrown a regime which the United States had been supporting with money, with arms and with all her moral backing.

Cuba, under Batista, was a happy hunting-ground not only for the gambling syndicates, the crooked real estate operators, the hotel owners, bar keepers, prostitutes and pimps, but for investors also.

The economic hold that the United States had over the Cuban people can be judged by these figures. Prior to the revolution the United States controlled

	80%	of Cuban	utilities
	90%	" "	mines
	90%	" "	cattle ranches
(almost)	100%	" "	oil refineries
	50%	" "	public railways
	40%	" "	sugar industry
	25%	" "	bank balances

United States firms received 40 per cent of the profits on sugar, a crop that represented 89 per cent of all Cuban exports.

None of this benefited Cuba. In 1957, total U.S. earnings on direct investments in Cuba amounted to $77 million, but these only employed a shade over 1 per cent of the Cuban population. From 1950–1960 the trade balance in favor of the United States was one billion dollars.

The loss of all these profitable undertakings was serious enough, and from the moment it became clear to American policy makers that Castro was determined to carry through a genuine social revolution, it became the set policy in Washington to overthrow his regime.

But there was another aspect of the Cuban Revolution

that concerned Kennedy and the ruling groups around him even more than the financial loss that United States commercial interests had sustained. The establishment of a *successful* socialist state in Cuba would encourage the revolutionary movements throughout Latin America. Let a Cuban-type revolution start in a large country such as Brazil and it would sweep like a prairie fire throughout Latin America. The danger of this was enough for Kennedy to go forward with the disastrous invasion plans which ended in the fiasco of the Bay of Pigs.

Kennedy knew what conditions were like in Cuba. It was Kennedy who said in a campaign speech in Cincinatti (before he became President):

> ". . . We refused to help Cuba meet its desperate need for economic progress. . . . We used the influence of our Government to advance the interests and increase the profits of the private American companies which dominated the island's economy. . . . Administration spokesmen publicly hailed Batista, hailing him as a staunch ally and a good friend at a time when Batista was murdering thousands, destroying the last vestiges of freedom and stealing hundreds of millions of dollars from the Cuban people. . . . Thus it was our own policies, not those of Castro, that first began to turn our former neighbour against us.[17]

Conditions in Cuba, Kennedy knew quite well, were no worse than in many other Latin American countries, and U.S. exploitation just as rampant. (70 per cent of Brazil's principal industries are foreign-owned and even *Time-Life* is getting into the act by buying out a major T.V. station. Cuba all over again.) Something therefore had to be done to diminish the likelihood of an eruption of a series of Cuban-type revolts throughout the continent. (Shortly before his death, Kennedy told Jean Daniel that the accumulation of United States' errors in Cuba "has put all Latin America in danger.") For almost nothing had been done in

Latin America by the U.S. except outright exploitation of her resources. During the fifteen years after World War II the U.S. had granted more aid to Franco's Spain than had been given to *all* of the Latin American countries combined. Now, thanks to Castro, the United States had to act quickly.

Thus, in March, 1961, with great fanfare, the "Alliance for Progress" was launched. "Let us transform the American continents into a vast crucible of revolutionary ideas and efforts," declared Kennedy, "an example to all the world that liberty and progress walk hand in hand."

The rhetoric was luminous. The results were nil. It is now universally agreed that the "Alliance for Progress" has been a gigantic flop.

Under this program the United States committed itself to utilize during the next ten years $10 billion in U.S. Government funds and $300 million annually in U.S. private investment capital in Latin America to finance economic growth of 2.5 per cent. In committing these funds Kennedy stressed the absolute necessity of social reforms, including land and tax reform, for "unless the great mass of Americans share in our increasing prosperity—then our alliance, our revolution and our dream will have failed."

And fail of course it did, for the program was never intended to be a revolutionary program, but a program to *prevent* revolution. Kennedy may have hoped that some sort of land and tax reform might blunt any incipient revolutionary movements. The local ruling elites would have none of it. They would rather do without the aid than relinquish their prerogatives.

Colombia ranks third in Latin America in total U.S. assistance, the vast bulk of the aid going to large commercial farmers at the expense of social progress. In 1969, the Senate Foreign Relations Committee sent experts to study Colombia as a case history in U.S. aid. Their report represents the most thorough study of its kind yet made. Here are some of its findings:

- After seven years of aid from the· "Alliance for Progress" the per capita gross national product has risen only from $276 to $296 a year.
- In this period the number of functional illiterates *went up* from 5 to more than 6 million. (In a population of under 20 million).
- Land reform has provided land titles to only about one-tenth of the half-million landless families, whose number is increasing by 10 per cent a year.
- The major emphasis, the report points out, has been the giving of aid to large commercial farmers "at the expense of social progress."
- The social structure of the country "remains essentially unchanged, with close to two-thirds of the population not participating in the economic and political decision-making process."
- In the course of the seven years the Colombian peso depreciated from 8.50 to the dollar to 16.45. (This means that any commodity bought from the United States costs a Colombian almost twice as much as formerly, and what he *sells* to the United States will bring him in only half of what he got before. The economic benefit to the United States of this devaluation of Colombian currency probably does much more than offset all the "aid" that the U.S. had granted to that country).
- U.S. aid, the report says sombrely, helped successive Colombian governments "postpone making more basic changes."

Thus the Alliance for Progress in the end did not provide any help to the mass of the Colombian people. Quite the reverse. All such "aid" programs are bound to fail in their supposed objective, for their purpose is not "aid" at all but to maintain a *status quo* which is highly profitable to the United States.

Aid—The Stranglehold of Debt

All underdeveloped countries receiving aid from imperialist countries are chronically in debt because with aid received their indebtedness continually increases. It is a giant millstone around their necks preventing economic advance. In 1956, the estimated medium- and long-term foreign public indebtedness of the underdeveloped countries was estimated to be $9.7 billion. By 1967, it was $41.5 billion.

This fourfold increase in public indebtedness of the poorer countries also means, of course, an increase in the interest payments and other charges that are required to service the debt. In 1956, the cost to the poorer countries of servicing this indebtedness was $800 million; by 1967 this had risen to $3.9 billion! *In 1966, 44 per cent of all aid flowing from the advanced to the underdeveloped countries was utilized merely to finance past and present debts.*

This is taking the underdeveloped countries as a whole. Some of them, however, are in a worse predicament, finding themselves in the fantastic position of paying out more to the United States in interest on past indebtedness than they are receiving in aid. For example, during the years 1962 to 1966, the average annual service payments on external public debt of all Latin American countries was $1,596 million. During these same years the average annual assistance from the United States in the form of both loans and grants amounted to $1,213 million. *Thus American "foreign aid" did not even cover the interest payments on past "aid"!*

Why are the underdeveloped countries unable to meet these interest charges? Why are they not able gradually to pay off their past indebtedness and free themselves from this oppressive burden?

The answer is simple—*because they cannot.*

Foreign aid must be paid off in the currency of the country that has granted the "assistance." The only way of accumulating such currency is to attain a surplus of exports over imports. Since World War II the income received by the underdeveloped areas for their exports is largely controlled by the very countries that have granted them the "aid" and which, of course, find it in their interests to keep these prices as low as possible.

This is not the only reason why the underdeveloped countries can never shed their burden of debt. Aside from the enormous interest payments to the United States government there are the still greater amounts payable abroad to U.S. corporations, to cover the huge profits that they have made on their investments. These profits must also be paid in the currency of the investing country. U.S. corporations do not want pesos or cruzeros, they want *dollars*.

So what do we find?

The burden on the underdeveloped countries represented by the cost of "aid," plus the exports necessary to pay for the profits of the foreign capitalist enterprises, represents an *economic stranglehold which prevents the underdeveloped countries from advancing*. For example, for every dollar of foreign exchange earned by Mexico by the sale of products abroad, sixty cents has to be earmarked for the servicing of her foreign debt and for interest payments and profit of foreign investors (mostly, of course, to the U.S.). This leaves Mexico with only forty cents for her own essential imports —a situation true, to a greater or lesser extent, in all underdeveloped countries. Unable to accumulate sufficient capital for their own industrial and economic development, the underdeveloped countries, though providing enormous wealth for the investing countries, are kept in a permanent state of stagnation, mass poverty and subjection.

With insufficient foreign currency to pay the interest charges, they are compelled by their Washington "benefactor" to continue *borrowing,* and go still deeper into debt. (The only organizations that are prepared to extend loans to underdeveloped countries such as the World Bank, are controlled chiefly by the U.S.A.) Increasing their total indebtedness merely tightens the economic stranglehold of the richer country. Just as a loan shark in Harlem prefers to keep his victims permanently in debt rather than have his loan repaid, so the chronic indebtedness of the underdeveloped countries unquestionably suits the United States and the lesser imperialist countries. Through *debt* their control of the poorer countries can be maintained.

* *

Summary

We are now in a position to summarize our conclusions in regard to the foreign aid policies of the United States.

- Aid: assisted the European countries to revive their economies within the capitalist framework; it kept them capitalist.
- Aid: under the pretext of providing "protection from communism," enabled the United States to establish a powerful and permanent military presence in Europe.
- Aid: deflected a depression in the United States by providing the purchasing power to other countries with which they could buy American commodities.
- Aid: provided a useful means of dumping U.S. surplus products.
- Aid: is a concealed subsidy for U.S. foreign exporting corporations, a subsidy paid by the American taxpayer.
- Aid: is a means by which the United States can exert political and economic blackmail over other countries.
- Aid: provides a means of encroaching on the interests of competitor capitalist countries and ousting them from markets that they had formerly dominated.
- Aid: helps to open up the underdeveloped countries to American investors.
- Aid: is used to force other countries to grant bases and other facilities for use by U.S. military forces.

Aid: does not help the poorer countries to become less poor, it makes them relatively poorer.

Aid: helps to keep the poor countries permanently in debt and thus perpetuates their state of backwardness.

Aid: does not lead to the growing independence of the poorer countries but makes them more dependent.

Aid: is a means of maintaining tyrannical oligarchies in positions of power and through them suppressing every movement that attempts to liberate the people from foreign and local oppression.

Aid: is a tool for economic, political and military domination of other countries.

Aid: IS A FRAUD!

NOTES

1. John F. Kennedy, April 2, 1963. In 1968 modifications were made in loan contracts which made "aid" an even better deal for U.S. corporations (see page 130).
2. Howard Rusk, a member of a special committee appointed by the President. *New York Times,* International edition, 5 April 1963.
3. *New York Times,* 19 July 1967.
4. Howard Rusk, *Ibid.*
5. For these and the following quotations I am indebted to Victor Perlo's book *"American Imperialism"* (New York: International Publishers, 1951). There is a wealth of useful material in this book—I recommend it to all who wish to make a more detailed study of American imperialism as seen in the earlier post-war years.
6. *Ibid.,* p. 151.
7. *Ibid.,* p. 152.
8. From an address quoted in the *Harvard Business Review,* January–February, 1968, p. 63, and referred to by Harry Magdoff in the *Monthly Review,* November 1968, p. 32.
9. *Life,* Atlantic Edition, 15 April 1968, p. 46.
10. A meticulously researched study, *The United States and Bolivia,* was prepared for the Haslemere Group in Britain by Laurence Whitehead, an Economic Fellow of St. Antony's College Oxford.
11. John D. Montgomery, *Foreign Aid in International Politics*

(Englewood Cliffs, N.J.: 1967), p. 16. Quoted by Harry Magdoff, *Monthly Review,* November 1968, pp. 21–22.

12. Testimony before the House of Representatives, Committee on Foreign Affairs, *Hearings on the Foreign Assistance Act of 1967,* Washington, D.C., 1967.

13. *Ibid.*

14. Congressional Record 24 May 1965.

15. "The Domestic Dividends of Foreign Aid," *Columbia Journal of World Business,* Fall 1965, p. 25.

16. *New York Times,* 19 July 1967.

17. *New York Times,* 7 October 1960.

4

The Plunder of the Poor
Nations—I.

Why Are They Poor?

Despite all the vaunted technological and economic
progress of modern times, there are probably more
poverty-stricken people in the world today than there
were fifty years ago.

DR. EUGENE STALEY, of the
Stanford Research Institute

Why?

Why are the poor countries of the world still so poor?

We have seen how the "aid" granted by the Western
powers has not helped the underdeveloped countries to advance, because it was never *intended* to help them.

But what about the huge amounts of capital that have
been poured into the underdeveloped countries by foreign
business corporations? What about the factories that these
corporations have set up, the plantations and mines and oil
wells that they have developed? Surely this inflow of wealth,
this development of their resources, must be helping these
countries?

The answer is the same as with the so-called "aid" programs. Foreign investment has not helped the underdeveloped countries because it is not *intended* to help them. It is intended to make *profit* for the investors—which is a very different thing.

The Face of Poverty

The facts of the world's poverty are familiar to us, so familiar that we tend to build our inner wall of indifference—of boredom even—whenever the topic is raised. Perhaps we could not otherwise bear the realization that for the vast majority of mankind life experience is one of grinding and unrelieved suffering. We are overwhelmed by the sheer magnitude of the problem this represents; we feel helpless before a situation about which as individuals we can do nothing. Perhaps, deep down, some people have a faint and fearful intimation that at least a portion of this suffering is due to what is being *done* to these countries; that we are in some way connected with it; that much if not most of the suffering is *avoidable*.

The facts are there, and we'd better look at them:

* The average annual *per capita* income in the United States is almost $3,000. On the other hand there are forty countries whose average *per capita* income is less than $120. This represents a difference of 2,500 per cent.
* The sum spent by American women *on cosmetics* every year is greater than the combined annual budgets of all the African states which have supposedly freed themselves from colonial rule since World War II.
* More electricity is consumed in New York City than is generated in all of the sub-continent of India.
* Four Western countries, U.S., Britain, Sweden and West Germany, together have an average annual per capita consumption of industrial steel of 564 kilograms. Six typically underdeveloped countries, Pakistan, Thailand, Nigeria, the United Arab Republic, Brazil and Peru, together have an annual per capita consumption of twenty kilograms.

• In India alone 5 million children die each year from lack of food.[1]

A news story from Bolivia, in the *New York Times:*

Down a creaking, narrow-gauge track, two Indian miners strained to move a rusted cart full of tin ore.

The ore would eventually find its way to Huanuni, in the valley, then to the concentrating mill near Oruro twenty miles away, then to smelters in the United States or Britain, and then, perhaps, to tin cans for the convenience of housewives and, finally, to garbage heaps to be buried again in the earth.

The Indians pushing the cart, whose basic wage is $25 per month, had probably never eaten anything that comes in a tin can. Their cheeks bulged with their staple food—coca leaves, from which cocaine is extracted.

Bolivian miners chew the leaf, which costs five cents for a double handful, because it dampens hunger and gives them energy for work in this thin air.

Behind the one cart, a tiny girl no more than six years old trudged along. Her infant brother peered out from the tattered shawl that held him to his sister's back. The little girl's feet were bound in mud-caked rags. Her legs were blue.

She was looking along the track for pieces of ore shaken loose from the carts. If the ore is of high grade, it can be exchanged for food in illicit stores.[2]

That is an example of life as experienced by countless millions in those countries directly or indirectly under imperialist control.

The Underdeveloped Countries Are Not Poor

One of the grotesque paradoxes of our world is that the backward countries are really enormously rich. *It is indeed because of their wealth that they* are *colonies.*

Take Latin America:

It has more cultivable, high yield tropical soil than any other continent, at least three times as much agricultural land, per capita, as Asia, the biggest reserves of timber in the world. Buried in it are uncalculated but vast reserves of oil, iron, copper, tin, gold, zinc, lead: the list is endless—it embraces virtually every metal, base and rare, and every industrial chemical known to man. With its oil and hydroelectric power it constitutes one of the greatest untapped reservoirs of energy; its annual population increase, hovering between two and three per cent, provides an inexhaustible source of future manpower.[3]

The natural wealth of the underdeveloped countries can be inferred from the huge amounts of agricultural products and raw materials that are extracted from these lands by foreign corporations. The advanced capitalist countries are highly dependent on imports from these supposedly "poor" countries, as can be seen from the following figures. The advanced industrial nations in 1962 obtained these amounts from the underdeveloped countries:

> 98% of their coffee
> 78% of their sugar
> 85% of their cocoa
> 94% of their tea
> 93% of their peanuts
> 99% of their copra
> 61% of their cotton
> 76% of their rubber
> 96% of their jute
> 49% of their raw lumber
> 93% of their crude oil
> 65% of their phosphates
> 49% of their iron
> 74% of their manganese
> 58% of their copper
> 86% of their tin
> 46% of their zinc
> 43% of their lead
> 88% of their bauxite (for aluminum)

How is it that nations with such rich resources, supplying such vast quantities of the world's essential materials, remain so appallingly impoverished? Peru has some of the richest and most diverse mineral deposits in the world—but three-quarters of its population are subsisting on the border-line of starvation outside the money economy. Two hundred million people live in Latin America. One hundred million of them are illiterate, one hundred million suffer from endemic disease, one hundred and forty million are poorly fed. Forget about official "aid," which we have seen is a gigantic fraud. United States private corporations have invested $11 billion in Latin America. "It is a curious thing," writes Carlos Fuentes wrily, "we have always received your investments, and we are still poor . . ."

The People of the Underdeveloped Countries Are Not Congenitally Incompetent

One of the more arrogant illusions indulged in by Westerners is that the underdeveloped countries are underdeveloped because their peoples are backward, incompetent and lazy; that they are inherently incapable of utilizing and developing their natural resources and therefore other people must do it for them. Westerners never learn. Chinese soldiers were looked down upon with derisive contempt by U.S. Army officers working with Chiang Kai-shek—but before long Chinese soldiers fought the U.S. Army to a standstill in Korea and proved themselves to be better gunners than the Germans. Soviet science was looked upon with a sneering sense of superiority—until the sons and daughters of peasants and workers sent up the world's first satellite. When the British were ousted from Suez they were convinced that the Egyptians were incapable of running the Suez Canal and would have to call the British back to run it for them. It soon turned out that the Egyptians were running it with greater competence than the British ever did.

A senior United States official in Hong Kong expressed surprise to see on a suitcase that I had bought in Shanghai fittings that were chrome plated—he was surprised because he didn't think the Chinese knew how to do chrome plating, and this at a time when the Chinese had already developed their own advanced computers! It is a constant source of surprise to Westerners that "natives" can master the intricacies of large-scale industrial production as readily as themselves, that they can fly jet planes with superb competence, and that some of their medical techniques are equal to—and in some instances in advance of—Western techniques. The fact is that nowhere in the world has it been shown that people in the underdeveloped countries, if given the opportunity of learning the necessary skills, are innately less able to master modern technology. However, the myth dies hard. It dies hard because it is deliberately propagated so that the reverse myth can be sustained, the vicious myth of Western racial superiority.

The Silent Invasion
There are two ways of conquering a foreign nation. One is to gain control of its people by force of arms; the other is to gain control of its economy by financial means.

JOHN FOSTER DULLES

When the sovereignty of a country is threatened by military force, everyone in the world will soon know about it. If fighting starts, reporters will rush to the spot, emergency meetings of the Security Council will be called, the air will ring with denunciations, attempts will be made to mobilize world opinion against the aggressors.

Economic invasion, on the other hand, is silent, largely invisible, undramatic, un-newsworthy. It is often accomplished so gradually that the ordinary people of the invaded country are not even conscious that it has taken place—at least not at first. *They even accept the word of the invader that he has come as a benevolent friend to do them good!*

The general theory put forward by the apologists for foreign investment (which is the most important aspect of economic invasion) is that without it the backward countries would remain industrially underdeveloped, and therefore poor. The investing country (so the argument goes) places part of its surplus capital at the disposal of the receiving country and by doing so will hasten its economic development. For this, the investing country will receive interest on its money, or dividends from enterprises set up with its capital. In due course, out of the increased production made possible by the investment, the receiving country will repay the amount originally invested. Everyone benefits. The receiving country has advanced its productivity, the investing country has received a fair return on its capital, which can now be invested elsewhere. In due course, by this method, the discrepancy between the rich countries and the poor will even out and social and economic advance will be enjoyed by all.

What a hope!

That assistance *can* be given in this way is shown, for example, by the loans made by China, which carry either a very low (usually 2.5 per cent) rate of interest or often no interest at all and are repayable after a set period of time. With loans such as these the receiving country has to repay only the amount of the original loan plus the low interest charges (if any).

Most important of all, the mines and factories and other productive enterprises set up by means of these loans belong to the country receiving the loans and thus they add to the country's economic growth.

This is not, however, the way it works out when investments are made by capitalist corporations. Not by a long shot! All the talk about "mutual benefit," and "helping the underdeveloped countries with our know-how" and so on are downright lies. Why, if there were "mutual benefits," are the poor countries today relatively *poorer* than they were? If the system works according to the idyllic plan as described by the apologists, how is it that after millions have been (very profitably) invested by U.S., British and other corporations in India since the war, India's standard of living, which in 1935 was one-seventeenth that of the United States, by 1962 had dropped to one-thirty-fifth?

The truth is that investment by foreign capitalist corporations has always accomplished precisely the opposite of what the theory claims. Whatever short-term local stimulation of business and rise in employment and wages might initially take place, the *long-term* consequences are *invariably* that more wealth is taken *out* of the underdeveloped country by the foreign corporations than they invested in it. This is the whole point of such investments. Thus foreign investments do not diminish the disparity in the rate of development between the advanced and underdeveloped countries but aggravate and increase it.

To see why, let us take a typical example. A private U.S. corporation sets up a subsidiary in a foreign country and earns a yearly profit of 20 per cent—a rather modest return on foreign investment as these things go. In five years' time the full amount of the original investment will have been repaid. From then on, the receiving country will be *paying out* wealth it never received in the form of investment. In another five years it will have paid out *twice as much as* it received, in ten years three times . . . and this export of wealth continues *indefinitely*. There are many corporations in the United States today whose original investment has been paid back ten, fifteen, twenty times, but who are still drawing profits from the original investment.

To this process there is no end except by the nationalization or socialization of the foreign enterprise—and this is of course precisely what the United States is doing everything in its power to prevent.

The Octopus

A new stage in the expansion of U.S. foreign investment began almost immediately after the end of World War II. At the end of the war in 1945, U.S. foreign investment was a mere $11.6 billion; by 1966 it had risen to a staggering total of $50.1 billion.[4] By 1967, in spite of restrictions imposed on the export of capital, it had risen still further to about $59 billion; and in 1968 to over $65 billion.[5]

Money has poured out of the United States, grabbing any opportunities to make the most profit. Like the tentacles of some hungry octopus searching for food, American capital has fingered its way into every crevice. It does not matter how far away, how onerous the physical conditions, how destructive of local customs or local enterprises—where money is to be made, there you will find American capital making it. American money digs for oil, for gold, for copper, for tin. It buys up local enterprises or builds its own. It purchases huge cotton, coffee, sugar plantations and makes them American; it builds railroads and harbors and dams; it sets up banks and credit agencies. And the profits, the fabulous profits, are sucked back into the United States or are used to enlarge still further the range of foreign enterprises for yet greater profits in the future.

This flood of capital has enabled the United States to secure control over the economies of nations that today are sovereign and independent in appearance only. Argentina and Uruguay depend largely on their export of meat—the meat industries of these countries are now in the main owned by the three largest meat-packing houses in Chicago. Chile is dependent on its export of copper—controlled largely by American copper companies. Brazil, Colombia, Guatemala, Haiti depend on their exports of coffee—and their coffee industries are controlled by the great U.S. buying corporations such as General Foods, Maxwell House and A&P. The United Fruit Company to a large extent controls the economy of Guatemala.

> Along with the sophisticated markets in Europe and Canada . . . globalization [of U.S. capital] is also stretching out to developing markets in Africa, Latin America and the Far East. A total of $11.4 billion has been invested in Latin America, where U.S. companies make and sell everything from automobiles to Mexican peanut butter. Another $10 billion has been committed to Africa and Asia. For example, the Gillette Co., which already controls 60 per cent of the European razor-blade market and which last week took over the big West German appliance firm of Braun, is now moving in on Africa with its Nacet blades. Gillette offers shaves to Africans who have previously trimmed their whiskers with knives . . .
>
> (*Time*, December 29, 1967)

By 1963 over 3,300 U.S. companies had established their own manufacturing bases overseas, or had purchased already established local industries. Leaving aside for the moment the economic invasion of Europe, almost every U.S. corporation with a household name has invested some of its profits in the underdeveloped areas of the world—from Kaiser Aluminum in Ghana to Bristol Meyers in South Africa; from Proctor and Gamble in India to Bethlehem Steel in Venezuela. And, of course, the U.S. oil companies are everywhere.

By 1967, according to the U.S. Department of Commerce, the number of U.S. companies doing business overseas had risen to 4,200. Their assets averaged no less than $9 million each (as against the average assets of corporations within the United States, which were $1.6 million each). In 1966 alone $5.3 billion was invested by American companies abroad. Of this, IBM contributed $1.5 billion; Ford, $230 million; General Motors, $290 million; Standard Oil of New Jersey, $640 million; Mobil Oil, $680 million. In 1967 investment rose by another 20 per cent.

According to the report to the stockholders, about 55 per cent of all the declared income of Standard Oil of New Jersey in 1966 came from outside the United States. The oil companies provide the best-known and the most outrageous example of the plundering of the colonial countries' irreplaceable natural resources. The expansion of United States' automobile corporations has been almost equally dramatic. For example, the Chrysler Corporation, weakest of the three large car companies in the United States, only got into foreign expansion in 1958, when it bought Simca Automobiles, then the third largest French producer, for $147 million. Then for $75 million it acquired Rootes Limited of Britain. Today Chrysler makes cars in Argentina, Australia, Britain, France, Greece, Mexico, the Netherlands, the Philippines, South Africa, Spain, Turkey, Venezuela. All this in a brief twelve years!

While the amount invested by the United States in the more advanced industrial countries is greater than that invested in the poorer countries, the economic grip that Western countries exercise over the latter is far greater, for they control a substantial portion of the resources of the poorer countries.

Today, dominant Western nations have acquired control of more than three-quarters of the known major mineral resources in Asian, African and Latin American countries, and about four-fifths of the total output of twenty-two kinds of important raw materials in these same countries.

The United States Government does all in its power to assist this global take-over by American private investors. As principal giver of "aid," as principal buyer, as principal investor, the United States, through its government agencies, is in a marvelous position to wring from the poorer countries the best possible terms for the U.S. private investor.

This is what Dean Rusk had to say on this matter when he was Secretary of State:

We don't challenge in the strictest constitutional sense the right of a sovereign government to dispose of properties and people within its sovereign territory. . . . We do think as a matter of policy it would be wise and prudent on their side to create conditions which would be attractive to the international investor. So our influence is used wherever it can be and persistently, through our Embassies on a day-to-day basis, in our aid discussions and in direct negotiation to underline the importance of private investment.[6]

Time Magazine of March 19, 1965 spells out what this State Department "influence" can accomplish. After pointing out that U.S. investments in Latin America had risen from $64 million in all of 1963 to $175 million in the first nine months of 1964, *Time* continues:

The State Department has negotiated detailed agreements with fifteen Latin American countries guaranteeing investors against loss from expropriation, currency inconvertibility, war, revolution or insurrection—the very losses they fear most in Latin America . . . Dow Chemicals, General Motors and Chrysler, all . . . are building large new plants. U.S. Steel, Union Carbide and Alcoa are considering multi-million dollar expansion there . . .

These private U.S. investments in the underdeveloped countries have paid off very handsomely.

Just *how* handsomely we can see by the returns United States corporations enjoyed from their investments in Latin America between 1950 and 1965.

In these fifteen years U.S. private corporations invested $3.8 billion in Latin America. Part of the profits were retained in Latin America to increase the total investment of the companies concerned; part of the profits were remitted to the United States. From this investment of $3.8 billion no less than $11.3 billion in profits were remitted home to the U.S., while the profits retained locally increased the investment of $3.8 to $10.3 billion.[7]

Thus, from the $3.8 billion invested was derived $17.8 billion in the form of remitted profits and increased local investment—a cool 469 per cent!

Those in the United States who wonder why the people with money seem so little interested in investing it in, say, low-cost housing construction in Chicago, should ponder those figures. What could the people with money do with it in the United States that would give them comparable returns?

Capital, we have said it before and will say it again, has no patriotism, no loyalty but to itself. The profits are in Latin America, in the Middle East, in Labrador, in Australia, in Europe, in South Africa—not in the ghettos of American cities, not in the Appalachians or in Mississippi, nor in hospitals or community centers or in cleaning up the polluted rivers and air, not in providing decent housing or a half-way humane medical service for the poor. Profits and super-profits are not to be found there, and it is towards profit that capital will always move and to nothing else.

"Here in Venezuela," said a U.S. businessman quoted by *Time* Magazine, "you have the right to do what you like with your capital. This right is dearer to me than all the political rights in the world!"

And no wonder.

> Profits are enormous. So much money can be made so easily in Caracas real estate that a speculator would be a fool to piddle around with 10–12 per cent profits in industry and commerce. Fifty per cent seems to be the minimum acceptable. A glass bottle factory was dismantled because it made only 80 per cent, and there was bigger money to be made elsewhere.[8]

One year Standard Oil's Venezuela subsidiary, Creole, made a profit of $167 million. This works out that the corporation in this one year made *$9,630 profit on the labor of each of its employees.* And where did this profit go to? The United States! We can now begin to see why the fundamental need of backward countries, if they are to become less poor, is to accumulate capital for their own advancement by stopping the outflow of their wealth in the form of super profits to foreign investors. Only when they have stopped this outflow will these countries be able to develop their own economies for their own peoples' benefit.

The economist Gunder Frank perhaps expressed the situation most clearly:

> The metropolis expropriates economic surplus from its satellites and appropriates it for its own economic development. The satellites remain underdeveloped for lack of access to their own surplus . . . One and the same historical process of expansion and development throughout the world generated —and continues to generate—both economic development and structural underdevelopment.[9]

The great American octopus, with its grasping tentacles drawing in its sustenance, its profits, from every corner of the non-socialist world, is insatiable. It is always ready (under foolproof guarantees, of course) to move into what at first glance might seem the most unpromising areas. Those American lads who are fighting for "freedom" in Vietnam, and those who have died there by the thousands, should perhaps have asked themselves before they went what the real purpose of that war was. For "freedom" they should have read "free . . . enterprise." Vietnam to these G.I.'s is just a bloody mess. To the handful of big banks, big corporations, big armament manufacturers in America it has been a bonanza—not only in the money they are making supplying the weapons and the ships and the planes, but in the *profits* they are making and hope to make by investment. Listen to this from the *Nation's Business* of February 1968. It is worth quoting at some length:

> The best thinkers on the subject in business and Government agree that magnificent business opportunities await in Viet Nam, Thailand, Laos, Indonesia, Malaysia and Singapore. As

the military situation in Viet Nam improves, they expect the flow of business to double, triple and guadruple.

. . . nothing is foreseen that would keep Southeast Asia from becoming an industrial business outpost of the first water . . . Many well known American businessmen are in Southeast Asia, even in Viet Nam—Bank of America and Chase Manhattan bank, Foremost Dairies, Caltex, Esso, American Trading Company, Landing Brothers and Co., Brownell Lan Engineering Co., American Chemical and Drug Co. . . .

But that's only a handful compared to the number that could be there. AID people insist, especially in view of the protection provided for American investments and the concessions offered by Southeast Asian governments to get foreign business.

After quoting a Rand Corporation report which indicates that the most enormous profits have been made in South Vietnam by American companies in recent years (some get their initial capital back in three, some even in two years), the article goes on:

American business being established in Viet Nam, through investments, acquisitions, partnerships or subsidiaries, will find an expanding network of communications, highways, waterways, docks and airports every one of which could be useful to industry and commerce.

In the past few years, six new deepwater ports have been built, eight shallow draft ports, eight jet air bases with twelve new 10 thousand-foot runways, eighty smaller fields, scores of bridges and hundreds of miles of roads, tanks and pipelines, storage and maintenance facilities and housing for 325 thousand soldiers, much of it convertible into housing for industrial workers . . .

Viet Nam is beyond doubt one of the prime investment points for American know-how in Southeast Asia . . .

If you have a boy slogging it out as a G.I. in Vietnam who writes and asks what the hell the U.S. is doing there, send *that* to him! And you could tell him at the same time what Major General Smedley D. Butler of the United States Marine Corps—you will find it on page 106—said about making China safe for Standard Oil.

The Octopus doesn't change its nature, it only grows bigger.

* *

We mentioned earlier in this chapter how some 4,200 U.S. corporations have established subsidiaries in other countries. These multi-national corporations are a relatively recent development. Some of the larger ones are scattered across the world, in the rich countries and the poor. The directors of these corporations think globally. To them national frontiers (within the "free" capitalist world) are not much more important than the boundaries between the states at home. Raw materials are purchased wherever they are cheapest; capital is shifted to whichever unit in the international complex can use it to give the greatest returns; production and sales schedules are set to provide the maximum benefit to the complex as a whole. George Ball (a great believer in the "global" approach), writing in *Fortune* in June 1967, put it this way:

> . . . the structure of this mulit-national corporation is a modern concept, designed to meet the requirements of the modern age; the nation-state is a very old-fashioned idea and badly adapted to serve the needs of our present complex world.

But it is not, of course, the "needs of the present complex world" that has given birth to these giants or determines their decisions—it is to serve their *own* complex needs. There is one important advantage that these multi-national companies enjoy—they can escape control by national governments. They can, for example, minimize taxation by shifting profits from high-tax to low-tax countries; they can limit production in one territory while enlarging it elsewhere; and by all kinds of bookkeeping manipulations they can conceal from any single government authority the true financial position of their company. In other words, these large corporations are able to outflank control by national governments without coming under any equivalent supranational control. Smaller single-nation companies are thus in a position of serious competitive disadvantage.

The compulsions that initially gave rise to the multinational corporation can be stated briefly. In their earlier stage of development, United States corporations were normally concerned with the manufacture of a single line of goods—cars, sewing machines, books, food or whatever it might be. But as the domestic market for these goods began to reach saturation and the need for further capital investment began to diminish, corporations began to look around to see what other manufacturing activities in the United States they could move into which would keep their available capital profitably employed. A company which formerly made a single product began to involve itself in an often bewildering variety of quite unrelated activities. A soap company reaching a plateau in its profit returns might go into the radio manufacturing business, or book publishing or ladies' stockings. What it went into was not important provided it gave a good return for the capital investment. This, of course, could only go on so long, for these secondary production activities would sooner or later also move towards saturation where no further capital could be profitably used for their expansion. So corporations began to look abroad. An article in *U.S. News & World Report* in June, 1964 put it this way:

> These businessmen are increasingly deciding that markets abroad—and not those in this country—offer the biggest potential for future growth. The feeling grows that the U.S. market, while huge, is relatively "saturated."

This same issue quoted a comment by an official of Colgate Palmolive Company:

> You're in a saturated market here in the U.S. where new products are the only answer to growth. Abroad there are millions of people each year who reach the stage in their cultural, social and economic development where they buy soap, toothpaste, other things we sell.

External economic expansion had therefore become a necessity for capitalist enterprises. The American economy had reached the point where it had to expand overseas if it was to survive. Mr. Sean Gervasi, Research Fellow in Economics at Oxford University, has concluded that:

> The profitable operation of the 500 largest corporations, which account for a large proportion of total assets, would probably be impossible without the extensive foreign markets which have developed in recent years.[10]

Some economists dispute this and maintain that the United States is not in any important sense dependent on foreign markets. They point out that U.S exports (about $35 billion) amount to less than 5 per cent of the Gross National Product of $850 billion. The figures are correct. But the viability of the American economy cannot be judged only by the flow of *goods* from the U.S. to other countries. It is on sustaining the level of *profits* that the American economy ultimately depends. The multi-national corporation is but another method of sustaining the level of profit of the home-based corporation by selling goods abroad through its subsidiaries. For though these corporations have become "global" in their operations they are not organizations without a nationality. In the final analysis they are operated in the interests of the parent company. To judge U.S. dependence on foreign markets, one must concern oneself not only with those goods that are shipped physically from the United States but the goods made and sold abroad by U.S.-owned corporations. These latter sales in 1965 amounted to no less than $45 billion—and they have undoubtedly increased substantially since then. Exports from the United States *and* sales of U.S.-owned companies abroad amounted that year to no less than $80 billion. It is quite misleading to repeat (as is done so often) that the United States is not dependent on its foreign markets because exports only represent such a small proportion of the GNP. The GNP, we must remind ourselves, includes all manner of services which have nothing to do with the value of the physical commodities that are produced. In 1964 the value of total movable *goods* manufactured in the U.S. was $280 billion and it was probably not very different in 1965. If we now relate that figure to the value of the goods exported from the United States plus the goods sold by American corporations abroad, we find that the total figure of $80 billion of foreign trade represents almost 30 per cent of all goods manufactured in the U.S. With this figure in mind, we can now see why the U.S. economy is *enormously* dependent on foreign trade.

Capital continues to pour out of the United States in ever growing volume. Foreign investment has increased more than 350 per cent in sixteen years. A fraction of $65 billion invested abroad could have utterly transformed America and solved most of the nation's social problems. But under the built-in imperatives of capitalism this was impossible. Always seeking its own maximum enlargement regardless of wider social consequences, expanding capitalism at home must develop into expanding imperialism abroad.

NOTES

1. *Newsweek*, 17 June 1963, reporting on the World Food Congress held in Washington under the auspices of the United Nations.
2. *New York Times*, 25 August 1967.

3. Paul Johnson, in *Whither Latin America?* (New York: Monthly Review Press, 1963), p. 25. Mr. Johnson is Editor of the *New Statesman* of London.

4. *The Times* (London), 29 November 1966.

5. U.S. Dept. of Commerce, *Survey of Current Business,* October 1969.

6. U.S. Senate, Committee on Foreign Relations, *Hearings on Foreign Assistance Act of 1968* (Washington, D.C., 1962), p. 27.

7. Mr. Harry Magdoff in the *Monthly Review* (November 1966). These figures were extracted from official sources. The figures are summations of data presented for 1950 to 1960 in U.S. Department of Commerce, *Balance of Payments Statistical Supplement,* Revised Edition (Washington, D.C., 1963). The data for 1961 to 1965 appear in the review of articles on foreign investments in various issues of the *Survey of Current Business* from 1962 to 1966.

8. *Time,* 21 September 1952.

9. Harvey O'Connor, "Venezuela, A Study of Imperialism," in *Whither Latin America?* (New York: Monthly Review Press, 1963), p. 93.

10. In a private paper entitled "Arrested Development and the Multi-National Corporations." I am much indebted to Mr. Gervasi for showing me this paper and I have drawn freely from it in the latter part of this chapter.

5

The Plunder of the Poor
Nations—II.
A Case History

There is no end to the variety of methods that foreign corporations have employed to extract wealth from the poorer
areas of the world. It may be instructive to examine just one
example.

The case in question concerns the activity of an American mining company in the island of Cyprus. A remarkable
article appeared in *Business Week* on October 10, 1964,
which describes the operations of this company. There was
political trouble in Cyprus at the time when the article appeared; it was titled HOT SPOT THAT PRODUCES PLENTY OF
COLD CASH.[1]

The Cyprus Mines Corporation, an American corporation with headquarters in Los Angeles, has been operating
in Cyprus since 1912. A turning point in the history of the
Cyprus Mines Corporation came when, in the early thirties,
the company opened another copper mine, also in Cyprus,
known as Mavrovouni. "We had a bonanza mine in Mavrovouni," said Henry Mudd, the company's president.

What with the low wages paid in Cyprus and the boom in

copper prices after World War II, Mavrovouni proved fantastically profitable for the Cyprus Mines Corporation. Postwar net profits from operations in Cyprus amounted to $100 million—80 per cent from the Mavrovouni mine. From the facts reported by *Business Week* it is clear that almost the whole of the net profits were remitted to the United States. Cyprus Mines Corporation became the largest employer in Cyprus, with a payroll of 2,400 and the largest taxpayer. It was known, however, that the Mavrovouni mine would be exhausted within a few years, but while the copper ore lasted enormous sums of money were being made.

What has been done with these huge sums of money extracted from the copper ore of Cyprus?

Partly, they have been distributed to stockholders, enabling among other things, the Mudd family to retain (in the words of *Business Week*)

> . . . its position as one of the keystones of philanthropy in Southern California. Harvey Mudd College in Claremont—"it was built by Mavrovouni"—occupies much of Henry Mudd's time. Other benefactions: a philosophy building at the University of Southern California, gifts to Pomona and Claremont, an engineering building at Columbia University in New York.

But more important, the profits extracted from Cyprus have enabled the Cyprus Mines Corporation to build up an entirely new economic complex, both in the United States and abroad. This new empire began to be put together in the early fifties when the profits from Cyprus were rising to their peak but when it was already clear that the mines were nearing their exhaustion.

Among the new ventures built with the profits made in Cyprus were:

> An iron mining company in Peru.
> A copper mining company in Arizona.
> A shipping company in Panama.

A cement plant in Hawaii.
Two chemical plants in the Netherlands.
An iron mining company in Australia.

These are no doubt bringing back handsome profits into the coffers of the Cyprus Mines Corporation in Los Angeles, will allow the company to spread its activities still further afield, and will enable the Mudd family to sustain their position as one of the "keystones of philanthropy."

But what about the people of Cyprus? What about the little island from which this stupendous wealth is drawn?

Like many American companies abroad, the Cyprus Mines Corporation prided itself on its enlightened labor policies. It paid high wages by Cyprus standards ($4.62–$5.60 a day). The company "has poured millions into housing, schools, recreational facilities, a modern hospital, a program to provide milk and yogurt for the children." *Business Week* quotes the company's vice president as saying: "We could have been just an episode in the island's long history, but we are trying to create something worthwhile to leave behind."

But what does the company leave behind?

It leaves behind an island with a reduced tax revenue; it leaves behind 2,400 unemployed workers; it leaves behind in the minds of poor children memories of the time when they were given free milk and yogurt.

As the *Monthly Review* commented,

Imagine where Cyprus could be today if it had been able to borrow the capital to exploit Mavrovouni as a 2.5 per cent twelve-year loan, similar to those which Cuba has received from the Soviet Union and other socialist countries! The loan would long since have been paid off, and the $100 million which has gone into the Mudd philanthropies and the new empire for the Cyprus Mines Corporation could have been used to build a viable and rapidly expanding economy. And Harvey Mudd College under another name could have become one of the great educational institutions of the Mediterranean and Middle East.[2]

But that possibility is gone; the wealth of the island has been plundered. This great opportunity has gone for good and Cyprus *has almost nothing to show for it.* Whatever the company vice president might say, the Cyprus Mines Corporation *will* be just another "episode in the island's long history," and a disastrous one.

NOTES

1. We are indebted to the *Monthly Review* for drawing its readers' attention to this article and for their comments on it in the issue of January, 1965.
2. *Ibid.*

6

The Plunder of
the Poor Nations—III.
Some Techniques Of Looting

Foreign capitalist enterprises are concerned only with maximizing their profits. They are not concerned with the national economy of the underdeveloped country except in so far as it will directly or indirectly further their own objectives.

That is only a fancy way of saying that a foreign investor coming into an underdeveloped country will grab the most profitable, the most needed and the most valuable business opportunities for himself. He has the money, the management skills and the production know-how; he has the State Department behind him with the leverage of granting or withholding "aid." These foreign corporations are not interested in integrating their business in a long-range plan for the country's economic advancement and eventual economic independence. They want profits, *super* profits, and they want them quickly. Foreign investment of this kind would have no place in an economically independent country; and therefore it is in the interests of the foreign investor to *prevent* advance towards independence by creating all kinds of barriers against the country's foreign trade.

At first glance it might seem a wonderful help, say, to Chile to have General Motors establish an assembly plant there. It will of course give employment to many and will also eliminate the need to spend foreign currency for the importing of cars from abroad. But these undoubted advantages must not mislead us into supposing that a foreign plant of this kind can help Chile to meet its basic problem of accumulating a surplus for its own advance. Nor does it aid this country to develop an export trade, for General Motors will not allow these cars to be exported to Brazil, Australia or Europe, where the company already has plants. General Motors does not want to compete with itself.

How *little* foreign-owned manufacturing enterprises help the local economy to earn the needed foreign exchange is seen in these figures: in 1965 U.S.-owned manufacturing firms in Latin America exported to the U.S. only 1.8 per cent of their products; sold only 5.7 per cent to other foreign countries; but sold 92.5 *per cent of their products locally* which, of course, did not bring into that country any foreign currency. Thus, far from helping a country accumulate foreign currency, foreign enterprises as we have seen, will *extract* it in the way of profits and interest that must be remitted abroad.

Objection to foreign investment goes far beyond its failure to provide an underdeveloped country with foreign exchange. That is but one aspect. Foreign investment must be challenged, as we have said earlier, on the more basic ground that it extracts the surplus value of a country for the enrichment of those with capital; that it represents unequal and therefore unjust trade; that its primary objective is not to help the underdeveloped country but to rob it.

Extraordinary pressures are brought to bear on underdeveloped countries to prevent any activities there that might be in competition with U.S. interests. Chile, for example, is not allowed to refine the copper produced by U.S.-owned mines—the copper must be sent to refineries in the U.S. In the same way, Bolivia is prevented from refining its own tin, which must be sent to the tin refineries in the U.S. or Britain. Measures such as these do not only benefit the imperialist countries but prevent the underdeveloped country from achieving its economic independence.

The imposition of tariffs is another weapon that the U.S. doesn't hesitate to use to help its own enterprises and to discourage the underdeveloped countries from processing their own goods if it can be done in the U.S. Tobacco, leather, bananas, cocoa beans, dates, lumber, etc., are all examples of commodities that come into the U.S. *duty free* if they are *unprocessed*. If they are treated in any way, tariffs are imposed. These U.S. import duties make it difficult for local producers in the underdeveloped countries to start manufacturing or processing in their own country.

The Terms of Trade—Another Stranglehold

We have already given several reasons why the poor countries remain poor. There is another reason to add to the list. It can be stated very simply. In their dealings with the underdeveloped countries the capitalist countries are able to manipulate prices so that they *buy cheap and sell dear*. It is as simple as that; but the consequences are disastrous for a country trying to pull itself up by its own boot straps.

As of 1968 the trade between the underdeveloped countries and the advanced capitalist world flowed at the annual rate of approximately $25 billion a year. While trade between the capitalist countries covers hundreds of thousands of items, mostly manufactured goods, the number of items that the underdeveloped countries have to sell is very small. The Dominican Republic, for example, relies on only five items for 91 per cent of its exports; Libya relies on only one item for 99 per cent of its exports. Among thirty-seven underdeveloped countries only two—Paraguay and Peru—have as many as six items which could be considered among their "leading exports."

This reliance on only a very few items—mostly agricultural produce and raw materials which are normally available from many alternative sources—places these countries in a hopelessly vulnerable position. There is no elasticity in agricultural production. The wealthy countries, with their concentrated power as buyers, are in a position to impose conditions of trade which will *always* be to the disadvantage of the underdeveloped countries. And this is precisely what they do. Over the last decade the prices the advanced countries are ready to pay for what they buy from the poorer countries have *decreased,* the prices they make the poorer countries pay for the manufactured goods have *increased.*

So narrow is the margin on which the underdeveloped countries operate that even a small drop in the world price of a commodity can cause untold hardship to the country whose main source of external revenue is that commodity. Six countries in Latin America—just to give one example—rely greatly on their export of coffee. It has been estimated that a drop of only one cent per pound in the price of green coffee results in an annual loss to the Latin American producers of $50 million. And since 1954 the price of coffee has fallen by more than half! It is not the rich owners of the plantations who suffer—they undoubtedly have enough tucked away in the bank to tide them over without the slightest hardship. The brunt, as always, will be borne by the peasants and the workers, whose already near-starvation wage might be cut 30 or 50 per cent, or they may be thrown out of work altogether, until the world price of coffee recovers, if it ever does.

This steady deterioration in the terms of trade prevents the underdeveloped countries from ever accumulating sufficient foreign currency to buy enough trucks and tractors, machine tools, mining equipment, locomotives and the dozens of other minimum essentials that are necessary for these countries to help overcome their economic stagnation. It cancels out any increase of purchasing power that "aid" might temporarily provide. In 1962, for instance, Colombia was given $150 million under the Alliance for Progress program—but that year it lost $450 million due to the drop in the price of coffee. As only a fraction of the saving is passed on to the ultimate consumer, it was the coffee importing companies in the United States which stood to benefit and the peasants of Colombia who stood to suffer.

United Nations' economists who have studied this problem carefully have concluded that if prices (both imports and exports) had remained the same as they were in 1950, the total purchasing power of the underdeveloped countries in 1962 would have been $2.3 billion greater than it was. By 1966 the position had deteriorated still further. The loss in purchasing power due to the worsening of the terms of trade was no less than $2,752 billion. *The Economist* estimated that if the external *per capita* purchasing power of the Latin American countries (excluding oil-rich Venezuela) in 1928 is represented by the figure one hundred, by 1965 it had dropped to thirty-two! [1]

What does this mean in practice?

It means that if the *per capita* terms of trade had remained stationary and not moved against her, Brazil could buy a given number of tractors from the U.S. for 1,000 bags of coffee instead of the 3,000 she has to ship today. It means that the Bolivians, to buy equipment for a hospital, have to ship three times the tonnage of tin ore to pay for it. It means that the United States is acquiring the produce—the wealth —of Latin America at one-third the cost that she would otherwise have had to pay.

And this is not the whole story.

Devaluation

If the deteriorating terms of trade do not already make it hard enough there is still another gimmick that makes the predicament of the producer country yet more desperate and, of course, acts as a benefit to the American entrepreneur—*devaluation of currency.*

Since World War II, for example, there have been at least fifteen successive devaluations of the South Korean *huan* relative to the U.S. dollar. Each devaluation was on the order of 25 per cent or 50 per cent. If his currency is devalued by 50 per cent it means that a Korean must work twice as long and sell twice as much of his produce to earn enough foreign currency to buy a bag of fertilizer or a sack of cement from the U.S. or from any other country linked with the world dollar currency. The Korean peasant has no control over this . . . all he knows is that with each successive devaluation the cost of living rises and he becomes poorer.

This works splendidly for the foreign purchaser who can now buy the products he needs from Korea for only half of what he paid before devaluation.

We have used devaluation in Korea merely as an example. There is hardly a poor country, dependent on the sale of its primary products to the affluent West, that has not suffered from the consequences of devaluation. There are some nations that have had to devalue to a drastic extent. In June, 1967, President Joseph Mobutu of the Congo announced the devaluation of the Congolese franc. It was replaced by a new "heavy" monetary unit to be called the *zaire*. As a result of this devaluation one U.S. dollar could buy 500 old Congolese francs instead of the 150 that it was worth before the devaluation. What this meant was that any U.S. goods bought from the United States cost 333 per cent *more* than before devaluation, but any Congolese goods purchased by the United States (such as the uranium bought by the Rockefeller interests) cost the United States' purchaser 70 per cent less than before.

The poor nations which have been exploited by the wealthier and more industrially advanced countries are, as we have already seen, chronically in debt, both on account of interest charges payable on the "aid" they have received and the drainage of their resources to pay the high profits made by the foreign concerns who have invested in these countries. This chronic indebtedness makes it almost impossible for the debtor nation to resist the pressures brought to bear on them to "devalue" (and thus, supposedly, to "rationalize" their economy). This enforced devaluation of currency is a modern form of piracy—far more insidious and profitable than raiding overland caravans or highjacking gold-laden ships on the high seas. The eyes of the old pirates would boggle, they would be drunk at the very thought of the riches, the billions of dollars that all the devices of imperialism, from "aid" to devalution, have brought to the giant corporations in the wealthier countries.

Do we still need to ask why the poor nations remain poor?

NOTES

1. *The Economist*, 25 September 1965, p. 8.

7

The Plunder of the Nations—IV.

Three Questions and Some

Conclusions

Question 1. Why, if aid and foreign investment can provide no solution, do the governments of the under-developed countries continually clamor for more foreign aid and more foreign investment?

To find the answer we must understand the impact Western capitalism has on the structure of society in most of the underdeveloped countries. Capitalism, Carlos Fuentes says, was

> superimposed on the feudal structure without destroying it. It abandoned to their fate the great masses of peasants and workers, and reserved progress for an urban minority. It ended by crystallizing a dual society in Latin America: the modern capitalistic society of the cities and the feudal society of the countryside. The minority society became richer at every turn, face to face with a majority becoming more miserable at every turn . . .[1]

Who is it in these countries that clamors for "aid" and ever more foreign investment? It certainly is not the peasants! It is the small upper class, the elite, the rich, the group that governs, and the lesser social groups that surround them and make up the complex of the upper urban communities. They, like the *compradores,* all get their share of the loot. It is always the same . . . the few rich, the many poor.

From a report in *Newsweek:*

> Just a few hours by jet from New York or Chicago live more than 200 million people in the vast reaches of Latin America, and it is doubtful whether one-tenth of them know what it is like to go to bed with a full stomach. The great cities glitter opulently—Rio de Janeiro, Buenos Aires, Mexico City; but beneath the glitter and in the hinterland are odious and despondent slums where liquid-eyed Indian children scrounge for scraps and handouts while their parents labor for wages of twenty cents a day or less. This is the wasteland of the Western hemisphere, a land of misery whose poverty is as stark as any in the world . . .[2]

The rich in these countries have shown themselves to be indifferent to the wretched conditions in which most of their fellow-countrymen live. They are not at all indifferent to any threat to their position of wealth and power. They are fully aware of their danger. The atmosphere is charged and they feel it. They hear the growing demands for social justice. They are frightened by the dark and rising bitterness among the poor, which one day must explode. Of course *they,* the elite, want aid—especially "military assistance" which allows them to surround themselves with an army and security forces and police and informers—the whole paraphernalia of suppression. They need American "aid," their very survival depends on it. They know that without it they wouldn't last a month.

Investments too. This wonderful influx of dollars—quite a bit of it to be secretly put away in Swiss banks ready for the day! And the professional classes in the cities—the lawyers and bankers and members of the Chamber of Com-

merce, the hotel owners and liquor importers and car deal-
ers, the night club owners, the pimps and the "B" girls and
the dubious tourist guides . . . they all benefit from this
pumped-in wealth from overseas.

Money . . . money . . . good American dollars; and
the streets of the capitals alive with a show of "progress."

> At the Bolivar Hotel (wrote Paul Johnson after his visit to
> Peru), I got Cooper's Oxford Marmalade for breakfast and
> could stroll around the amply stocked store of Sears-Roebuck
> (Peru) Inc. Nearby, workmen were erecting a ninety-foot
> Cinerama screen believed to be the biggest in the world.

"Aid" and investments make all this possible. No wonder
they ask for more and more—and they get it; but what does
it do for the great gray hinterland?

> Across the river was the other side of the story: the diseased
> warrens of slums; and, once outside the tiny coastal plain,
> the desolate misery of a man-made lunar landscape.[3]

> *Question 2. Why has the "granting of independence" to the
> former colonial countries not benefitted them
> economically?*

After World War II, the imperialist countries, especially
Britain, which had the largest colonial empire, were confronted with the determination of the colonial peoples to be
rid of their foreign masters. The era of colonialism was
over. This was not at first recognized. The Dutch, the
French, the British in Malaya, all tried to hang on with military power as long as they could. Eventually they realized
that any attempt to continue colonial rule would not be tol-
erated. But would they relinquish the enormous benefits of
colonialism? Confronted with the insistent demands of the
colonial peoples they devised a new stratagem prepared by
the shrewd men in Whitehall. "All right," so it went, "we
will grant these people their independence, but we'll be
damned sure to hang on to control in a less obvious form.

And of course we will do it in style." So if it is a British colony a member of the royal family will fly out to be present at the great "independence" celebrations and to be photographed (see, we are all equal now!) dancing with the "natives." To whom is British power "handed over"? Not to the people—but to a local elite. Guns are fired in salute, the Union Jack is lowered, the new flag is hoisted, . . . and another "free" nation is launched towards a glorious future. And back at home the people will never cease to pride themselves on their wisdom and magnanimity for giving back what they should never have taken in the first place.

But the fact is that Britain and the other colonial powers did not give up much—the form, the glory—while keeping the substance. They have given up their headaches, not much more. The British today are taking as much profit out of India and Kenya and innumerable other former colonies as they ever did, and without the trouble of administration.

The continued control of a former colony through economic and other means is the essence of neo-colonialism.

The new state, though nominally "independent," finds itself still shackled by debt. It must continue to use its precious foreign exchange to pay interest and profit to foreign investors. The glorious future does not arrive, for political "independence" has left the former colony in no better position to retain its surplus, to build up capital or to break down the feudal structure of its society. And the mass of the people are left with their age-old poverty. For 95 per cent of the people in the former colonies, "independence" has not made one scrap of difference. They are as hungry and poor as they ever were.

As with the granting of "aid," the elite (the small class of urbanized wealthy and their hangers-on and the large landowners) will stand to benefit from "independence." They can now operate without the physical presence of their former overlord. They can continue to exploit their own people as they always did before, and sometimes even more.

They gain enhanced status, they are the top boys now. They have access to the country's local finances; many of them having been educated abroad can now exert, untrammelled by the presence of foreigners, the power that comes with superior education and the knowledge of Western ways.

The peasants and workers of the former colonial countries have always had two enemies to fight—their foreign masters and their own ruling elite. And they still have.

To the imperialist countries, the granting of "independence" to their former colonies has brought another advantage. It may at first glance be assumed that though the "independence" is largely fictional this new status must provide at least *some* new opportunities for maneuver which are not available to a country under direct colonial rule. And this may be true in peripheral and non-essential areas. As Laurence Whitehead has pointed out,

This increased autonomy must, in some ways, be an advantage—but with it goes the disadvantage of reduced consciousness of the real distribution of power. Neo-colonialism may be a *more stable system of domination,* because it is more flexible (but still fierce in defense of essentials) and because it can so often transmute a conflict between metropolis and colony into a domestic dispute among the dominated. To unite a people against neo-colonialism is far more difficult than to rally them against an explicitly colonial regime . . .[4]

The imperialist powers have sometimes shown great shrewdness in the way they have manipulated the giving of "independence" to their own advantage.

Here are two examples.

The first concerns the trade treaty which the United States entered into with the Philippines. Under this treaty both countries agreed not to discriminate against each other in any manner. It *sounds* splendid. So fair, so just. Both the United States and the Philippines were to be treated on a basis of absolute equality.

The disposition, exploitation, development, and utilization of all agricultural, timber, and mineral lands of the public domain, waters, minerals, coal, petroleum and other mineral oils, all forces and sources of potential energy, and other natural resources of either Party, and the operation of public utilities, shall, if open to any person, be open to citizens of the other party . . .

The United States corporations under this treaty are free to set up any business in the Philippines, can buy up the mineral rights and oil wells and agricultural lands and lumber, can exploit "all forces and sources of potential energy" there, can operate the public utilities, etc. The big bear can eat the little bear. *And the little bear is also free to eat up the big bear.* So Philippine companies can do the same in the United States. They are quite free to come over and buy up Westinghouse and General Electric, take over the oil companies, get a controlling interest of the Bell Telephone Company, buy up the agricultural lands and so on. Big deal! The very spirit of equality!

Harry Magdoff has pointed out another angle to this "equality" which would escape most people. The words "mineral lands of the public domain" have here a rather special meaning, for the Philippine law follows the Spanish, rather than the Anglo-Saxon tradition on mineral rights. This means that in the Philippines minerals in the subsoil are in the public domain and do not belong to the private owner of the land as they do in the U.S. Thus U.S. business firms are free to develop mines anywhere in the Philippines. And in return Philippine companies can exploit any U.S. land that is in the "public domain"—Yellowstone National Park perhaps, or Yosemite! A marvelous "equal" treaty! (United States investors were quick to realize the advantage they had gained. U.S. investments rose from $375 million in 1962 to $529 million three years later.)

The second example is the agreement entered into by cer-

tain European powers with the African states that were formerly their colonies. This was a convention signed at
Yaounde[5] in July, 1963 between the six European members of the E.E.C. (known as the Common Market) and the
eighteen African states which had formerly been colonies of
one or the other of the European countries. (Only Luxem-
bourg of the E.E.C. countries had not previously possessed
African colonies.)

Under the Yaounde agreements, the actual details of
which are complicated and need not be discussed here, the
eighteen African states must provide the greatest freedom to
the citizens and companies of the six European countries to
set up business inside the eighteen African states—and in
return, of course, the African states are equally free to set
up their industries and business in Europe! The Convention
further stipulates that the eighteen African states will not
introduce any exchange restrictions affecting investments.
The Eighteen of course are also free to invest on an equality
with the Six. What this means in practice is that the Eighteen in Africa and the Six in Europe have set up what
amounts to a free trade area—business and capital can flow
freely in this huge trading area. As the European six have
enormous funds for investment and the African eighteen
have none, it isn't difficult to see which direction this
"equal" flow will take. This "equal" treaty will perpetuate
the present division of labor, for without tariff barriers to
protect them the African states will find it impossible to start
new industries against the competition of the advanced European countries. The semi-colonial, underdeveloped countries will continue to supply the basic raw materials—and
remain poor. The advanced countries will continue to have
access to raw materials on their own terms—and continue
to become richer.

The fact that the eighteen "representatives" of the African countries signed the Convention gives the whole ar-

rangement an aura of legality and mutuality. But how "representative" were they of the masses of peasants in their countries? [5]

These two treaties are both examples of what is meant by *neo-colonialism*—of how the advanced countries, though granting nominal "independence," have not given up the economic advantages that colonialism provided, but through various devices have contrived to perpetuate it under a different mask. The great tentacles of imperialism have not been cut loose.

> *Question 3. What can be done? What form of development*
> *would be best for the underdeveloped countries?*

There is a prevailing assumption that the only path to economic advance for the underdeveloped countries is for them to set up industries so that they can develop an export trade in manufactured goods. Only in this way, it is said, can they earn the foreign exchange necessary for their own economic development. Thus, for example, Harry Magdoff (with whom in so many other areas I find myself in agreement) writes:

> The real hope for developing larger export markets and thereby getting out of the debt bind lies in exports of manufactured goods. This is the buoyant area in international trade.[6]

But *is* this the first priority for an underdeveloped country? To make exports of manufactured goods a primary target would result in distorting the whole process of industrialization as the basis of an independent economy. To manufacture goods to be sold *outside* the country in question would involve gearing capital investment to the needs of the market in the rest of the world—either in advanced industrial countries or in underdeveloped countries. In either case, these manufactured goods (produced inevitably at first at a low level of efficiency) could not compete with the

products of highly industrialized countries. If a country did
set up some factories and was able to produce manufactured
goods—who would it sell them to? Suppose' Malaya was to
make tires out of its rubber, could it compete with the highly
advanced tire manufacturers in the U.S. and Europe?
Should it even try? If it did try, the capitalist manufacturers
would kill within five minutes any market that they did capture—and the capital invested in the home country to produce these export commodities would be wasted. Harry
Magdoff himself gives examples of how every attempt, however tentative, on the part of underdeveloped countries to
develop industries that might compete with the advanced
countries is at once crippled, if not destroyed. (One example he gives is an attempt on the part of Brazil to use the
broken coffee beans, that Brazil is not normally able to sell,
for the manufacturing of instant coffee. As soon as Brazil-
ian-made powdered coffee came into competition with the
U.S.-made powdered coffee, it was declared to be "unfair
competition" and all manner of restrictions on it were imposed.)

The main task for an underdeveloped country wanting to
develop an independent economy is not to compete with the
advanced and established capitalist countries *but to supply
the needs of their home population through the development of their own resources.* Some imports will of course be
needed. Colonial countries with a history as exporters of
raw materials will not find difficulty in procuring necessary
foreign exchange once the immense drain on the foreign
currency represented by the interest and profits of foreign
corporations and the repayment of "aid" loans is brought to
an end. The needs of each country will vary but it is generally true to say that when a country has secured real independence from foreign economic control and has been able
to meet the needs of its own people by establishing local
industries to produce goods for local use, then, and then
only, is the time ripe to develop an export trade in manufac-

tured goods. To do so at an earlier stage would be wasteful and futile.

The needs—the urgent and desperate needs—of the underdeveloped countries are very easily defined. No one has done so more clearly than Senator Mike Mansfield, when he addressed himself to the basic problems of Latin America (and what is true of Latin America is true of all other underdeveloped areas). His prescription for an underdeveloped country is excellent:

1. It must act, at once, to alleviate the most glaring inadequacies in diet, housing and health from which tens of millions of people suffer.
2. It must improve agriculture by diversifying crops, broadening land ownership, expanding cultivable acreage and introducing modern agricultural techniques on a wide scale in order to increase production, particularly food.
3. It must bring about the establishment of a steadily expanding range of industries.
4. It must wipe out illiteracy within a few years and provide adequate facilities to educate an ever increasing number of highly trained technicians, specialists and professionals to provide a whole range of modern services.
5. It must end the relative isolation of the beachheads from the interiors and the parts of the interior from one another by a vast enlargement of existing systems of transportation and communications.[7]

Experience has indicated that there are three other necessary steps, not, for obvious reasons, mentioned by the Senator:

1. No underdeveloped country should under any circumstances permit foreign corporations to own and operate enterprises within its borders. By their very nature, these enterprises can never be instruments for the country's economic development; they are pumps designed to suck up the country's wealth and transfer it abroad.

2. Where enterprises owned by foreign corporations already exist they should be nationalized. Foreign investors have no moral claim to compensation, none whatsoever. Rather the reverse. A claim for compensation could with justice be entered by the underdeveloped peoples against those countries that for decades have been draining their wealth away.

3. The only acceptable assistance from abroad is in the form of technical help and loans (never investments) without strings and which vest the ownership of the new enterprises developed with these loans wholly in the hands of the receiving country.

But how are these objectives to be achieved by a people controlled economically and politically by a foreign power, acting in collusion with a local elite?

Obviously, under these conditions, they cannot be achieved; they never have been achieved under such conditions and they never will be.

The first priority, then, for any underdeveloped country, before it can begin the economic and social development most appropriate to the needs of its people, is the seizure of power by the masses and the total destruction of the control and influence of the foreign power and the local exploiting elite. Without this, nothing is possible.

Until this first step is taken every effort at advance will be frustrated. And why should we expect it to be otherwise? It does not matter how many admirable speeches are delivered by Mr. Mansfield or other Senators in Congress, or by British M.P.'s in the House of Commons; the very nature of capitalism impels it always to seek the maximum gain for itself, and by every trick and device to prolong its control.

And always it is the poor who suffer. Basic social reform and private investment simply don't mix. Under imperialist exploitation even the most fundamental needs of the indigenous population are neglected for the sake of profit. Under the French, for example, Indochina became the largest exporter of rice in the world. In 1939 she exported 40 *per cent* of her rice production, but the people remained utterly impoverished and were actually consuming 30 *per cent* less rice *per capita* than they had been in 1900! Three-fifths of the imports into Vietnam under the French consisted of cars, perfumes, textiles, and luxury goods used by the resident colonialists and the small Vietnamese elite. What is true of Vietnam is true of all colonial countries, and it remains true wherever the economy, even after "independence," is still planned to benefit the foreign capitalist investors and the local elites.

The historian Arnold Toynbee has made his views on this matter very explicit:

> America is today the leader of a world-wide anti-revolutionary movement in the defense of vested interests. She now stands for what Rome stood for. Rome consistently supported the rich against the poor in all foreign communities that fell under her sway; and, since the poor, so far, have always and everywhere been far more numerous than the rich, Rome's policy made for inequality, for injustice, and for the least happiness of the greatest number.[8]

And some people still wonder why in every underdeveloped country in the world there is an active and growing revolutionary movement!

The list of objectives put forward by Senator Mansfield is a good list. Why, he should ask himself, was it only *after* the Chinese Revolution that the Chinese people could begin to achieve precisely the objectives he presented? Why was it only then that they could "broaden land ownership" and increase their food supply? Why only then that they could eliminate—as they did so quickly—illiteracy and could offer educational facilities to all? Why was it only then that the Chinese people could begin to eliminate the "glaring inadequacies in diet, health and housing"? Why only then that they could establish a "steadily expanding range of industries"? And, it is legitimate to ask, what was the Senator doing while the Chinese were accomplishing with almost unbelievable human effort the very ends he declared to be essential? He was joining in with all the other Senators in their chorus of abuse and vilification of the Chinese people!

And not only China. Why was it only *after* the people of North Korea threw out the foreign exploiters and the local elite that the country could develop, so that today North Korea has one of the fastest growth rates in the world and trades with over forty countries? Why was it possible only *after* the Cuban people overthrew the bloody Batista regime and his American-paid army and stooges, and only *after* they took over the enterprises owned by foreigners that the Cuban people could begin to establish schools and hospitals, to plan the diversification of agriculture, to eliminate illiteracy and unemployment—and this in spite of every hindrance put in their way by the United States?

Under the French only two children out of every hundred in Vietnam ever went to high school, and modern medicine for the people was all but non-existent. Why was it possible only *after* they threw out the French and foreign investors that the North Vietnamese were able to institute a land-reform program, to provide schooling for all their children and to establish a magnificent nation-wide medical service —while in the South, still under the domination of foreign capital and a local elite, land reform remains a farce and the schools and hospitals are to this day a national disgrace?

These are pertinent questions; they involve in the most intimate and important ways, the lives and happiness of countless millions of people.

The people of an underdeveloped country—whether it is nominally "independent" or not—are not able to advance while foreign enterprises drain away the wealth of their country. And why should we expect the foreign investor to leave? History does not offer us a single example of an elite voluntarily giving up its position of power and privilege. *Their overthrow can be accomplished only by force.* With no channels for peaceful reform; no participation in government; no machinery for the redress of grievances, an ever growing number of patriots within the underdeveloped countries have been forced to recognize—often against their deepest inclinations—that much as they would wish it, *there is no alternative.* The solution, the only solution, is a revolutionary solution.

The ruling circles in the United States know this, and they know the battle is engaged. That is why they are stockpiling napalm in Bolivia; that is why the United States finances tyrannical oligarchies, equips and trains their military, and is preparing a myriad different strategies to meet every kind of revolutionary outbreak.

American imperialist rhetoric ("the defense of freedom and democracy" etc.) was astonishingly successful in concealing the extent to which the United States was giving her military and economic and moral support to some of the most revolting dictators in Latin America (Batista, Trujillo, Duvalier, Jiminez et al.). The American public never protested, never rose in sheer disgust at the unspeakable barbarities committed by these regimes. Dulles even held the Jiminez regime (one of the bloodiest) up as an example for other Latin American countries to follow.

> Venezuela has adopted (he said) the policies which we think other countries of South America should adopt. Namely, they have adopted policies which provide a climate which is attractive to foreign capital.[9]

Under Kennedy, the tone changed a little. The Administration occasionally expressed "regret" at particularly brutal acts of tyranny and would even withhold (though only for a very short time) military and other aid after some more blatant seizure of power. Under Johnson, however, things went back to normal and the realities began to appear through the façade. Assistant Secretary of State Thomas C.

Mann (in charge of Latin American affairs), speaking to a meeting of U.S. diplomats on March 18, 1964, announced frankly that the United States "would no longer seek to punish military juntas for overthrowing democratic regimes." He said that "rightist and military" dictatorships are acceptable providing that their program included "the protection of $9 billion in U.S. investments in Latin America" and "opposition to communism." [10] Could anything be more frank? Or give a clearer signal? Just fourteen days later the military in Brazil overthrew the constitutionally elected government of President Goulart (and were applauded by Washington for doing so) because among other things Goulart supported trade unionism, relationships with communist states and a program of reforms by means of which Goulart (in the words of *The New York Times*) "began to curry favor with the poorest peasants." [11]

But Washington is playing a losing game—its support of Chiang Kai-shek was a losing game, as was the support of Batista, and the Korean War, and the Bay of Pigs and, of course, the costliest losing game of all, Vietnam. It will be a long and bloody struggle. There will be local victories for the elites and the foreign investors; and for the military and the C.I.A. A military coup here, some effective bribery there, the landing of marines some other place, assassinations, imprisonments, torture. All in the name of "freedom." But in the long run it will not work, for the exploited people of the world will not let it work. How many more Vietnams can America handle, when she cannot even cope successfully with one? The American Empire, and all the lesser empires which it supports, are now at last on the losing side.

NOTES

1. Carlos Fuentes, "The Argument of Latin America," in *Whither Latin America?* (New York: Monthly Review Press, 1963), pp. 11–12.

2. *Newsweek,* 27 August 1962.
3. Paul Johnson "The Plundered Continent," in *Whither Latin America?* (New York: Monthly Review Press, 1963), p. 36.
4. Laurence Whitehead, *The United States and Bolivia* (London: Haslemere Group Publication, 1969), p. 3. Emphasis added.
5. A fuller analysis of the Yaounde Convention can be found in Pierre Jalée's excellent book *The Pillage of the Third World* (New York: Monthly Review Press).
6. *Monthly Review,* November 1968, p. 42.
7. *New York Times Magazine,* 4 December 1960.
8. *America and World Revolution* (London: Oxford University Press, 1961).
9. Quoted in Robert F. Smith, *The United States and Cuba* (New York: Twayne Publishing Co., 1962).
10. *New York Times,* 19 March 1964.
11. *Ibid.,* 2 April 1964.

8

Imperialism in Action: Guatemala

Guatemala, known formerly as "The Banana Republic," was at one time virtually controlled by the United Fruit Company. Today many American companies have invested in Guatemala. Ninety-two per cent of the $117 million of foreign investments in Guatemala comes from the United States. There are no restrictions on the transfer of foreign-owned assets, dividends or interest—there is no amount of profit that must (as in some other countries) be reinvested in Guatemala. All the loot, in other words, can be remitted home. Foreign industries need not pay any duty for ten years on the importation of construction materials, machinery and equipment; foreign businesses need pay no taxes for five years and they are given a 50 per cent reduction for the next five years. A number of new American companies are taking advantage of these benefits. International Nickel, for example, has started a mining project that is likely to become a $60–$80 million investment.

U.S. AID is granting loans to Guatemala for her industrial development, but under strict conditions. Guatemala must not for example use these loans to assist companies that would be in competition with U.S. companies, though they can be in competition with other foreign, but non-U.S. companies. Industries which, by means of this aid, could increase their purchases from the United States are, of course, eligible. Trade relations between the U.S. and Guatemala have been unfavorable to Guatemala. In 1964, for example, Guatemala imported $38 million more than it exported; $36 million of this unfavorable balance was with the United States.

The only three years since 1947 to the present when Guatemala had a favorable balance of trade were the years 1952–1954, the years when Jacobo Arbenz was the legally elected President of Guatemala. (In the elections of 1950 he received 72 *per cent* of the votes.) In Guatemala, as in all of Latin America, one basic problem was land ownership. In Guatemala (counting each foreign corporation as a person) 98 *per cent* of the land was owned by 142 people. As a step towards correcting this situation Arbenz instituted a mild land reform program. This involved taking over 200 thousand acres of idle land owned by the United Fruit Company. Little did he know what the consequences of this were to be! The land was not confiscated, but was to be paid for with 25 year bonds. The Guatemalan Government, as the basis for compensation, accepted the valuation of the land that the United Fruit Company itself had made for purposes of taxation—namely $600 thousand. Though this was the company's own valuation, it was rejected as not being "just compensation" and the United States Government on behalf of the United Fruit Company entered a claim for $16 million.

The actions of the Guatemalan Government were looked upon with extreme disfavor in Washington and on June 18, 1954 a Guatemalan Colonel, Castillo Armas, invaded Guatemala from neighboring Honduras. The United States supplied the arms and military equipment as well as planes and pilots. The Arbenz Government was overthrown. In Washington Mr. Dulles declared that the success of this wholly illegal invasion added "a new and glorious chapter to the already great tradition of the American States." [1]

The justification for this invasion (as could be expected) was that "international communism" had "gained a political base" in Guatemala—although the State Department itself in an official White Paper admitted that the number of communists in the country was probably not more than 3,000–4,000.[2] No cabinet members were communists.

That the U.S. was directly responsible for this invasion and overthrow of a constitutionally elected government cannot be doubted. Some years later, chiding President Kennedy for not having taken similar strong action against Cuba, Republican Thurston B. Morton described the scene at the White House when the decision was taken to intervene in Guatemala.

> As Morton recalled the scene, President Eisenhower reviewed the Central Intelligence Agency's plans for toppling the regime of Guatemalan President Jacobo Arbenz Gusman. Then Ike said: "I want all of you to be damn good and sure you succeed."
>
> Beside Morton, those present included Secretary of State John Foster Dulles and Secretary of Defense Charles E. Wilson . . . as well as Allen Dulles, then Director of the C.I.A., and the Joint Chiefs of Staff . . .
>
> . . . Ike is close to Morton . . . and probably won't quarrel with Morton's recollection that the General declaimed: "When you commit the flag, you commit it to win." [3]

(A year earlier, on April 16, 1953, this same Eisenhower made a quite different declaration. "Any nation's right to a form of government and economic system of its own choosing is *inalienable* . . . Any nation's attempt to dictate to other nations their form of government is *indefensible*." [4] Do we listen to the words or watch the actions?)

After the *putsch*, the military junta suspended the land reform program, disenfranchised the "illiterate masses" and seized the property of peasants. All the lands expropriated from the United Fruit Company were restored to the company. The junta also abolished the taxes on dividends and profits payable to investors living outside the country, "as a result of which $11 million cascaded into the lap of a single foreign-owned company." [5]

Two United States writers, familiar with the events, had this to say about the new government:

> The Castillo Armas regime . . . was a brutal dictatorship. Hundreds and perhaps thousands of peasants and workers were killed in a wave of revenge on the part of employers and landlords.[6]

(*For the Record:* The United States intervened in Guatemala on behalf of the United Fruit Company. John Foster Dulles, U.S. Secretary of State at the time, had for a long time been the legal adviser to the United Fruit Company; his brother Allen Dulles, Director of the C.I.A. at the time, had been president of the United Fruit Company; Henry Cabot Lodge, the U.S. Ambassador to the United Nations at the time, was on the Board of Directors of the United Fruit Company; John Moors Cabot, then Assistant Secretary of State for Inter-American Affairs, was a large shareholder in the United Fruit Company; and Walter Bedell Smith, Director of the C.I.A. before Dulles, became the president of the United Fruit Company after the Arbenz Government was overthrown. The day after the invasion an urgent request was made by the Guatemalan Government that the United Nations Security Council be called into session to deal with the events. The request was turned down by the then President of the Security Council, who happened to be the same Mr. Henry Cabot Lodge. All these facts may, of course, be purely "coincidental.")

Other items of interest:

U.S. AID in 1961 (with the Export-Import Bank) provided $12 million for the construction of a road. The $12 million in principal, plus roughly $5 million in interest charges, must be paid back to the United States *in dollars* (a great drain on the nation's slender foreign currency reserves.) The machinery for the construction had to be purchased from the United States, and the contractors, engineers and supervisors were all from the United States. (One of the companies building this road—a U.S. construction company—also built the U.S. air base at Retalhuleu, from which United States planes took off for Cuba at the time of the Bay of Pigs invasion.)

Another AID project was a loan to Guatemala for the purchase of fifty-four Ford cars specially equipped for fighting guerrillas. (The archbishop was photographed giving his public blessing to these Ford cars in the Central Plaza of the capital.) AID also gave 300 bullet-proof vests to the Guatemala police.

Of the Guatemala budget, $12 million on average is spent annually on buying U.S. military equipment, most of it surplus. *Meanwhile, Guatemala has an illiteracy rate of 75 per cent and the average per capita wage is less than $200 a year!*

NOTES

1. For those wanting a far more complete account of this event and its consequences we recommend the chapter "Guatemala" in David Horowitz's *Free World Colossus* (London: MacGibbon and Kee, 1965), pp. 163–186.
2. Department of State *Intervention of International Communism in Guatemala* (1954), p. 33.
3. *Newsweek*, 4 March 1963.
4. Horowitz, *Free World Colossus*, p. 163.
5. David Graham, "Liberated Guatemala," *The Nation*, 17 July 1956.
6. Charles O. Porter and Robert J. Alexander, *The Struggle for Democracy in Latin America* (New York: Macmillan Co., 1961), p. 70.

9

The Satellization of the Rich

In the last few chapters we discussed the plunder of the poor countries. But it is not from the poor countries that the tentacles of the great American octopus has sucked its greatest nourishment. Raw materials are drawn from the underdeveloped countries, and the returns from invested capital there are handsome, but the wealth—the really large-scale looting—has come as a result of the invasion of the more industrialized countries, especially of Canada and Western Europe.

A report by the Common Market Commission published in August 17, 1970 shows clearly the huge expansion of American investment in Europe. U.S. investment in Common Market countries has now reached $30,000 million. American investment has trebled between 1958 and 1966 and, according to this authoritative report, will increase by 25 per cent in 1970 alone. More than 80 per cent of the big American companies now have branches in Europe. The report noted that it was principally Europeans who financed the American investment in Europe. "A company such as General Motors has not exported a single dollar from the United States to realize its foreign investments during the past twenty years." But how many millions (or billions) of dollars of profit has that company drawn out of Europe and remitted back to the United States during these twenty years?

American capital certainly knows when it is on to a good thing!

* *

Some Facts to Ponder

- Standard Oil of New Jersey (Esso Europe) sells more oil in Europe than it does in the United States and its sales there are expanding three times as fast.
- More than half of the automobiles made in Britain are made by American companies.
- Sixty-five per cent of the French telecommunications industry is controlled by American firms.
- In the five years 1961 to 1966 American corporations in Europe doubled the annual total of their investments and they did this in large part out of their profits rather than from loans.
- The world's third largest industrial economy (after the United States and the Soviet Union) consists of the overseas operations of United States corporations.

From *Newsweek*, March 8, 1965:

In the two years prior to March 1965 American companies opened 500 new operations in France. U.S. firms now control almost the whole of the French electronics industry, 65 per cent of the petroleum distribution, 90 per cent of the production of synthetic rubber, 65 per cent of the farm machinery production.

From *Time* Magazine, December 29, 1967:

Americans now control 80 per cent of Europe's computer business, 90 per cent of the microcircuit industry, 40 per cent of its automaking. In Britain, U.S. companies own half of all modern industry . . .

Startling figures. What do they mean?

They mean that Europe is being invaded and is on its way *to becoming an economic satellite of the United States.*

The ironic of all this is that the American invasion of Europe, as we have seen, is being largely financed by Europeans themselves. American firms in Europe, because of advanced technological and managerial skills, are able to squeeze 50 per cent more profit out of their invested capital than European firms. Europeans thus are finding it more profitable to lend their spare cash to American firms in Europe by buying interest bonds, than investing in European firms. Only 10 per cent of the capital required for American expansion in Europe is in the form of direct dollar transfers from the U.S. The rest comes from the profits that American firms have already earned in Europe and from Europeans lenders. The European financial elite have sided with the invaders. In other words, Europeans are helping to finance their own satellization!

If it were only a question of razor blades and canned soup, the problems created by the American invasion would not be too important. But it goes deeper than that, with far more ominous portents for the future.

In the last chapters we saw how United States corporations in the underdeveloped countries grabbed first those sections of the economy that were most profitable and showed the greatest promise of expansion. The same is true of their invasion of the more industrialized countries. American corporations are now firmly in control of those sections of the European economy that are the most technologically advanced. And to see what this means we must understand the new industrial revolution that is just about to shatter all our former conceptions.

The arrival of the *computer* signals a change of magnitude which we are only just beginning to grasp.

What are computers? And why should they cause a new industrial revolution?

Computers are a new form of communication, more drastically different than a modern high-speed printing press is
different from medieval handwriting. Computers are able to
store, classify and coordinate a vast amount of information
and make it available in seconds in the precise form that is
needed to be usable. They can almost *instantly* provide answers to mathematical problems that would take hundreds
of man-hours to work out. It is estimated that soon the
speed of computers will be increased to the level of one billion operations a second.

What can be done with these new machine-brains?

Here's one example:

Today, about 100 thousand technical reports are published in the United States *every year*, in addition to about
900 thousand articles in scientific and technical journals,
plus about 7 thousand new technical books. This vast
amount of information would be immensely valuable to industry if it could be used. But however carefully it is classified and catalogued, the sheer volume is too great to cope
with. Computers alone can find the precise information that
is required, and find it quickly.

Mr. William Knox, who until 1967 was Presidential Adviser on this area of technology, said in an address:

> There appears the possibility that by 1980 a small number
> of computers will replace *all the written documentation exist-
> ing in the world,* and that they will work in "real time"—
> replying to questions with information at the speed of human
> conversation.

Modern electronic technology of this kind has not only
immeasurably widened the gap between the industrialized
nations and the underdeveloped world—it is also creating a
gap between the industrialized nations who have mastered
the new technology and those that haven't.

> It is now conceivable (said Mr. Knox in the same address)
> that we may no longer be able to communicate—simply com-

municate—with those who have not kept pace in their own technology with scientific advancements we have incorporated in our own industrial structure and which are changing their nature.

In 1955 there were 1,000 computers in the U.S. By 1975 there will be 80 thousand. Computers are now being made that will answer questions from scores, or even hundreds, of users simultaneously.

The development of the direct-access, time-shared computer system, with remote terminals, such as teletypewriters and dial phones, is the revolutionary development of the future. The user will not need to write, or print, or even punch a keyboard; he need only speak to the computer, which will answer at the speed of a business conversation.

An industrial concern able to control the flow and timing of a huge factory with the aid of computer-supplied information; able, immediately and with precision, to obtain answers to a series of complex production, marketing and supply problems has an enormous advantage over any rivals or groups of rivals that have no access to such machines. The human user has, in effect, coupled his intelligence with the computer's fantastic memory and calculating speed.

It is precisely in this area of advanced electronics that the United States has already secured a virtual stranglehold over its competitors. In Europe in 1965, 62 per cent of all computers were American-made. Since then, General Electric has taken over the computer section of the French Bull Company and the computer section of the Italian firm of Olivetti, so the share of American-controlled computers has risen to 80 per cent. The only non-American computer firm of any size in Europe is the British ICT Company which in 1965 supplied only 9 per cent of the computers in Europe. What, perhaps, is even more significant is that American corporations control 95 per cent of the market for the integrated circuits which are a crucial component of computers.

The United States may, in the field of electronics, have secured a lead over all others, but it will find that it has caught a bear by the tail. The arrival of the computer will soon confront the United States with a whole host of problems. The inner contradictions of capitalism will be more clearly revealed. The arrival of the computer will accelerate the production of commodities but at the same time will reduce the number of employees required to produce them. The consequent unemployment will withdraw purchasing capacity from a large segment of the working population, will increase redundancy, and will increase yet more the concentration of manufacturing facilities and wealth in yet fewer hands.

The contradictions posed by the computer revolution are insoluble within the context of the capitalist economy.

As a century and a half ago only the bourgeois-democratic revolution could solve the problems created by the industrial revolution, so today the advanced electronic revolution can be carried through and used for the benefit of mankind only after a socialist revolution.

Industrial Europe and industrial U.S.A. have approximately the same population, but Europe is lagging far behind. Although the six Common Market countries do not constitute Europe, we can learn something by comparing the American share of the total world production of certain items with the share of the Common Market countries.

In *automobiles,* the U.S. produces 76 per cent[1] of the world's production, the Common Market countries 13 per cent.

In *oil,* the U.S. controls 73 per cent of the world's production, the Common Market countries 13 per cent.

In *electronics,* the U.S. produces 68 per cent, the Common Market countries 14 per cent.

In *chemicals,* the U.S. controls 62 per cent, the Common Market countries 21 per cent.

What can the European nations and peoples do about it? Not much.

Bringing their industries under "national ownership" is no answer, for who "owns" the nation and for whose benefit will such nationalized industries be run? Only if nationalization is part of a total social-economic change can it be a step towards freeing a nation from outside domination.

The dilemma of the European nations can be stated simply. If the U.S. invasion of Europe continues, Europe's whole economic system will be controlled by the U.S. In Mr. Harold Wilson's words, there is danger of "an industrial helotry under which we in Europe produce only the conventional apparatus of a modern economy, while becoming increasingly dependent on American business for the sophisticated apparatus which will call the industrial tune in the seventies and eighties." *Economic control implies political control.*

To accept satellization—that is one possibility.

The other is for Europe to impose restrictions on U.S. investments; but the effect of this might only be to slow her own development and make her even less able to compete with the U.S. in other parts of the world.

There would be a second consequence of the barring of American investments from Western Europe—it would result in an increased flow of American *products*. An American company, making, say, tape recorders, finding that it was not permitted to set up its own factory in Europe, would seek to send its U.S.-made tape recorders into the European market. Barriers against U.S. capital would have to be followed by barriers against U.S. commodities. Capital, unable to enter Europe, would find other areas of the world ready to accept U.S. investment—and Europe would then have to compete with American commodities outside of Europe.

To Europeans, their future as an impoverished and impotent appendage to the American economic machine does not hold out much enchantment. The United States will go on buying Europe's best scientists and doctors, chemists and inventors, and will continue to drain the surplus wealth of Europe as she is draining the surplus wealth of the poorer countries. The ruling circles in Europe—just as the elites in the underdeveloped countries—will identify their interests more and more with the United States. They have offered surprisingly little resistance, for they regarded American power as too great for resistance to be effective. They feared also that too sharp a struggle with the United States, too divided a capitalist world, would encourage anti-capitalist revolutionary movements abroad. Their concern was not the welfare of their own country ("capitalism has no patriotism") but to find ways of entering into collaboration with the Americans to preserve, as much as possible, their own interests. As long as it *pays* them to sell off their industrial holdings for American cash, they will go on doing so. As a result they, the financial elite, will continue to do well, while the general economic malaise of Europe will grow worse.

There is no immediate *economic* answer to the American invasion of Europe while America has its own Fifth Column, the capitalists, who are only too ready to sell the pass for a bit of cash; but sooner or later there will be a *political* answer. Just as today the Vietnamese people are fighting the military invasion of their sovereignty and are ready to die to regain it, so the workers of Britain and France and Italy and West Germany will realize that *their* sovereignty has been invaded too, and that it is *their* wealth, the workers', that is being drained away. When this is realized, and when American workers understand that they, also, are being gypped—and on a grand scale—the workers of Europe and the workers of the United States will fight together to overthrow a system that brings benefit only to a very few. This sounds, in today's context, visionary and unreal. And it will remain visionary until the present system cracks up (as it will) and makes it impossible to go on in the old way. While it is important for us to see why capitalism is moving towards its own dead end, it will only be the worsening of their conditions that will teach the workers in capitalist countries everywhere that the time has come for a change.

It will come in Europe as a result of a significant number of individuals realizing that the problem is not the "satellization" of Europe by the American economy (or competing with it on its own terms as J.-J. Servan-Schreiber suggests in his book "The American Challenge"). For capitalism is not only faced with an objective economic crisis, but a crisis *within the consciousness of man himself.* The increasing mechanization and dehumanization of man's experience, and the identification of technological progress with human progress have stripped man of his individuality. Man can no longer express himself in his work, and is less and less able to shape his life in accordance with his own choices. For Europe to "Americanize" itself would be only to plunge into the same extremity of social conflicts and lawlessness that the United States is facing today.

The answer for Europe, as we hope to show in a later chapter, is to extricate itself from the bondage of a system that is certainly not meeting the human needs of its victims, nor even of those who are supposedly benefitting from it most.

* *

This chapter would not be complete without some mention of what the British choose to call their "special relationship" with the United States.[2]

There still lingers in the minds of many British people a romantic notion that between the United States and themselves there exists a strong bond of friendship. The United States is pictured as a country essentially democratic and progressive, closely knit to Britain by ties of blood, language and common ideas of law, and sharing many similar attitudes to the problems of the world. The United States is being presented to British people as being fundamentally friendly and helpful in spite of occasional frictions which, the British people say to themselves, are the kind of minor disagreements that "occur in any family."

Many of these ideas about America—its democracy, its attachment to peace and aversion to militarism and bureaucracy, and its special regard for Britain as the "mother country"—derive from a much earlier era. They have no validity whatever today. But these are attitudes which help America achieve its imperialist aims, namely, to *use* Britain, to control, as much as necessary, Britain's international policies without this becoming too obvious, and to take over any British enterprises which might be profitable to herself.

At Potsdam, Britain still figured as one of the "Big Three," but she soon was seen to be a much weaker power than either the United States or the Soviet Union. As other capitalist powers recovered from the war and Britain's relative position weakened still further, Britain aspired to a position of a lesser partner of the United States. Britain did all she could to cultivate this "special relationship" with the United States to conceal as far as possible her own growing weakness. But this role too was lost. When Kennedy became President in 1960 he made it clear that Britain was to be treated as no better than one capitalist country among a number and all were expected to toe the American line. If anything the United States began to regard West Germany, rather than Britain, as America's most useful junior partner.

After World War II, with all her allies (who were also her potential rivals) impoverished, the United States deliberately and consciously set out to take over global power—largely at Britain's expense. Canada, with 70 per cent or more of her industry acquired by the United States, was pulled into the U.S. orbit; Australia and New Zealand were linked to the United States in the military ANZUS Pact, from which Britain was ostentatiously excluded; Britain was displaced in the Middle East as the dominant imperialist power; in 1949 the U.S. forced a 30 per cent devaluation of

Sterling and insisted on the loosening of British exchange and trade controls in order to facilitate her commercial and economic penetration.

No one saw and expressed more clearly the United States' global ambitions than Mao Tse-tung. In August, 1946— three years before the successful conclusion of the Chinese Revolution—he talked to the American journalist Anna Louise Strong. This was at the start of the United States' cold war against the Soviet Union. In the course of this conversation Mao said:

There are two aspects to the propaganda about an anti-Soviet war. On the one hand, U.S. imperialism is indeed preparing a war against the Soviet Union; the current propaganda about an anti-Soviet war . . . is political preparation for such a war. On the other hand, the propaganda is a smokescreen put up by the U.S. reactionaries to cover many actual contradictions immediately confronting U.S. imperialism. There are the contradictions between the U.S. reactionaries and the American people, and the contradictions of U.S. imperialism with other capitalist countries and with the colonial and semicolonial countries . . . Both Hitler and his partners, the Japanese warlords, used anti-Soviet slogans for a long time as a pretext for enslavement of the people at home and aggression against other countries. Now the U.S. reactionaries are acting in exactly the same way . . .

The United States and the Soviet Union are separated by a vast zone which includes many capitalist, colonial and semicolonial countries in Europe, Asia and Africa. Before the U.S. reactionaries have subjugated these countries, an attack on the Soviet Union is out of the question. In the Pacific the United States now controls areas larger than all the former British spheres of influence there put together; it controls Japan, that part of China under Kuomintang rule, half of Korea and the South Pacific. It has long controlled Central and South America. It seeks also to control the whole of the British Empire and Western Europe. Using various pretexts, the United States are making large-scale military arrangements and setting up military bases in many countries. The U.S. reactionaries say that the military bases they have set up and are preparing to set up all over the world are directed against the Soviet Union. True, these military bases are directed against the Soviet Union. At present, however, it is not the Soviet Union but the countries in which these military bases are located that are the first to suffer U.S. aggression.[3]

Despite all the efforts and apparent successes of the Americans, the balance of forces on a world scale since the end of the war have swung against them.

First, their relative economic preponderance has declined. While in 1945 America's industrial output was twice that of all the other capitalist countries, today the others together equal hers; and the socialist countries, which from 1949 have included China, account for nearly one-third of total world output.

In spite of the United States' relatively declining global power the British ruling class continued to seek support from the United States. American support meant for them, concretely, not merely loans and supplies but also the deployment of American forces in appropriate areas. This is why the British after the war not only connived at American cold war propaganda but helped to promote it. The cold war was a pretext for spreading American power over the world.

To some extent the British imperialist policy worked as they expected. They received financial and some political and military support from America. But British political influence was downgraded. The Suez attack in 1956 was a milestone on this road of British decline. It was the last attempt on the part of Britain to act independently of the United States. She was quickly brought to heel. The lesson sank in. Since Suez the British ruling class has never ventured to challenge the Americans on any major question.

This gives rise to a fundamental political question: to what extent is there today a separation between British and

American imperialism? Are the two so closely linked that for all essential political purposes they are inseparable? Who is the main enemy of the British people today? British imperialism? American imperialism? The two jointly? The close ties between the British imperialists and American imperialism are seen more and more clearly as time goes on. Each successive British government now obeys the Americans with complete servility. They talk of long-term policies to strengthen Britain but their actual short-term policies of continued overseas spending and domestic deflation make Britain weaker not stronger. The help that the British Government is being given by other imperialist powers is extended on terms that ensure that no change in Britain's policies can be made, and hence Britain's decline is accentuated. The position of the British ruling class is dependent on the closest possible collaboration with American imperialism and they will do all they can to maintain it.

Although American direct investment in the United Kingdom has grown, the total volume of U.S. investment is less significant than its character. American influence in the United Kingdom is based not so much on direct investment as on the way U.S. interests have interlocked themselves with British. For example, the British and American oil companies act in many ways as a joint international cartel; there are many links in chemicals, non-ferrous metals, machinery, consumer goods and so on. There is very close collaboration between the "City" and the United States over banking, insurance and investment.

The out-and-out collaborators with U.S. imperialism, those committed to an unshakable alliance with the United States, are a relatively small number of the biggest capitalists. They are small but extremely powerful.

On the other hand other British interests feel themselves directly and immediately challenged by America and are anxious to resist its control before it is too late. Two examples are the British aircraft and automation industries.

Other British groups which are predominantly concerned with overseas trade tend to collaborate with the Americans in the belief that they can obtain support which, on balance, is worthwhile. Many capitalists, including smaller industrial concerns, are fearful of American competition not merely in overseas markets but in their share of the United Kingdom market itself. For example, drugs, toiletry and cosmetics, food processing, some non-ferrous metals and so forth.

But what is the position of the British worker?

Great numbers of the British people already have strong feelings against United States' domination. These feelings are given little or no expression by any of the political parties. A very wide section of the British people, however, for many different reasons and with differing degrees of understanding, realize that Britain must resist the increasing United States dominance over her affairs. Particularly those who want to see a genuine socialism established in Britain must realize that this is impossible until Britain can settle her future free from outside interference. A great task at this stage for the British people is to build up a wide alliance of those who stand for British national independence and a resistance to American imperialism and its British partners.

* *

Those who still cling, in spite of all the evidence, to the comfortable belief that the United States is Britain's "friend" should read a report written by Mr. Richard Neustadt for circulation among official circles in Washington which was printed in the *New Left Review* in their September–October 1968 issue. Neustadt was a presidential adviser to both President Kennedy and President Johnson. He was sent to Britain shortly before the Labour Government took office to assess what their reactions would be in regard to the Multilateral Nuclear Force policy which was then being pushed by Washington. This report reflects clearly the attitude of patronizing contempt with which Washington views British influence and power and how cynically they view their relationship with the British political leaders. Talking, for instance, of a forthcoming visit of Mr. Wilson to Washington, Neustadt wrote:

> As Prime Minister I would expect him to arrive in Washington with recollections of the Anglo-American relationship and hopefully his own personal relationship which are quite different from perceptions of reality held by many American officials. Numbers of things can be done on the cheap to avoid shocking his sensibilities. For one, the President might ask his advice on the short list of replacements for [Ambassador] David Bruce. For another Averell Harriman might figure prominently among his hosts. If these don't serve there are sure to be others. They are worth thought and attention.
>
> These suggestions all rest on the one underlying premise that it will be worth our while to ease the path for Wilson, pay him a good price, leave him no possible excuse we can foresee for failing to proceed toward MLF in company with us and with the Germans . . . if we get over this hurdle in good style the stage will be well set . . . for effective Anglo-American relations . . . I can think of nothing likelier to speed a Labour Government's approach toward the European and Atlantic attitudes *we* favor, than productive, firm relations both with Washington and Bonn.

The "royal reception" of Mr. Wilson on one of his more recent visits with an honor guard and all the trappings on the White House lawn, indicates that the American officials are still looking for things "that can be done on the cheap to avoid shocking his sensibilities."

This is about all that is left of Britain's "special relationship" with the United States.

NOTES

1. From a table compiled by the Compagnie Lambert of Brussels, quoted by Jean-Jacques Servan-Schreiber in *The American Challenge*.

2. I am indebted to Mr. Adolf Silver for allowing me to read and make use of a paper on the subject which he wrote for private circulation.
3. Mao Tse-tung, *Selected Works*, Vol. IV.

U.S. Imperialism's Not-So-Junior Partners

We now need to correct a misplaced emphasis.

Our stress in this book so far on *United States* imperialism will be greatly misleading unless we remind ourselves that other imperialisms still exist. It is a fairly common present-day error to think of the United States as almost the *sole* imperialist power, with Britain, France, West Germany, Japan, limping weakly and dependent, far behind. It is true, of course, that the United States today is by far the most powerful and dominant of the imperialist nations but these other countries play an important role as well.

Take Britain—always in financial difficulties, with an almost chronic balance of payments problem and a rate of growth that lags far behind most other industrial countries. She has been called "the sick man of Europe."

But just how sick is she? And if she is, why is she?

In 1966, Mr. Jack Revell, senior research officer of Cambridge University's Department of Applied Economics reported the results of an eight-year study in which he and his colleagues attempted to determine Britain's true financial position. Among other things, this report assessed British overseas assets as of December 31, 1961 (the latest date for

which Revell could gather reasonably comprehensive information). The figure he came up with was £7,364 million
or (at the then rate of exchange) $20,619 million.[1] The
United States overseas investments at the time were approximately $36,000 million.[2] From this we can see that British
overseas assets were at that time over 57 per cent of those of
the United States. (With a U.S. population about four times
that of Britain we arrive at the rather startling conclusion
that British *per capita* overseas investment was well over
twice that of the United States.) The relative position of the
two countries may since have altered somewhat, but the
overall picture remains true, namely that Britain is still a
very big foreign investor. (British investment in Malaya, for
example, runs as high as $120 per head of the Malayan
population.)

U.S. investments in the underdeveloped world are only
about half of her investments in Canada and Western
Europe. As Britain has been pumping investments into the
underdeveloped world for over a hundred years it is not surprising that her investments in those areas are proportion-
ately greater than those of the United States.

British overseas capital, therefore, is of direct relevance
to the liberation movements. By an overemphasis on *American* imperialism the position of Britain in relation to the
world revolutionary struggle can be lost sight of. And add to
British overseas investment that of West Germany, France,
Japan and Belgium and we will see that the United States is
by no means the only imperialist power.

If Britain has these enormous overseas assets, why is she
in a chronic balance of payments crisis? Partly, of course,
due to her adverse trading position—she consistently buys
more commodities from abroad than she sells abroad. But
this adverse balance would be made up by invisible exports
—shipping, insurance, etc.—and by profits and interest on
overseas investments. The real cause of British balance of
payments difficulties is that the British capitalists are still ex-

porting capital, still expanding their overseas investments, are still determined to derive from abroad the super-profits that cannot be made at home, regardless of the damaging consequences this may have on the British economy as a whole. (Add to this Government military spending overseas to defend Britain's imperial interests.)

Britain, like the U.S., has a "foreign aid" program, but of British development aid 66 per cent is tied to the purchase of British goods. British "aid" in 1962 was £163 million, in 1966 it had risen to £209 million.

With U.S. capital encroaching into Canada and Western Europe, tensions have arisen within the capitalist world. The exploiters are finding themselves exploited by the larger predator—the U.S. These inter-imperialist struggles can only grow sharper. France's open hostility to U.S. penetration has been clear for some time; and Canada and other countries talk of taking some steps to protect themselves from still further U.S. economic invasion.

Britain recently has become a net importer of capital (more U.S. and other foreign capital is coming *into* Britain than Britain is sending overseas). Large amounts of capital coming into Britain (mostly U.S.) enable Britain to export capital, allowing British imperialism to expand its own exports of capital. The result of this of course is the growing "colonization" or "satellization" of Britain; in the end it will make Britain totally subservient to the United States. A similar process is taking place in the other West European countries. So, one might say that the United States has *developed colonialism to a new level,* bringing into its sphere of control not only Europe, but *through* Europe, those areas of the underdeveloped world that traditionally have been in Europe's sphere. She is thus colonizing the colonialists. U.S. imperialism through this "colonialism at the higher level" is in fact attempting to move towards a global system of imperialist powers in which she remains the dominant partner but in which one part is inseparable from the others.

If this appears a somewhat far-fetched concept, one need only read how some influential leaders of the United States envisage the future. A good example is an article in *Life* magazine written by Mr. George W. Ball, who was Under Secretary of State under Presidents Kennedy and Johnson and is one of the most respected, and is considered one of the most "moderate," members of the American ruling elite. Mr. Ball in this article presents his plan for a "new world system." He calls for a tightly knit alliance of "3½ super powers"—the United States, a United Europe, the Soviet Union and (the "half" power!) Japan. Ball's general thesis is that the discontent of the poor nations is not a serious threat if the powerful nations stick together.

> Shameful as it undoubtedly is, the world has lived at least two-thirds poor and one-third rich for generations. Unjust as it may be, the power of poor countries is limited. They . . . do not have the capacity to precipitate major world conflict . . .
>
> Our first priority must be to build a modern structure of power in the industrialized North.

Under the impact of this super plan Mr. Ball believes the attitudes and policies of the communist countries will "erode." Japan, and by implication the Soviet Union, would, he says, "wear the club tie." (China, with almost a quarter of the world's population, is hardly mentioned.) American enterprises are to lead the way towards "realizing the total promise of the world economy."

> By gearing their policies to a world economy—with respect not only to sales but also the procurement of raw materials, production, investment and financing—the great American world companies provide man with a fresh and hopeful vision: the possibility of utilizing resources in accordance with a single, objective standard of efficiency.[3]

What a noble, what a truly inspiring vision for the young people of the world to thrill to! A global empire of 3½ super powers, Americanized, "efficient" and holding their own against the world's poor!

Today, the United States is not the only imperialist nation, and we must remember that; but if Mr. Ball and his colleagues have their way, the identity of these national imperialisms will gradually disappear as they become absorbed into a single world imperialist system.

One cannot help wondering how the Japanese will take to being a mere half-power in Mr. Ball's spacious plans. Or what they think of the arrogance implicit throughout his article. A quarter of a century ago on the U.S.S. *Missouri,* Japan signed her admission of total defeat. Her cities were in shambles, her country lay in ruins. Her recovery at first was painfully slow. Today she has pushed Britain out of third place in industrial production, and she is the largest ship-builder in the capitalist world—she is in fact building half the world's total. In the production of cars and trucks, electronic and optical goods she is now second only to the United States. Her capitalists are pushing into South Korea and South Vietnam, into Hong Kong, into Malaya, into Australia. She may still be a junior member in Mr. Ball's global club, but she is certainly not likely to remain junior very long.

In spite of Mr. Ball's long experience in high office I do not think that we need place too much confidence in his powers of vision. How little these people learn! It was the same Mr. Ball who, in 1962, was expressing his views on the Vietnamese National Liberation Front in a State Department publication:

> The guerrillas . . . are poorly trained and equipped and are not motivated by deep conviction. Rather, they are merely unsophisticated villagers or peasants who have been conscripted by terror or treachery . . .[4]

Eight years and many, many thousands of lives later, Mr. Ball's poorly trained, ill-equipped, terrified, unsophisticated, unmotivated peasants had fought the most powerful military nation in the world (the nation that was to lead the super global empire) to a standstill and brought it to total political defeat!

You were 100 per cent wrong then, Mr. Ball . . . and you are again 100 per cent wrong with your dead business-man's "fresh and hopeful vision." Bitter inter-capitalist rivalries will never allow the neat little arrangement that you envisage. Even if, for reasons of sheer survival, the capitalist powers could for a while submerge their rivalries, your plan will still not work because the ordinary people of the world —yes, especially the poor two-thirds who you say are so powerless—are fully determined that it never will.

NOTES

1. Stephen Arls, "How Much Britain is Worth," *The Sunday Times* (London), 1 May 1966.
2. Computed from figures in *The Times* (London), 29 November 1966, which were based on U.S. Department of Commerce statistics.
3. *Life,* Atlantic Edition, 15 April 1968.
4. Department of State, *Vietnam, Free-World Challenge in Southeast Asia* (Washington, D.C., 1962), p. 15.

II

The Military Madness—I.
"What We Have We Hold"

Don't forget, there are two hundred million of us in a
world of three billion. They want what we've got—*and
we're not going to give it to them!*

PRESIDENT JOHNSON
in a speech to G.I.'s
at Camp Stanley in Korea

I consider the Department of Defense to be a Department of Peace.

PRESIDENT NIXON
February 6, 1969

Among the "survival imperatives" of the new American
Empire which we listed earlier was a global network of
bases from which United States military power can be deployed. Given that the preservation and extension of
America's "free enterprise" system is paramount, overriding
all other national considerations even if in the end it leads to
disaster, the military policies of the ruling circles of the
United States take on the appearance of a certain short-term
rationality.

The new American Empire *is* in danger, but not quite in the way Mr. Johnson related it. It is not threatened because the rest of the world "wants what the United States has," but because the people of the poorer nations are increasingly determined to throw out the foreigners who have been exploiting them. They are passionately determined to run their own countries themselves and they are now quite persuaded that they will never receive their fair share of the wealth that they produce until they do. "Social justice," said Arnold Toynbee, "is the first item on the present agenda of at least three-quarters of the human race."

The roots of this world-wide movement, according to Toynbee, lie in the failure of the bourgeois-democratic revolutions to share the benefits that resulted from them with the poor majority of mankind. (Of course there was never any intention to share the benefits.) The industrial revolution had raised the living standard of some, but the great majority of mankind experienced no appreciable improvement in their conditions. For most of them all that happened was the replacement of a landlord oligarchy by a bourgeois oligarchy. The great masses remained as poor as they ever were.

> By far the greatest and most significant thing that is happening in the world today is a movement on foot for giving the benefits of civilization to the huge majority of the human race that has paid for civilization, without sharing in its benefits, during the first five thousand years of civilization's existence.[1]

For the United States this world-wide movement poses problems, for the revolutionary peoples are learning that power grows out of the barrel of a gun. A new technique of empire, with less obvious political coercions, has had to be improvised. But whatever their appearance, all empires are in the end sustained by force, and in the case of America military power on a vast scale was an essential. The United States was consolidating her empire precisely at the time when a growing political consciousness and rising nationalism was making it increasingly difficult to hold peoples in subjection.

To a nation compelled by the survival necessities of its system to keep the largest possible area of the world within the capitalist orbit *any* political change *anywhere* was almost certain to be a "threat." The United States therefore took over the championship of the *status quo*. She became the prime defender of things as they are and the leading opponent of revolutionary change. The very continuation of the free enterprise system to which the United States is committed depends on the prevention of socialist revolutions, for they would shrink still further the areas of the world in which American capital and business can retain a foothold.

As Baran and Sweezy point out:

> . . . policing the empire and fighting socialism are rapidly becoming, if they are not already, one and the same. For the threat to the empire comes from revolutionary movements which . . . are sparked by a deep-seated yearning for national independence and are fueled by an increasingly urgent need for economic development, which experience is proving cannot be achieved by underdeveloped countries today except on the basis of public enterprise and comprehensive planning —in short, only if their national revolutions are socialist revolutions.[2]

For those in the United States who benefit from their country's position as the world's top dog, number one imperialist power, socialist revolutions in the underdeveloped countries raise a direct and unacceptable challenge; and they attempt to scare the American people with a picture of the nightmare consequences if they were allowed. W. W. Rostow, who was one of President Johnson's principal advisers on international affairs, gave this testimony to a joint Congressional committee:

> The location, natural resources, and populations of the underdeveloped areas are such that, should they become effectively

attached to the Communist bloc, the United States would become the second power in the world . . . If the underdeveloped areas fall under Communist domination or if they move to fixed hostility to the West, the economic and military strength of Western Europe and Japan will be diminished, the British Commonwealth as it is now organized will disintegrate, and the Atlantic world will become, at best, an awkward alliance, incapable of exercising effective influence outside a limited orbit, with the balance of the world's power lost to it. In short, our military security and our way of life as well as the fate of Western Europe and Japan are at stake . . .[3]

We are all familiar with the picture, but we should at least briefly remind ourselves of the formidable military power that the United States has developed to prevent these calamities.

The sheer magnitude of the U.S. global network is difficult to grasp.

A few years ago, basing my remarks on a short paragraph in *U. S. News & World Report,* I mentioned in a public lecture that the United States was operating no fewer than 3,328 foreign military bases around the world. This figure was immediately challenged as being a "ridiculous exaggeration." Repeated attempts to obtain specific figures from the Pentagon and the State Department proved fruitless. The replies I received were evasive. To some of my letters I received no reply at all.

Eventually some figures did come to light. In a *New York Times* dispatch from Washington dated April 9, 1969 (printed in the Herald Tribune International Edition on April 10), the number of overseas bases operated by the U.S. was made public. My previous figure proved to be wrong. *It was too low.* The United States actually operates 3,401 overseas bases.

In this dispatch, *The New York Times* reveals details of a 1,200-page survey for "alternative U.S. defense strategies for the coming decade and the overseas military bases that each strategy would require."

The survey was completed by a team of thirty senior civilian and military experts just before the Nixon administration took office.

It reveals that a quarter-century after World War II the United States still maintains 429 major and 2,972 minor military bases throughout the world.

These bases, according to an expert study, comprise 4 thousand square miles in thirty foreign countries—and Hawaii and Alaska. Stationed on them are apparently 1 million American servicemen, 500 thousand dependents and 250 thousand foreign employees. The cost of these bases ranges between $4 billion and $5 billion annually . . .

Those who have had access to it report its broad conclusions as follows:

• There is little likelihood of early or substantial cutbacks in U.S. bases overseas so long as the United States intends to honor its treaty commitments to its allies.

• Even such developments as the huge C5A air cargo plane or nuclear-powered warships still require substantial numbers of overseas bases and skilled personnel to run them.

• To relinquish the distant overseas bases and concentrate army or marine corps divisions, air force and naval units nearer—or even inside—the continental United States, may cost more than keeping them where they are, on bases long since paid for.

. . . the study is said to have found that, over ten years, it would cost approximately $400 million to shift an army division from the Western Pacific to a permanent location in Hawaii, where modern facilities exist. To shift the same division to [areas] . . . where facilities would have to be built, might cost $800 million or more.

The study is also said to indicate that it would cost approximately $10 billion over ten years to relinquish all existing U.S. Army, Navy and Air Force facilities in Japan and Okinawa and replace them in say, Guam, Wake, Hawaii or the Continental United States . . .

In other words—the U.S. military are not going to give up their foreign bases. *No, sir!* For according to their tortuous reasoning, to reduce the number of their expensive bases would cost too much!

Add to these three thousand-odd overseas bases:

- a navy larger in total tonnage than all the other navies of the world combined,
- a thousand hardened intercontinental ballistic missile silos dotted around the United States, each missile armed with a nuclear warhead, each pre-programmed to strike specific targets in the Soviet Union and China and each with a count-down time of under thirty seconds,
- three and one-half million men in the armed services,
- seventy Polaris submarines, nuclear powered and nuclear armed prowling under the seven seas,
- the largest bomber force, the largest fighter plane force, the largest helicopter force in the world,
- a military establishment that has the most advanced and sophisticated electronic devices of any nation in the world,
- a whole array of biological and chemical agents designed to spread disease and kill off entire populations with toxins against which there are no known cures, and to destroy and make unusable large areas of fertile agricultural land crops,
- an arsenal of nuclear weapons which adds up to the equivalent in explosive power of fifteen tons of TNT for every man, woman and child in the world.

The financial cost of keeping this monstrous military establishment going is something over $216 million every twenty-four hours. Twenty-two thousand firms, among which are virtually all the biggest, are classified as "major defense contractors." *The annual military budget is larger than the net incomes of all the nation's corporations put together.*

A single figure can perhaps best convey the sheer magnitude of the military machine that has been created to "protect" the American Empire. During one year an average of *30 thousand defense contracts were signed on every work-*

ing day of the year—a total for the year of 7,500,000.[4] Just *contracts!*

As we shall see in a later chapter the dominance of the military establishment has altogether altered—and for the worse—every aspect of the nation's life. It has also effectively prevented the implementation of urgently required social programs. Translate the cost of the weaponry into the things that the United States needs:

- For every bomber . . . 500 school classrooms could be built.
- For every destroyer . . . nine school buildings.
- For every nuclear powered submarine . . . fifty modern hospitals.

The resources invested in manufacturing the prototype of a new bomber could:

1. pay the salaries of 250 thousand teachers for one year,
2. maintain for one year thirty university science departments with one thousand students each,
3. build seventy-five hospitals with one hundred beds each,
4. and there would still be enough money over to make 50 thousand farm tractors.[5]

"Every gun that is made," declared Dwight D. Eisenhower, "every warship launched, every rocket fired signifies, in the final sense, a theft from those who hunger and are not fed, those who are cold and are not clothed. We pay for a single fighter plane with a half-billion bushels of wheat. We pay for a single destroyer with new homes that could have housed more than 8 thousand people . . . Is there no other way the world can live?"

Yes, General, there is. But you didn't do much about it while you were President. It can't be done while those who make the decisions are committed to controlling a worldwide empire in defense of vested interests—*their* vested interests. For the ordinary people who must pay and die for them, empires come dear.

NOTES

1. *The Economy of the Western Hemisphere* (London: Oxford University Press, 1962), pp. 3–4.
2. Baran and Sweezy, *Monopoly Capital* (New York: Monthly Review Press, 1966), p. 206.
3. Subcommittee on Foreign Economic Policy of the Joint Economic Committee, December 10, 12 and 13, 1956.
4. James McCartney, report from Washington for the *Miami Herald-Chicago Daily News* wire service, 19 November 1961.
5. Labor Research Association, *Economic Notes* (April 1959).

The Military Madness—II.
"The Fake Alarms"

> Our government has kept us in a perpetual state of fear
> —kept us in a continual stampede of patriotic fervour—
> with the cry of a grave national emergency. Always
> there has been some terrible evil at home or some mon-
> strous foreign power that was going to gobble us up if
> we did not blindly rally behind it by furnishing the ex-
> orbitant funds demanded. Yet, in retrospect, these dis-
> asters seem never to have happened, seem never to have
> been quite real.
>
> GENERAL DOUGLAS MACARTHUR
> to the stockholders of
> Sperry Rand, 1957

Since World War II, the United States has spent about
$1,000 billion (yes, one *million* millions) on its military
establishment.[1] With just a fraction of this astronomical
amount of money the nation could have rebuilt every slum
in the country.

We have seen, however, how the militarization of the
economy was necessary if the capitalist system was to survive. But it is only fair to ask whether, apart from this economic compulsion, the United States during these years was

in such danger that this expenditure was in any case necessary for the nation's security? And if the U.S. was in no such
danger, if the military expenditure was primarily an economic and not a security policy, how were the American
people conned into paying such fabulous amounts of money
for a military machine that wasn't really needed?

The answer to the first question is: No. The United States
since the war has at no time been in danger of attack.

World War II ended, as we have seen, with all the main
protagonists, except for the United States, enormously dam-
aged and exhausted. The Soviet Union suffered possibly the
greatest physical destruction of all and lost the greatest proportion of her young male population, but even before the
war ended the American people were persuaded to look
upon that country with the most profound fear and suspicion. A myth was conveniently disseminated soon after the
war (and it is even now widely accepted as true) that after
the war the Soviet Union (unlike the United States) kept its
military forces intact so that it could be ready to spring at
the throat of a disarmed West. In actual fact, as P. M. S.
Blackett pointed out in his *Studies of War,* the U.S.S.R.
made a very big reduction of her armed forces after the war,
reducing them to 25 per cent of the 1945 figure, compared
to the U.S. reduction to 13 per cent. (Mr. Blackett, scientific adviser to the British government, presumably knows
what he is talking about.)

> Considering that the U.S.S.R. had long and potentially hostile
> frontiers, in Europe, the Middle and the Far East, whereas
> the U.S.A. had atomic bombs and no potentially hostile fron-
> tiers bordering the U.S.A. itself, the 1948 total Soviet man-
> power figures of 2.9 million would hardly seem excessive from
> a purely military standpoint, when compared with the Ameri-
> can 1.5 million.[2]

As for American fears of attack by the Soviet Union, this
is what George F. Kennan (former U.S. Ambassador to the
Soviet Union) wrote in 1956:

The image of a Stalinist Russia poised and yearning to attack the West, and deterred only by our possession of atomic weapons, was largely a creation of the Western imagination, against which some of us who were familiar with Russian matters tried in vain, over the course of years, to make our voices heard.[3]

This "creation of the Western imagination" did not arise spontaneously. It was quite clearly in the interests of those who felt it was essential to launch the United States upon a large military expenditure program to establish an adequate justification. It would be difficult to persuade a skeptical American people to support a global extension of military power to keep the world safe for American investors. It was therefore necessary to convince the American people that they were *in danger,* that a devilish external enemy was out to overthrow the United States. And not only the United States—but the whole Western world. The destiny of the United States was to save civilization.

To make people afraid is always easy.

President Truman in his *Memoirs* was later to write:

The demagogues, crackpots and professional patriots had a field day pumping fear into the American people. . . . Many good people actually believed that we were in imminent danger of being taken over by the Communists and that our government in Washington was Communist riddled. So widespread was this campaign that it seemed no one would be safe from attack. This was the tragedy and shame of our time.[4]

Writing this some years afterwards it was easy for Truman to blame the "demagogues" and "crackpots," ignoring altogether the fact that he was himself greatly responsible for initiating this national hysteria, and that if he had wished, he could have nipped it in the bud. J. Edgar Hoover (whom Truman retained as head of the F.B.I. throughout his administration) had already told the people that communists were at work "at every level and in every organization." On March 12, 1947 Truman virtually declared war on "international communism" with his Truman Doctrine speech, in which he announced a global anti-communist policy.

Thirteen days after making this speech Truman initiated the first of a series of orders requiring 2.5 million government employees to undergo new "security" checks. Thus began the era of the loyalty oath. The social and political implications of this were enormous. It was the first step towards the disintegration of Americans' trust for each other. From that moment the mass of the American people were to see the world in the lurid light of *conspiracy*—external and within.

> At one stroke of the pen (wrote Professor D. F. Fleming) the assumption that American citizens were loyal was destroyed. All government employees became second class citizens, living under the shadow of F.B.I. dossiers whose contents could never be revealed to them on the ground of protecting secret informers.[5]

When Truman signed the order it applied to 2.5 million employees, but soon it was extended to 3 million members of the armed forces and three million employees of defense contractors. From then on, including their families, about 20 million American citizens had secret police dossiers, and as others entered and left investigated employment the numbers who had such dossiers increased year by year. Thus was the fear of "communism" engendered.

In 1949 the success of the Chinese Revolution came with a shattering impact on the American consciousness. It was put down, not as the final culmination of great historic forces that had for long been at work within China, but as the result of "disloyalty" of public officials within the United States.

Then came McCarthy.

For four fatal years this man dominated the American

political scene. "No bolder seditionist," wrote Richard Rovere, "ever moved among us—nor any politician with a surer, swifter access to the dark places of the American mind." [6] McCarthy completed what Truman and the Republican Party had begun. He succeeded in convincing a very large section of the American people that the United States was the object (in his words) of "a conspiracy so immense, an infamy so black, as to dwarf the history of man . . . a conspiracy directed to the end that we shall be contained, frustrated and finally fall victim to Soviet intrigue from within and Russian military might from without."

To those in the ruling positions all this of course was known to be arrant nonsense. How was it possible then that this man gained such an ascendancy? Why—until his work of reducing the American people to paranoiac fear was accomplished—were so few voices raised against him? Why did President Eisenhower—whose national prestige was unassailable—refuse to speak out against McCarthy even when one of his closest friends, General George Marshall, was under McCarthy's savage and totally unfounded attack? It is impossible to believe that the ruling groups within the United States, with their influence over the mass communications media, could not have restrained this man much sooner than they did or reduced his fantastic demagoguery to ridicule. We must assume that they didn't do so because McCarthy was *serving their interests.* (It was only when McCarthy began to attack the loyalty of the army establishment itself that they had had enough and decided to get rid of him—and they did!)

In the general atmosphere of fear and suspicion that McCarthy generated, what need was there for any elaborate explanations about the economic compulsions that lay behind the cold war? No need to justify America's moral and economic support for some of the bloodiest and most tyrannical regimes. They were "against communism"—and that was surely enough for any patriotic American. And so it was that the American people were brainwashed into a total conviction that only by a gigantic expansion of military power could the country be rescued from irremediable disaster.

From that time on, the military-industrial consortium had it virtually their own way. Year by year mounting military budgets, each more stupendous than the last, were dutifully voted by Congress almost without discussion. What a glorious multi-million-dollar bonanza it proved to be! A bonanza for the military, a bonanza for the makers of all that miraculously complicated hardware that so often was obsolete even before it was delivered! And didn't the cold war keep several million young men in uniform off the labor market? What could they have done with them, with unemployment still not controlled in spite of "prosperity" booming away like mad? (The magnitude of the *wastage* this involved can be measured by the following: Gaylord Nelson [Congressman from Wisconsin] in his *Newsletter* of May, 1969 lists 41 missile systems that were never deployed or were abandoned in formative stages. The cost of these useless missiles was $23 billion—*over 6 per cent of the national debt.*)

The beauty of these self-generated fears is that they can be turned off or turned up as necessary. For example President Kennedy, during his election speeches, was warning the American people that there was a dangerous "missile gap" —that Russia was about to overtake the United States unless something drastic was done about it quickly. After he was elected he "discovered" that there was no missile gap at all. Similarly, the Nixon Administration in the spring of 1969, wanting to frighten the American people into supporting its Safeguard A.B.M. program, also "discovered"— suddenly—that the Soviet Union was preparing a first-strike or surprise-strike capability. Secretary of Defense Melvin E. Laird said he had "uncovered" new intelligence on the most modern Soviet rockets, the SS-9 intercontinental ballistic missile. "As we look over the development and the deployment of the SS-9," Laird told the disarmament subcommittee of the Senate Foreign Relations Committee, "it leads me to come to the conclusion that with their big warhead . . . this weapon can only be aimed at destroying our retaliatory force." He also said that the Russians with the SS-9 ". . . are going for a first-strike capability. There is no question about that."

Unfortunately for Laird a member of the Committee remembered that the Assistant Secretary of Defense for Systems Analysis, Dr. Alain Enthoven, had reported to the Senate Armed Services Committee that the SS-9 was a *retaliatory* weapon and could not be used effectively for a first strike. It was left to Senator Fulbright to accuse Laird of using "a kind of technique of fear to precipitate acceptance of a large program . . . Suddenly the Russians are becoming eight feet tall and they are about to overwhelm us!"

Fulbright should have been accustomed to this technique; it had been used for years.

When the ruling circles want to create *fear* they can certainly lay it on. This is what Nixon wrote to the *New York Times* in 1965 about the Vietnam war (we have added the italics): ". . . victory for the Vietcong . . . would mean ultimately the destruction of freedom of speech *for all men for all time* not only in Asia but in the United States as well."

Nothing less!

NOTES

1. Dr. Ralph Lapp, as quoted in I. F. Stone's *Weekly,* 8 July 1968.
2. P. M. S. Blackett, *Studies of War* (New York: Hill & Wang, 1962), p. 242.
3. Quoted by David Horowitz, *The Free World Colossus* (London: McGibbon & Kee, 1965), p. 23.
4. Harry Truman, *Memoirs,* 2 vols. (New York: Doubleday, 1955–1956), 2:291.

5. *The Cold War and Its Origins,* 2 vols. (New York: Doubleday, London: Allen & Unwin, 1961), p. 1,067.

6. Richard H. Rovere, *Senator Joseph McCarthy* (New York: Harcourt, Brace, 1959).

Imperialism's Home Base

I

The Mythology of American "Success"

Until recently the assumption that the United States' economy, based on "free enterprise," has been a resounding success was so deeply ingrained that it required a certain boldness to challenge it.

The achievements are there, for all to see. The giant factories, the millions of automobiles, a living standard that is the envy of the world with (for some) its undreamed-of luxury; the super abundance of food, even if it never reaches all. So long a period without a serious recession is a record never before experienced by a capitalist country. This surely is an overwhelming answer to the arguments that socialists level at capitalism—that it cannot control its own destiny and is bound, by the laws of its own nature, to experience disastrous periodic depressions.

How can anyone deny these tangible evidences of success?

I deny them. And more and more Americans are beginning to deny them. It is obscuring the issue to call America's economy a "success" without further qualification. That America's capitalist economy has been a success in the true sense that it has benefitted the American people as a whole, can be challenged both on economic and on social grounds.

We examined at the beginning of this book the quality of life that this supposedly successful system has offered to the majority of its people. Here we will examine only one aspect of the "American way of life" and on this alone it stands condemned: namely that *the American economic system needs and creates enemies.*

* *

The wheels of American industry are today kept going only by a fantastically high level of military expenditure— *and this is true regardless of whether the country is at war or not, or even in danger or not.* The U.S. Government has already warned that even if the war in Vietnam should end there will be no cutback in the military budget; that indeed there will be an increase. " . . . A cessation of hostilities," the Under Secretary of the Treasury declared on June 25, 1968, "would result in great pressures to rebuild stock in military supplies and equipment to a more acceptable level." He went on to say, "We have been fighting this war on a very, very lean budget."

Only $80 billion!

While Nixon's first announced "cut" of $1 billion in the 1970 military budget was not really a cut at all, only a cut in the projected $4.1 billion *increase,* there seems at the time of writing some likelihood that there will be *some* modest cutback. The cost of the war in Vietnam was expected to drop in 1970 by $3.5 billion.* This sum was not allocated to welfare or to clearing the slums but was allocated to military expenditure unconnected with the Vietnam war.

In other words, regardless of the state of the nation's rela-

---

* By 1970 a number of leading industrialists and financiers had joined the ranks of those who want the Vietnam war brought to an end—not, needless to say, because of the illegality or immorality of the war, but because its enormous financial cost, its inflationary effect and its impact on the balance of payments were beginning to weaken the international position of the dollar.

tions with the rest of the world, a high expenditure on armaments is to continue. A permanent war economy has been
institutionalized.

It is customary to give the figure of 10 per cent as the
proportion of the Gross National Product that is devoted to
military expenditure, and even this would seem, especially
in peace time, to be an excessive deflection of the nation's
wealth. But in actual fact this figure grossly underestimates
the economic significance of military expenditure. If one
takes into account what economists call "the multiplier
effect" one arrives at a figure showing that close to 25 per
cent of the G.N.P. and of employment is attributable to military spending (military spending puts money in the pockets
of workers who in turn spend it on food, clothing, housing
etc.). Some have estimated that as far as employment is
concerned no less than 36 per cent of America's labor force
is dependent, directly or indirectly, on military expenditure.

The United States military budget is very great by any
standard. It is of course relatively easy for economists to
show how this expenditure could be allocated for non-
military and socially productive purposes, for a cut back in
taxes and the shortening of working hours. There is no
theoretical reason why this money could not be spent on the
alleviation of poverty and suffering, on schools, hospitals,
communications, the cleansing of the rivers and the air and
the general beautifying of the land. However, within America's "free enterprise" system neither major political party
specifically opposes the war economy. Those who today
have a vested interest in the present arrangement (that is,
those who gain financially from it and whose social status is
dependent on it) are precisely those who wield the controlling political power. Why was it that (until the opposition
to the Vietnam war made even the Pentagon vulnerable to
attack) the huge (and often blatantly unnecessary) financial demands of the military were always acceded to without question by the Congress, while those who asked for

funds for schools, slum clearance and so on were rarely given even the pittance for which they asked?

Robert P. Wolff, Instructor in Philosophy at Harvard University, raised the real question in a letter to *The New York Times:*

> . . . Does the United States really wish to disarm . . . ? Of course we wish to disarm, you will say, but I wonder.
>
> What Senator or Representative . . . would announce himself in favor of the immediate cancellation of all military electronics contracts? How would the powerful aircraft industry greet a proposal to discontinue the production of all warplanes and missiles? How many Congressmen could watch with equanimity as two million [now 3.5 million] soldiers, sailors and airmen were released to flood the job market?
>
> How would the Pentagon react to the prospect of closing down West Point, Annapolis and the newly-created Air Force Academy, pensioning off the officer corps, and sending home the Chiefs of Staff? Just how great would be the rejoicing as community after community, industry after industry saw itself deprived of the contracts, installations, subsidies, which have meant economic life or death for the past twenty years? . . .[1]

The questions answer themselves. A significant cutback (let alone the virtual elimination) of military expenditure is not economically possible under the present system; it would lead to financial chaos unless the slack were taken up within an overall, government-supervised and government-planned economy—in which case it would cease to be "free enterprise."

The supposed "success," therefore, of the capitalist system in the United States today is directly dependent on the continuation of a high level of military expenditure—the most socially wasteful form of expenditure. What is more, however "peaceful" the United States declares its policies to be, a high level of military expenditure cannot help but lead to international tension, for other nations quite understandably feel threatened by America's ever mounting military arsenal. The steps they take for their own protection then provides those in the United States who benefit from it with the justification for a yet further increase in military expenditure. Thus the vicious spiral continues . . .

It is sometimes argued that if the U.S. is inescapably tied to a continuation of a huge military establishment, this must be true also of China and the Soviet Union.

Everything we know about the economy of socialist states indicates that even a far-reaching curtailment of military expenditure would *not* lead to economic chaos. A socialist economy has already at hand the machinery of governmental planning on a national scale and could very rapidly redeploy the newly released capital and manpower to improve the nation's agriculture, housing, medical services, communications, education and so on. Unlike the United States, socialist nations are under no *economic* compulsion to maintain any given level of military expenditure, and there are no economic vested interests to resist even its total elimination. No one would lose any money by such a step, no one's livelihood would be threatened by it, there are no powerful private corporations and shareholders whose profits would suffer. As far as political pressure is concerned, the military would probably resist steps which would deny them their present position of influence, but they would not have as allies the vast industrial interests which in the United States provide the military caste its political leverage.

Indeed, in general, the political pressure upon the leaders of the socialist countries is precisely *opposite* to what it is in the United States, for the success of the socialist system is intimately linked with its ability to provide the great mass of the people a steadily improving condition of life, and nothing would assist this more than a cutback in the socially unproductive and wasteful expenditure on the military services. In the United States military expenditure *sustains* the economy; in socialist countries it has the opposite effect—it *retards* the rate of economic growth.

The ever-mounting military power of the United States makes it impossible for either China or the Soviet Union to disarm unilaterally, much though it would be to their economic advantage to do so. The important point, however, is that the level of their military expenditure is determined *by an assessment of their military requirements* and not, as in the case of the United States, by economic compulsions which have nothing to do with the objective requirements of national security.

* *

There is enough evidence in the history of American capitalism in this century to arrive at the conclusion that the economy has always tended to drift towards stagnation and depression—that the *norm* of capitalism is stagnation. Chronic depressions are against the interests of both the capitalists and the workers, but apparently these depressions can only be overcome by a massive expenditure in the public sector. This *could* of course, as we have said, be spent for the public welfare—social services, education and so on, —but expenditure of this kind runs counter to the interests of the privileged classes. The overall betterment of the conditions of the workers diminishes the special rights and privileges of the rich, and—what they would consider even more important—reduces the economic return on their capital. If a large expenditure on *welfare* does not meet the needs of the upper classes a large and ever growing expenditure on the military establishment certainly does. It buttresses and supports the existing class structure, gives marvelously generous returns on investments, and it is easy to obtain public approval for expenditures that are ostensibly for national "security." It is anyway essential for policing the American

Empire overseas. The American system has, so far, been a great success for the ruling class. That is why the warfare policy met very little criticism. It was a "non-partisan" policy supported by all sections of the ruling elite; it was essentially a policy shaped to meet *class* interests. (This was also true, of course, of British foreign policy.)

But is it true that the American economy would stagnate if it were not for these large public expenditures?

The history of the United States since 1900 would suggest that it is military expenditure that has saved the United States' economy from a depression that would otherwise have been chronic. Even before the inter-capitalist clash of the First World War, the United States had been through three severe economic crises—1900, 1907 and 1914. World War I saved the United States from a major depression. The end of the war ushered in a *general* period of crisis —that is, a crisis of the entire capitalist system. Between the two great wars the capitalist system failed altogether to solve its major economic problems—it failed to provide work for millions of people and it failed to make full use of its productive capacity. At the beginning of 1929—though this was the highest point of the post-war "prosperity cycle"— there were still several million people in the United States who could find no work, and only 70 per cent of the industrial capacity was being used. After the 1929 crash things became worse. By 1932, U.S. steel production was back to where it had been in 1902; in Britain it was back to 1897. In agriculture—though at this time millions of Americans were on the very edge of starvation—billions of dollars worth of food were being destroyed. The inherent dynamics of capitalism made it impossible for this food to be channelled to those who were desperately in need of it.

The Great Depression following 1929 was not solved by Roosevelt's New Deal measures. In 1940, 15 per cent of America's labor force was still unemployed, the G.N.P. had barely regained its 1929 levels. It was World War II that ended this depression. By 1944 war spending accounted for 42 per cent of the G.N.P.

A similar sequence followed the end of World War II. Having emerged from World War II with an industrial capacity that had all but doubled, the American system was confronted with even greater problems of "over production" than in the thirties. After an initial post-war boom based on civilian demand accumulated in the war years and the Marshall Plan, the economy once more moved into a period of decline. Industrial output between November, 1948 and June, 1949 fell by 14 per cent and the crisis overshadowed all of 1949 and part of 1950. By February, 1950, over 4.5 million Americans could find no work, and these official figures do not include those who could only find part-time work or the many who had given up registering for work as useless. Capitalism again showed its incapacity to meet the most basic needs of the people; again it was war —this time the Korean War—that came to the rescue.

Capitalism learned its lesson. After the Korean War the American economy was put on a permanent military footing. It did not require the outbreak of actual war to keep the economy going, the "cold war" did just as well. From that time on the public expenditure on the military establishment expanded, and this has continued to the present day, enormously accelerated by the war in Vietnam. Thus only as a *war economy* can the "successful" American system survive.

An economic-political system which is compelled, regardless of military necessity, continually to increase its war expenditures, and is unable to use these resources for the obvious and even desperate needs of its people, cannot be considered a "success" whatever other benefits (such as a high standard of living for some of the population) the system may for a time bring along with it. An institutionalized war economy, which by its very nature must result in high tension or actual conflict with other nations, obviously cannot serve the long-term interests of the people. Sooner or later the American system, which is devised and maintained to benefit private interests but which runs counter to the welfare of the people as a whole, is bound to precipitate the decline and fall of the United States as a world power.

Today, as one travels through America, one is conscious that the old, unbounded optimism in the future is fading fast. Too many people realize that something has gone quite dreadfully wrong, that the great American success story is ending as a gigantic tragedy. Today you hear few orators even on the most patriotic occasions extolling, as they always used to do, the wonders of the American way of life, for in too many hearts there has entered the first chill intimations of their country's inescapable failure. Many Americans—especially young Americans—are saying to themselves: If this is success, we can do without it.

NOTES

1. *New York Times*, 25 September 1959.

2

The "Successful" System— Successful for Whom?

GOOD LIVING BEGINS AT $25,000 A YEAR
Something thoroughly satisfying happens to people when they cross an income threshold of around $25,000 or more a year. Until then basic family wants tend to outrun income, but afterward income moves ahead of needs. The family pays off debts and stays out of debt . . . unrestrained acquisition is a new thrill . . . The ability to spend freely without worrying, to cope with financial demands, is a huge satisfaction and—to those who are new to it—a great relief. They are proud of it.

Fortune Magazine, May 1968

Earl Perkins is a black man who chops cotton on a white man's plantation:

The most he ever earns is $3.00 for a twelve-hour day in the fields, and usually he is paid off with a fraction of his actual pay in cash (the rest probably goes to the company store). To supplement the larder, Perkins sometimes hunts rabbits, not with a gun but by skewering cotton-tails in their warrens with a sharp stick . . . Perkins, his wife and eight children pay $10 a month rent for a dilapidated 'shotgun' shack, which has no

indoor plumbing, electricity or gas. Perkins' life is typical
of the more than 100 thousand Southern blacks in the
Delta whose mode of existence has changed little in
159 years.
> *Time* Magazine, May 17, 1968

Time explains that a shotgun shack is one you can shoot a
shotgun through without hitting anything—for there is
nothing in it to hit.

In the same issue of *Fortune* from which the first quotation was taken is another article, by Arthur Louis, titled
"America's Centimillionaires."

> The U.S. has become so affluent that there is no longer any
> great prestige in being a mere millionaire. The very word
> 'millionaire' is seldom used nowadays; indeed it has almost
> a quaint sound. It belongs to the era some decades back when
> a net worth of $1 million was considered a 'fortune'; a mil-
> lionaire was a member of a small class, and therefore a nat-
> ural object of curiosity. To have a net worth of $1 million
> today is to be, much of the time, indistinguishable from mem-
> bers of the omnipresent middle class.

The general impression conveyed by articles of this kind
is that the majority of Americans are rich, that some are
enormously rich; that only isolated pockets of poverty
remain, of which the American public in recent years has
belatedly become aware; and that thanks to the social security programs, unemployment relief, minimum wage laws
and the more recent "War on Poverty" legislation, poverty
in the United States will soon be a thing of the past. The free
enterprise system can then chalk up another victory.

Surveys to determine how the wealth of America is distributed have been made for years, but no one has paid too
much attention to them. Three recent high-level studies have
received somewhat more notice,[1] as has a report by the
Citizens Board of Inquiry into Hunger and Malnutrition in

the United States. Though varying in minor details, the findings of all these studies are essentially the same. Their verdict is unanimous:

1. That a very large number of American people live in dire poverty.
2. That the preponderant wealth of America is concentrated in the hands of a very few.
3. That the various social security measures, the relief programs and other attempts that have so far been made to alleviate the situation have been ludicrously, and tragically, inadequate.

What constitutes economic poverty? How is poverty defined when needs of families vary so greatly; when some families are "good managers" and others are improvident; when it takes more to live in cities than in rural areas, more in the West and East than in the South? The studies that I have mentioned allow for these variations and can therefore quite accurately help us to know how many people can accurately be called poor. To avoid plunging into the detailed statistics included in these reports it will be easier for our purposes to accept as a general rule of thumb the statement by Mr. Sargent Shriver, who was Director of the Office of Economic Opportunity in the Kennedy and Johnson Administrations. (And we should bear in mind that every government tends to give as favorable a picture as possible of the state of the nation.)

Mr. Shriver concluded that a family of four must be classified as poor if its annual income falls below $3,000, and an individual if his income falls under $1,500.[2] Mr. Shriver indicated that 35 million families are "poverty stricken" and are untouched by existing programs for assisting the poor.[3] If one assigns only three persons to each poor family (the national average is higher) it is clear that at least 105 million persons or *more than 50 per cent of the population live below the poverty line.*

Nor does this tell the full story.

There is a line even lower than the poverty line which has been called the "emergency level." Basing his findings on official figures, Dr. Kolko of Harvard shows that in 1957 no fewer than 27.5 per cent of all "spending units" (households) *lived below the emergency level.*[4] Ten years earlier, in 1947, the percentage of households living below the "emergency level" was precisely the same. Thus it can be seen that, contrary to the popular view, the proportion of the population living in desperate poverty did not diminish. Indeed, in absolute terms, taking into account the increase in the population, the number of people living below the emergency level increased during this decade.

"The fact remains," you will say, "that America is a rich country—the richest in the world. Indeed one of the arguments you make in this book is that the great wealth of this country has been drawn from the poorer nations of the world."

Yes, indeed; by any standards America is a wealthy country in terms of its national income and the overall accrued wealth of the total population. But the crucial question is, who gets this wealth? How is it divided? Who benefits from the American Empire and America's vast productive capacity? There is available in the reports I have mentioned and from a mass of official statistics irrefutable evidence that the large beneficiaries of the American "free enterprise" system are relatively few in number.

A quaint notion has been disseminated, by the rich themselves of course, that taxation for rich people is now so exorbitant that it is almost impossible today to become a millionaire, and that the number of the very rich is declining. In other words that the national income is slowly being more equitably distributed. The facts show otherwise. In 1944, for example, there were 13,297 persons who owned $1 million or more in wealth. Just nine years later, in 1953, the number had more than doubled to 27,502. By 1962, there were no fewer than 80 thousand millionaires and in 1968 they were so numerous that the numbers were no longer publicly announced. (Even allowing for the reduced value of the dollar, there has been a prodigious increase in the number of the very rich.)

But startling as these numbers are, the very rich still represent only a very small proportion of the total population. Here are some figures which are worth studying:

Assets
- Since World War II, one-tenth of the nation has owned two-thirds of all liquid assets.
- 1.6 per cent of the population own 32 per cent of all the personally owned wealth.
- The upper brackets of this 1.6 per cent own the lion's share. Thus in 1956, for example, one half of one per cent (one two-hundredth of the population) owned 25 per cent of all privately held wealth in the United States.
- The upper 1.6 per cent of the population in 1953 possessed an average estate of $186,265.00.
- In 1962, 200 thousand persons had assets in excess of $500,000.00.
- At the lower end of the scale 50 per cent of the adult population own only 8.3 per cent of the nation's wealth and had assets averaging only $1,800—hardly enough to cover clothes, furniture, a used car, a television set, a second-hand tricycle for the kid, a few battered pots and pans in the kitchen. *This is the average for half of all America.* Many had less. 5.7 million households had no assets at all or were in debt.

That is affluent America!

Income
- In 1966 the lowest 20 per cent of American families shared only 3.7 per cent of all personal income.[5]
- The top 20 per cent got 45.8 per cent of all personal income (a slightly larger proportion of the national income than they received twenty years ago).

- Break this down still more and the maldistribution becomes still clearer. The highest 10 per cent of the population received 27 per cent of the national income; the lowest 10 per cent received only 1 per cent of the national income.*

Savings and debt
- The lower 50 per cent of all income receivers in 1950 had a net savings *deficit* (that is they owed more than their savings) of 18.5 per cent.
- At the other end of the scale, the top 10 per cent of income earners owned 72 per cent of all savings.
- The public and private debt of the United States in 1960 amounted to $1,037 billion. By 1966 it had risen to $1,539 billion—an increase in six years of 48 per cent. This debt represents an amount of $7,692 for every man, woman and child in the country. Theoretically, on an average, a family of four—father, mother and two children—have hanging over their heads a debt of $30,768!

The farm subsidies paid out by the U.S. Treasury heavily discriminate against the poor in favor of the rich. In 1967, for example, only 4.5 per cent of the total farm subsidies went to poor farmers with incomes of less than $2500 a year. The huge farm corporations and food processing companies received 64.5 per cent of these subsidies. The Citizens' Report on Hunger and Malnutrition found that in 1966 *a quarter of a billion dollars* in farm subsidies were paid to one-fiftieth of 1 per cent of the population of Texas while the 28.8 per cent of the population living below the poverty line received less than $8 million in all forms of food assistance. That same year the U.S. Treasury paid almost $36 million in farm subsidies to one-third of 1 per cent of the population in Nebraska while it paid less than a million in surplus food allotments to the 26 per cent of the population of that state that lives in poverty. A single farm company in California, J. G. Boswell, was given

* Henry Ford's income in 1969, according to the French Press Agency 14 April 1970, amounted to $516 thousand or over $1,400 a day.

$2,807,633 in handouts by the Treasury that year while the enormously wealthy and powerful Hawaiian Commercial and Sugar Company got $1,236,355.

> Such are the huge hogs (wrote I. F. Stone) that crowd the public trough. Other even bigger corporations live on the gravy that drips from the military and space programs. We may never reach the moon—or know what to do with it when we get there—but the race for it has already created a new generation of Texas millionaires. The arms race and the space race guarantee the annual incomes of many in the country club set.[6]

And what of the others? Those not in the country club set?

On January 22, 1969, Dr. Arnold E. Schaefer of the United States Public Health Service gave evidence before the Senate Select Committee on Nutrition and Human Needs. He reported to the Committee the results of the first sampling of the National Nutrition Survey in Texas, Louisiana, New York and Kentucky. Other states will be surveyed later; the study is not yet completed except in Texas. The survey found that the nutritional level of the 12 thousand persons examined is as low as it is in Guatemala, Costa Rica, Panama, Honduras, Nicaragua and El Salvador, all of which were recently surveyed. "We did not expect to find such cases in the United States," Dr. Schaefer said. "In many of the developing areas where we worked—Africa, Latin America and Asia—these severe cases of malnutrition only rarely are found. They are either hospitalized or have died." Goiter, Dr. Schaefer told the Senate Committee, has staged a striking comeback and is endemic in certain areas—principally in a belt from the Great Lakes to Texas. Goiter is considered endemic when 5 per cent of the people have enlarged thyroid glands. Rickets, he said, is also increasing because a program to fortify milk with Vitamin D is stalled. The government requires milk to be fortified if it is going into American food programs overseas, but not if it is going to the poor in America itself. Both rickets and goiter were thought to have been wiped out in the 1930's, Dr. Schaefer said, but goiter is increasing because of lack of iodized salt in certain areas. In the "goiter belt" livestock is fed iodized salt, but people don't get much of it. Only 40 per cent of local markets in Texas stock it.

The Citizens' Board of Inquiry give heart-breaking accounts of what they found—people eating clay to ease the pain of hunger, children coming to school too hungry to learn and infants of the poor suffering from irreversible brain damage from protein deficiency.

This is a nation spending, as we have seen, over *$9 million every hour* on the military!

The industrial production of the United States is about the same as that of all other capitalist countries combined. Her agricultural production is so great that it costs over $1 million a day merely to *store the surplus.*

Why, in a nation so wealthy, with so enormous an industrial and agricultural productivity, are there any poor people at all?

To understand the meaning of this phenomenon we must grasp again that within a capitalist system wealth and poverty are part of a single process and are inextricably interrelated. Just as the inner dynamics of capitalism produce wealth for the imperialist countries and underdevelopment in those countries abroad which it can dominate, so capitalism generates both wealth and poverty at home. A certain section of the American population, relatively few, are disproportionately wealthy precisely because they have appropriated for themselves (or their fathers did before them) a surplus value produced by the workers and not distributed to them. The poor are poor because they (or their fathers) have been denied the value of that which they have produced and which was not distributed to them. This is a continuing process *that cannot be brought to an end within the terms of any capitalist economy.*

For a great number of citizens this process is concealed by the improvement of their conditions. An American worker sitting in his comfortable house (though it is probably not paid for), watching his favorite television program and with a reasonably modern automobile in his garage (that is probably unpaid for also) would consider it wildly absurd and somewhat insulting to his intelligence if he were told that he was allowing himself to be exploited *relatively* as much as the workers half a century ago were exploited. He has been given the impression, by all kinds of skillful propaganda, that the wealth of the United States is slowly but surely being more equitably distributed. That is not so. The distribution of the wealth in the United States has changed little; if anything the rich have become marginally richer. Those who have studied the national statistics most scrupulously have concluded that there is nothing in the statistics that would support the general belief that there has been some lessening of economic inequality in the United States in recent decades.

In slave and feudal societies workers were under the command of their overlord. In capitalist countries they are free to work for this employer or that and to bargain as best they can over the terms of their employment. But they are *not* free *not to work for others.* Most adult Americans are nothing more than employees earning money for someone else.

*   *

The system looks after the rich. "Good living," says *Fortune* Magazine, "starts at $25,000 a year." But with 56 per cent of the national budget allocated to the Pentagon and 10 per cent for the health, education and welfare of the people, the United States has become a warfare, not a welfare state. "No other Western country," says the Citizens' Report, "permits such a large proportion of its people to endure the lives we press on our poor."

NOTES

1. By Professor Robert J. Lampman of the University of Wisconsin, a study undertaken for the National Bureau of Economic Research; by the Survey Research Center of the University of Michigan; and by the Harvard historian Gabriel Kolko, presented in his book *Wealth and Power in America* (New York: Praeger, 1962).
2. Mr. Shriver later used slightly higher figures, namely $3,130 and $1,540 respectively.
3. *New York Times,* 27 May 1965.
4. *Wealth and Power in America* (see note 1 above).
5. Joseph Kraft, *Herald Tribune* International Edition, 11 February 1969.
6. *I. F. Stone's Weekly,* 13 May 1968.

3

Who Pays?

Nowhere has Karl Marx's dictum that governments are but
the Executive Committee of the ruling class been so clearly
vindicated as in the United States. How magnificently and
invariably the rich have been taken care of by every successive administration! The American economy is run by the
rich and controlled by the rich, and the laws are devised by
the rich to secure, and whenever possible to enhance, their
position of privilege. This is true to a greater or lesser extent
in all capitalist countries. America is no exception, but in no
other country since the overthrow of the French aristocracy
in the eighteenth century has the ruling class succeeded in
putting across swindles on such a gigantic scale—and all in
the name of the great American democratic system! And nowhere is this process of swindling taken to greater lengths
than in the manner in which money is collected for the national treasury. The wealthy have been extraordinarily successful in concealing the extent to which they have shifted
their share of the tax burden from their own shoulders onto
the shoulders of those who are far less able to afford it—
the workers.

If the propertied elite can enforce basic socio-political decisions—such as denying employment to large numbers of quali-
fied people on irrational ethnic grounds when the basic laws do
not support such discrimination—the experience of history
would suggest that they would go farther and also deal themselves enormous tax advantages. For down through history
the dominant classes . . . or political elites have always been
scrupulously prudent in avoiding taxes at the expense of the
lower orders . . .

It would be foolish to contend that there is a propertied
elite in the United States and then not be able to show that
this elite accords itself fantastic tax privileges down to and
including total exemption.[1]

In 1939 only 4 million Americans paid income tax. In
1968, 46 million Americans paid them. There is a prevailing impression that the wealthy are taxed with extreme se-
verity and that the bulk of the nation's revenue comes from
those in the upper income brackets. The reverse is true.
Eighty-six per cent of the national revenue comes from the
lower income earners, from the initial rate that all must pay.
The so-called "progressive rates" that hit the higher income
brackets contribute only 14 per cent.[2]

By means of a veritable medley of gimmicks—"dividend
credits," "depletion allowances," stock options, tax-exempt
bonds, "charities," expense accounts, medical allowances,
capital gains, undistributed profits and so forth—the rich
have been able to avoid paying their share of the nation's
costs. Some who are very rich have been able *legally* to
avoid paying any taxes at all. Here are some examples:

> *In 1959* five people with incomes of more than *$5 million
> each,* paid no federal tax at all. One person with an in-
> come of $10 million paid no tax at all.
> *In 1967,* according to the U.S. Treasury, twenty-one Ameri-
> cans with an income of $1 million paid no federal tax
> at all.[3]

In 1968, according to figures prepared by the Treasury, there
were 155 persons with incomes of $200 thousand or
more who paid no taxes, and eleven persons with incomes
of over $1 million who paid no taxes.[4]

In 1913 the Rockefeller family fortune was approximately
$900 million. (Today the Rockefeller empire—both of
profit and non-profit enterprises—has been estimated at
$5,000 million.) From 1913 to the present time the
Rockefeller fortune has not paid much more than $16.63
million in inheritance taxes.[5]

Philip Stern gives another example:

Eight real estate corporations amassed a total of $18,766,200
in cash available for distribution to their shareholders. They
paid not one penny of income tax.

When this $18,766,200 was distributed, few of their share-
holders paid even a penny of income tax on it.

Despite this cash accumulation of nearly $19 million, these
eight companies were able to report to Internal Revenue
losses, for tax purposes, totalling $3,186,269.

One of these companies alone, the Kratter Realty Corporation, had available cash of $5,160,372, distributed virtually
all of this to its shareholders—and yet paid no tax. In fact,
it reported a *loss,* for tax purposes, of $1,762,240. Few if
any of their shareholders paid any income tax on the more
than $5 million distributed to them by the Kratter Corpora-
tion.[6]

The wealthy, and their "Executive Committee," the government, are forever devising means by which they can legally avoid paying taxes.

President Eisenhower's Administration, for example,
worked out a "dividend credit" scheme intended, it was
said, to avoid "unfair multiple taxation." Under this scheme
a man with a tax bill of $2,020 and who had received divi-
dends of $500 could reduce his tax bill by $20. But for the
306 top taxpayers with an average dividend income of

nearly a million dollars the "dividend credit scheme" meant an average of $40 thousand in cold cash.

Tax-exempt bonds are another way in which the rich can avoid paying.

Tax-exempt bonds are a rich man's investment—the less well-to-do can invest their money in ways that provide a better return than those low-interest bonds. But for the rich they provide a marvelous tax avoidance bonanza. This is why 87 per cent of all tax-exempt bonds are held by the top 1.5 per cent of the population. As Mr. Stern worked it out, for the man in the $140 thousand–$160 thousand income bracket a 3 per cent tax-exempt bond is equal to a 15.8 per cent dividend on a stock; for people in the $300 thousand–$400 thousand income bracket these 3 per cent tax exempt bonds are equal to 30 per cent on a stock and everything above $400 thousand is equal to 33 per cent dividend on a stock.

No wonder these stocks are popular among the rich. In 1945 there were $17.1 billion worth of tax-exempt bonds outstanding; by 1963 there were $85.9 billion. This provides $2.577 billion of *untaxed* income every year—nearly all of it going to the very, very rich.

It is not generally realized that though corporations *apparently* pay income tax like individuals, they in fact pay nothing, for the taxes are merely passed on to the consumers. As the *Wall Street Journal* (5 May 1958) put it, the corporation tax is "treated by corporations as merely another cost which they can pass on to their customers." Corporations thus merely act as collection agents for the government. So many taxes, indeed, are passed on to the ultimate consumer that Eisenhower in an election speech complained that there were 100 different taxes on every egg sold!

As a vivid way of demonstrating how the tax laws *always* discriminate against the wage earner in favor of those with money—and especially those who live on *unearned* income —Philip Stern shows what happens to four men who each received $7,000 annual income.

> *The steel worker* paid $1,282 in federal taxes.
> *The man who got his income from dividends* paid $992.30.
> *The man who sold shares at a profit of $7 thousand* paid $526.00.
> *The man whose income came from state or municipal bonds* paid no tax.

Senior businessmen have available innumerable ways for avoiding tax and living a good life. Corporations will pay for their yachts, their hunting lodges, their country clubs— all they need do is to say that they were used more than half the time for "business purposes"! The dues on the big city clubs can be listed as "expenses," as can the dinner parties, the trips to Bermuda, the gifts of Cadillac cars. It has been estimated that upper sales personnel can siphon off up to $700 and $900 *a week* in "expenses" with no questions asked—and of course no taxes. By dodges such as these corporation officials can make things easy for themselves. Stern gives an example of a president of a small corporation who was paid a salary of $25 thousand on which he paid taxes of $8,300. His company paid for his apartment, his living expenses, his club dues, his trips abroad, giving him in all the equivalent of a salary of $98 thousand, on which he would have had to pay $62,600—nearly eight times the tax he actually paid.

A staff study made for Senator Proxmire, Chairman of the Joint Economic Committee of Congress, estimated that the more obvious tax loopholes enable the rich to drain off $11 billion a year from the U.S. Treasury. As I. F. Stone (13 May 1968) pointed out:

> If a rich man wants to speculate, he is encouraged by preferential capital gains and loss provisions which give him a 25 per cent cushion against losses and take less than half as much

on his speculative gains as on his normal earnings. But if a poor man on relief took a part-time job he had until very recently to pay 100 per cent tax on his earnings in the shape of dollar-for-dollar reduction in his relief allowance. Even now, after a belated reform in the welfare system, a poor man on relief must turn back to the Treasury 70 cents on the dollar while the rich man need pay the Treasury only 25 cents of every dollar he wins on the market even when his normal income tax is more than 50 per cent.

How can a man become rich enough to secure all these special privileges? It is not always necessary to have inherited wealth or go through the slow and tedious business of working up to the higher levels in some huge corporation. If, for example, you had invested only $1 thousand in General Motors common stock in 1908, your holdings in 1959 would be worth more than $1 million and *in addition* you would have received a total of $643 thousand in dividends—an average annual dividend income of nearly $13 thousand! (By 1970 these figures would have risen still more.) The original $1 thousand would have bought you only ten shares, but your holdings in 1959 (without you doing a single stroke of work) would total 22,897 shares as the result of repeated stock splits.[7] (The workers in the factories who created this wealth are of course among the 50 per cent of the nation whose total average assets amount to only $1,800.)

Lundberg in his massive study reaches certain conclusions which he expresses bluntly: "The tax laws," he says, ". . . grossly discriminate at all times and in all directions against salaried and wage workers. Grossly, grossly, grossly . . ."[8]

* *

It is difficult to persuade the 88 thousand millionaires (or even the 2 million-odd who are beginning to enjoy a "good life" on a paltry $25 thousand a year) that there is anything too much wrong with things as they are. It is unlikely that many of these people have spent much time in (I don't mean just driving through) the teeming slum areas of American cities or among the broken shacks that go for homes in the poorer rural areas. Not many of them have sweated out months and years in the assembly lines of the factories, only to find at the end of their lives that they have been able to save nothing. To people who only know the swimming pool life of suburbia, the dire poverty of America must appear as something remote, exaggerated, unreal, almost irrelevant—just as in the time of Britain's industrial revolution the dark hovels and the unspeakable degradation of life in the manufacturing cities must have appeared remote and irrelevant to the wealthy enjoying the social life of London.

The British poor at that period had no political representation; but how can a blatantly unjust division of a nation's wealth continue in a country such as the United States, where the affairs are supposedly run by the people themselves for the people's benefit? And this gross imbalance between the condition of the poor and the wealthy did not come about by mere chance or because of indolence on the part of the poor—it came about *intentionally*. As a result of his detailed examination of the tax laws, Lundberg became convinced that there was "(1) intent to deceive and (2) self-awareness of intent to deceive." And he goes on to ask: "How could nearly 99 per cent of a large population be put into such a wringer by some 1 per cent or less, as though the 99 per cent were the victims of a particularly brutal military conquest? How could such an apparently free population be reduced to the financial status of peasant slaves?"

The answer of course lies in the word "apparently."

* *

The facts we have given show how the privileged always look after themselves. From time to time, adjustments are made to conceal the more glaring abuses and to quiet opposition. That is why today we are seeing the liberals of America urging a reform of the tax structure so that millionaires will no longer escape paying their share. But they *will* escape, for however the tax laws are rewritten and however much these millionaires and the large corporations are made to pay, it is bound to be passed on to the people in the form of higher prices, which in effect means lower wages. Reapportionment of the tax payments of itself cannot eliminate the exploitation of American labor, nor the exploitation of the labor in underdeveloped countries; nor will it reduce by one iota the huge sums of money poured into the military establishment. To prevent the corporations merely passing on their share of taxes to the consumers, the corporations themselves must be controlled. Congress will never control them, for Congress is controlled by *them*. Even when (as sometimes happens) anti-trust or "consumer protection" legislation is passed it is largely window dressing, for the money made available for the effective enforcement of such laws is always ludicrously inadequate. The laws as a result remain largely inoperative.

But if Congress will not control the giants, who will? Who *can?* Who can challenge the great corporations, the banks and credit agencies, the network of interlocking industries and agencies that today manipulate the political and economic structure of the United States and other imperialist countries for their own enrichment? There is only one power large enough to do it: the people themselves operating through a people's government.

That most Americans genuinely believe that their economic system is the best that human wisdom has so far devised and that their political system is a "democracy" in which the interests of the people are paramount, is an indication of how profoundly they have been brainwashed by those who benefit from things remaining as they are—the very people, of course, who control the media of mass communication with which to do the brainwashing. Today, at last, an increasing number of young Americans are waking up to the fact that they are being swindled on a grand scale on every front—and not only through discriminatory tax laws. These young Americans are ignoring cliché and pretense and the demands of a phoney "patriotism" and are facing the realities of American life *and they don't like what they see*. For them, and for millions like them, the technology of capitalism has become a monster dominating the very texture of their lives. They have learned in their struggle against racial discrimination, and through their experiences of the Chicago Convention and in their local communities (and this is one reason for their volcanic anger) that *they are impotent* to correct the basic injustices of the system through the political procedures available to them. They are at last beginning to see that the present political structure itself—the famous American "democracy"—was itself devised to serve the interests of the privileged.

And they are learning, these young Americans, what so many others have learned throughout all history, that though the rich will from time to time (when they have to) make gestures to ameliorate the more intolerable injustices, they will *never* relinquish their economic privileges, or basically alter a political structure which protects them *until they are forced to*. It is never the rich who alter the basic character of societies, but the people, when they finally recognize their collective strength and take their future into their own hands.

NOTES

1. Ferdinand Lundberg, *The Rich and the Super-Rich* (New York: Lyle Stuart, 1968), p. 337. I am greatly indebted to this book for much information in this chapter; as well as to the book *The Great Treasury Raid*, by Philip M. Stern (New York: Random House, 1964). Mr. Lundberg was an economist with the War Production Board and War Shipping Administration during

World War II, was then with the Twentieth Century Fund. He is Adjunct Professor of Social Philosophy at New York University. Mr. Stern was Deputy Assistant Secretary of State in the Kennedy Administration and a former Harvard and Rockefeller Fellow.

2. These figures are derived from pre-1964 rates. Since then there might have been some slight modifications one way or the other. The basic story holds true.
3. *Time*, 4 April 1969.
4. Joseph Kraft, *Herald Tribune*, International Edition, 11 February 1969.
5. Lundberg, p. 595.
6. Stern, pp. 18–19.
7. *New York Times*, 3 February 1959.
8. Lundberg, p. 337.

SECTION FOUR

The Great Hang-Ups

I

The Bourgeois Mentality

We examined at the beginning of this book some of the more degrading and violent aspects of life in imperialism's "home base," the conditions which have developed in the nation which has built its social philosophies and actions more consciously and more fully than any other country on capitalist ideology. Other imperialist countries, Britain, France, West Germany, Japan, and so on, all display the same tendencies and characteristics, differing only in form and degree.

No one can live within the social climate of capitalist ideology (or any other ideology for that matter) without being deeply influenced by it. Our patterns of morality, our behavior to each other, our aspirations, our fears, our education, our religious beliefs, the very way in which we think, are all conditioned by the prevailing assumptions of the society (and by the class within the society) in which we are brought up. This is so obvious that it hardly needs laboring.

Yet we need to remind ourselves of it, for even those who are ready to take a scientific attitude towards every other aspect of human behavior find it difficult to accept how greatly we are conditioned human beings. For most people it is painful to discover that those characteristics which they consider peculiarly "their own"—their judgments and values, the mode of their thinking, indeed almost everything that goes to make up the fabric of their personalities—are not "theirs," arising out of their own independent being, but are largely reflections of their social and economic conditioning. What is more, we assume that our social environment and its institutions were determined by conscious decisions, but this is true only in a very restricted sense; the broad reality is that human consciousness and its "decision-making" process arise out of and are largely determined by environment.

What, then, are the primary conditioning factors that a bourgeois environment imposed on us? What is the consciousness that arises from the conditions of capitalist society?

The most immediately identifiable factor, of course, is the enormously important role that property and the possession of property plays in our lives, and the extent to which our lives are governed by the assumption that it is through wealth and the accumulation of possessions that we will find our fulfillment. As a result, an enormous proportion of our time and energies is spent in accumulating the means of living, regardless of what this does to the quality of living itself. Middle-class man, to an extraordinary extent, has identified himself, his *persona,* with his possessions, so that to lose his possessions is almost as great a calamity as losing life itself. It is in the defense of his property that bourgeois man will mobilize his deepest protective devices; and anybody that threatens his possessions will arouse his most passionate enmity.

We cannot here go into the vast ramifications of the bourgeois conditioning to which we have been subjected, the immensely complex and subtle way in which our minds and emotions have been distorted by capitalist ideology, and from which we must somehow extricate ourselves if a new society is to be established. Consider, for example, how deeply embedded in us is the notion that it is natural and right for one man to employ another and make money from his employee's labor, and that those who are employed are in some way beings "inferior" to those who employ them. Consider, also, how general is the assumption that men and women with intellectual capacities are superior to those who work with their hands and are rewarded accordingly. Again, it requires only a few moments thought to see the extent to which our response to "art" and "culture" has been largely conditioned by the tastes of the upper bourgeoisie of the eighteenth and nineteenth centuries and by what is pronounced "good art" by those who set themselves up as arbiters of "good taste." (How many people who today have a Van Gogh over their mantel would have bought one from the artist himself if he had come—hungry, ill-clothed and half-mad—to their door and begged them to buy one of his paintings?) Even in some socialist countries today we see, not the emergence of new artistic forms arising out of the people's own authentic revolutionary experience, but only too often a pathetic attempt to copy the ballet, the drama and the music that titillated the European upper classes under totally different social conditions. Take also the absurd extent to which the so-called elite circles in the larger cities of Latin America ape the manners, the clothes, the hair styles, the "culture" of Paris and New York, not recognizing at all that they are aping societies that are fast moving into decadence. So many of the educational procedures over the world (even, alas, in the newly developing countries that believe they have "liberated" themselves from their former colonial rulers) are still based on educational methods required by the class-oriented societies of Europe, an education that has no relevance at all to the needs of a socialist society—and which will, if allowed to continue, effectively undermine the basic goals of socialism.

Bourgeois attitudes to people, to "culture," to education,

to possessions, to "individuality," to family, were so deeply embedded even in a revolutionary society such as China that it required a second revolution, a Cultural Revolution and a national self-inquiry of a very profound nature, before the Chinese were finally able to throw off the false trappings of bourgeois conditioning. It is my belief that every individual and every society (even those which have rid themselves of the formal institutions of capitalism) must go through such a cultural revolution before the "new man" and the "new society" can arise.

Those who have the greatest power and influence and who gain most from a continuation of the capitalist social order of course do all they can to condition in us a defensiveness of things as they are, and many people are quite incapable of entertaining the idea that there might be preferable alternatives. Alternatives are presented to us always in the most frightening light; they are never shown as possible improvements. The obviously outrageous features of capitalist society—its inhumanity, its gross injustices, its violence, its hypocrisy, its lawlessness, the extent to which it favors a few at the expense of the many, its racism, its vulgarity, its inability to meet even the barest minimum needs of many of the population—all these are seen merely as correctable defects on an otherwise admirable system. They are not recognized as an integral and inescapable part of it.

When pushed to admit the quite obvious irrationality of the existing order, the bourgeois mind nevertheless defends it by falling back on the equally irrational assertion that "human nature is what it is and cannot be changed." This effectively undermines the idea that man can ever transform his society. As a result, bourgeois ideology has a built-in fatalism and cynicism; it is the ideology of pessimism.

We should at least examine those aspects of our bourgeois conditioning which have created the biggest mental hang-ups and which constitute the primary roadblocks that prevent the building of a new society.

2

The Religion Hang-Up

It is normal today among the young and the progressive to
deny the existence of God, and it may therefore appear
strange that we should list religious belief among the salient
features of the bourgeois mentality. We do so because,
whatever the current attitude towards a belief in God might
be, the ideology of religion is still sufficiently widespread
and still so deeply pervades Western societies as to constitute an effective barrier to the liberation of human thought.

From the earliest dawn of history man appears to have
speculated on the nature of reality. The search for "ultimate
truth" has been unflagging. Countless thousands of devoted
and gifted men have spent their lives attempting to prove
that this doctrine or that reveals the nature of reality. But
never has there been sustained agreement. From the same
facts different men have drawn quite opposite conclusions.
The prevailing beliefs of one generation are abandoned by
the next; and men everywhere continue to this day to
preach, argue, get angry and if necessary slaughter each
other on behalf of their particular belief system. Quite
clearly his system of beliefs form part of man's psychological security and he will mobilize almost as powerful a set of

defensive mechanisms to protect his beliefs as he will to protect his physical possessions.

Man has always had to live in a universe he only partially understands. He is confronted with forces and powers over which he can exercise only a limited control but which press upon his life and insist on conformity with their laws. In spite of the growing fund of knowledge about his environment, his knowledge is but a tiny beam of a pocket flashlight groping the dark expanses of an unknown desert. Man knows enough to formulate questions to which he can find no answers in experience. Answers to all the biggest questions still remain in the area of speculation.

Man's past response to this situation in which unknowns loom so large, in which natural laws are so inexorable and in which he knows that he, as an individual creature, is doomed to die—his past response to this total situation is what is called "religion"; and his attempts to formulate some intelligible and reassuring account of his relationship with the the mysterious and threatening world around him gave birth to the myths, the creeds, the dogmas, the "beliefs" by means of which men have attempted to find a measure of reassurance.

Western religions (unlike some in the East) take the divine origin of man as their starting point, and on this taken-for-granted basis have constructed the immense edifice of beliefs that have protected man from reality. Central to all Western religions is the concept of a divine "father" who has revealed what rules of conduct he wishes his human children to follow. That there was some survival usefulness in this concept of an extra-human lawmaker cannot be doubted. If a primitive society was to preserve its cohesion and to compel its individual members to conform to social customs it required a sanction outside itself. Thus the tribal rules of conduct became much more than socially useful rules, they became divinely ordained laws. And from the divine lawmaker there was no escape. However alone you were, however separated from your tribal group, the all-seeing eye was there watching you. In the very depths of the jungle, in the vast spaces of the desert you were being watched. As a technique to maintain social cohesion it was a useful device and perhaps in the earlier stages of man's development a necessary one.

Belief in an all-powerful, all-seeing father-god was an extension of the child's experience of his human father. To a small child his father appears godlike: he is omnipotent; he is the provider; in his arms one feels no fear; he brings protection, comfort, security, love. But the human father is also capable of terrible anger and has constantly to be propitiated. Every child is aware of the necessity to submit to his father, and this became later his submission to his father-god: "Thy will oh Lord not mine be done." Religion, in thus extending into later life attitudes appropriate to childhood, acted as a mechanism for the control of the adult.

During the past few generations an increasing number of people have rejected the concept of a divine father-god as no longer required by our human situation and not conforming to observable fact. But deep-seated beliefs die slowly. Though words such as "god" or "divine" have lost their power the notion that our customs, our mores, our patterns of morality are not merely relatively useful social regulations but have their roots in the cosmic order of things, lingers on. An enormous number of people who think they have abandoned their belief in a father-god nevertheless feel as if they have sinned, have broken an extra-human law when they deviate from some man-made rule.

Guilt is an immensely powerful weapon. If once you can make a man feel guilty, make him feel that there is something *wrong with him,* you have gained a psychological ascendancy over him. In the course of human history all manner of guilt producing techniques have been developed by those who wish to keep us in subjection. Organized Western religions are masters at producing guilt among their followers. "Be ye perfect as your father in heaven is perfect" is an example of a command which is humanly and psychologically meaningless, but it induces the feeling of guilt for just being what one is. The Christian churches have produced not only the concept of a god of absolute goodness (whatever that might mean) but also his son, a man-god, someone like us but also terribly unlike us in his perfection . . . and this man-god is placed before us as an example of what *we* must be! As counterparts to these rules, to fortify still further our sense of unworthiness, are such rituals as the Litany of the English church, in which believers must grovel on their knees and murmur "Oh Lord have mercy upon us miserable sinners." What better way could be devised to make a people vulnerable to control?

Guilt is a weapon often used on psychologically vulnerable people such as children. Very little children are peculiarly open to suggestion, as open as a photographic plate is to light. Small children have no value judgments of their own and absorb those of their parents, on whom they are dependent. Suggestions made to children often linger on with terrible tenacity. "What a wicked thing to do!" "You're a bad boy!" are the kind of casual exclamations that are often construed quite literally in a child's mind and accepted as true.

When an order is given to someone under hypnosis that he do something at a certain time after he is brought back to consciousness he will do his best to conform to the order however absurd it might be. If he is *prevented* from fulfilling the order he will have stirrings of acute guilt and anxiety. Most parents expect a great deal from their children when they grow up; some even want their child to follow a particular career whether he is suited to it or not. These suggestions made to children when very young have the same effect as a post-hypnotic suggestion—the child's whole life may be lived with an anxious feeling that he should be doing something other than what he is doing, that he should be a "better" person than he is, should be cleverer, more musical, a better athlete or whatever it might be. He is forever trying to live up to those early childhood commands and to obey suggestions given him when he was far too young to understand or evaluate them or even consciously to remember them.

The suggestions given to those made vulnerable by religious belief have the same potency. "Religious" people are almost always people with a high component of guilt and anxiety for they can *never,* in the very nature of things, live up to the "perfection" that is demanded of them.

We must now relate all this to the subject matter of this book. How does religion impinge on the question of capitalism and imperialism? What role does religion play in Western capitalist society?

That it clearly plays an important part is seen by the great amount of energy and money that is devoted to keeping the population in a "religious frame of mine"—for example the number of radio and television programs (both in the United States and Britain) that are devoted to religious broadcasts (and conversely how little opportunity is provided for those who wish to challenge the basic assumptions of religion). We can see also how contemporary religion seeks (as primitive religion did) to maintain a social cohesion by promoting the important ideological tie between the *ruler,* the monarch, the tribal chief, and "God." Even the President of the United States in taking his oath of office calls on God to help him. But above all, religion in bourgeois society today is used to keep people in a state of guilt, to mystify, to bamboozle, so that reality and myth, symbol and fact are all brought together in a veritable quagmire of mental and emotional contradictions, so that people are uncertain even about who they really are. Indeed, religion today might be called the ideology of confusion.

The human mind, under the influence of religion, has an astonishing capacity to accept as true all manner of mutually contradictory propositions. When dealing with the ordinary world around him a man will either accept the fact that the earth is round or that it is flat, he would not accept both at once and say they were both true. But in religion he is ready to swallow contradictory dogmas without turning a hair. He is asked to believe, for example (and if he is religious he somehow manages to do so), that the god he worships is both an infinitely patient, loving and forgiving god, *and* that he is a jealous god who will punish wrongdoers with hideous and everlasting torture. It was somehow possible (at least until recently) for highly sophisticated Japanese astronomers who would know in great detail the physical properties of the sun to believe that the Japanese Emperor was "descended" from the sun—and this in a literal and not a metaphorical sense. It was only a few years ago that the Pope reaffirmed the doctrine that the Virgin Mary ascended into heaven *physically,* that it was her material body and not her "spiritual" body that arose into the sky and went to heaven. Catholics—even Catholic physical scientists—presumably were able to accept this as true, though no astronomer has yet told us the location of this heaven which is ready to receive physical bodies in this astonishing way. It was belief in magic that led one of the American astronauts to take a rosary with him; another to quote the Bible while floating in space.

What all this indicates is the extent to which magic and mystery and obfuscation are part of the ideology of religion. What better weapon could those who want to control us have than to keep us in a world of fantasy? It is highly important for those who want to maintain the society as it is to prevent people from seeing and dealing with the realities of their conditions, for if they did so they would at once take steps to alter them. Whatever evolutionary and survival uses religion may have had in the earlier stages of man's development, with the emergence of class society religion became a *class weapon,* intended to obscure from the people the extent to which they were and still are being exploited. It is not *this* world that matters, we are told; *real* life, the life of joy and happiness comes when we are dead—but *only* if we remain docile and obedient ("blessed are the meek") in this! The celebration of High Mass is made to be more important to people than the condition of their earthly lives. Life *should* be a time of trial and tribulation—and the more trial and tribulation we experience the more credit we accumulate for our hereafter. "Blessed are the poor." The poor are extremely *fortunate* to be poor—for they will inherit everything, the whole earth—after they are dead!

Is it a wonder that so much effort, time and money goes into the religion business? Television programs, elaborate ritual, marvelous music, choirs, robes, vestments, diadems, angels, candles, every device that will bedazzle us and awaken in us the primitive yearnings from our ancient past. And with this go the reminders that we are miserable sinners, creatures unworthy of the infinite blessings that are ours!

The rhetoric of religion is also calculated to evoke deeply embedded responses—words such as "kindliness," "goodwill," "non-violence," "love." These words blunt the consciousness and obscure the need for *action* to secure change. For if indeed changes in society can be achieved by exhorting people to be *kind* to one another—why use more forceful means?

But religious rhetoric has another effect also. There is no one who does not long, in the deepest recesses of his heart, for a world in which kindness, lack of violence, goodness, thoughtfulness, love are the guiding motivations. To evoke such words then is an attempt to put the opponents of the religious ideology at a moral disadvantage, to put them in a position of embarrassment even within themselves, for they do not denigrate the concept of a world governed by moral law, indeed that is precisely what they themselves are most ardently hoping to achieve, yet they must deny the *func-*

tional reality of the words that the "religious" use in the defense of religion. But there are several aspects of the world they long for which differ profoundly from that of the "religious"; in their world there will be no place for a self-projected father-god; nor for the confusion of myth and symbol with reality which is always to be a part of the religious ideology; nor will an *induced sense of "sin"* be used as a means of social coercion. Religious ideology would no longer be used to suppress the liberating emotions and forces of man.

Christianity, which began as a revolutionary ideology, soon became a tool of oppression and myth.

The history of the Church of England provides an example of the extent to which the religious establishment identifies itself with the secular ruling class. Bishops in the House of Lords voted against the repeal of slavery; against the child labor laws at the end of the nineteenth century; and in World War II supported the use of indiscriminate bombing of civilian targets (saturation bombing); and the use of atomic bombs if used on the side of right and justice. There's no need to ask *which* side represented right and justice.

We began by saying that man had always sought answers to the meaning of his life, and he will continue to do so, for the unanswered questions will always beckon. The time has surely come in his evolution when he can stand the tension of *not knowing* rather than provide himself with the comfort of "beliefs." To the large questions of existence which still remain outside the range of his understanding he surely has reached the maturity to say, quite simply, *"We do not yet know."* And with that maturity he will be immune from the guilt producing, confusion producing techniques of religious ideology and can begin to direct his energies to the problem of how to make human society human.

3

The "Anything but Violence" Hang-Up

There is a group within the Protestant Christian community (and I, for a number of years, was among them) who take the absolute pacifist position. They argue that the use of violence to end violence is not only self-contradictory but that the use of violence is *morally* wrong, that Christianity forbids it, and that he who resorts to it, regardless of his motives or of any beneficial results he might achieve, is contravening a law of nature or of God.

Other pacifists are less concerned with "not sinning" but believe, rather, that the use of violence is always in the end self-defeating. They believe that the use of physical violence and oppression (which is another form of violence) inevitably breeds *more* violence and oppression, and that the only way to end violence and oppression is by confronting them with total non-resistance. They do not spell out clearly the causal connection between the two or explain the process by which nonresistance ends violence, except of course that a total *submission* to violence would eliminate the need for the violent man to use physical action against his victim.

But submission to violence does not *end* violence, it acquiesces in it; the victim becomes a partner of violence by allowing it to continue in a non-physical form. Some pacifists argue that sheer defenselessness will arouse pity and prevent violence. But is not this wishful thinking? It is very difficult to find instances where violence has ceased because pity has been aroused by the helplessness of the victim, while history records thousands of cases where the defenselessness of a people is precisely *why* they have been attacked. Did non-resistance of the Jews in Germany arouse Hitler's pity? Did the helplessness of the women and babies in Song My village in South Vietnam arouse the pity of the U.S. soldiers who butchered them in cold blood? If peaceful submission produces pity, how could slaveowners continue to own slaves?

In spite of the evidence of history, pacifism persists as a disturbing challenge to the liberal conscience. It is about the only emotionally charged belief left in Protestant Christianity. Its appeal is powerful, for the concept of a world without conflict evokes in all of us (just as the words used by the religious) a deep nostalgia for a society where violence and oppression no longer exist, where we can live humanly again, and where the nightmare of war and conflict are things of the past. Thus to challenge the position of the absolute pacifist induces in us a certain moral embarrassment, for *all* of us who see the need of a radical change in the social order, who see that the present violence and human exploitation must be brought to an end, wish with all our hearts that it could be changed *without* violence. In opposing and arguing against pacifism we half feel that we are arguing against some deep inclination within ourselves.

Pacifism has all the spurious appeal of *any* absolute position. We all wish that we could find some rule of thumb, some simple truth, one all-embracing theoretical standard to which we could conform and *know that we are right*. But what an evasion this is of the arduous task of finding our own relationship with the complex reality of the life around us! How enormously comforting to be able with a clear con-

science to tell the Jews in Germany or the villagers in Vietnam that by being murdered they were in some wondrous
way furthering the will of God!

In the harsh words of Christopher Caudwell:

> The fact that one participates passively in bourgeois economy,
> that one does not oneself wield the bludgeon or fire the can-
> non, so far from being a defense really makes one's position
> more disgusting, just as a fence is more unpleasant than a
> burglar, and a pimp than a prostitute . . . The bourgeois
> pacifist occupies perhaps the most ignoble place of a man
> in any civilization . . . He sits on the head of the worker
> and, while the big bourgeois kicks him, advises him to lie
> quiet . . .
> The pacifist is obsessed with the lazy lust of the absolute.[1]

What is the reality that the pacifist, the believer in non-
violence, must face? That two thousand years of futile Christian preaching of nonviolence has led to no diminution of
violence; that it is precisely those nations that claim to follow the philosophy of Christianity that are the most violent.
Those who drop the napalm bombs go to church. And why?
Why has the appeal of pacifism, which strikes such a deep
chord in all of us, so signally failed? *Because the roots of
violence have never been dug up.* Christian pacifism has appealed to our emotions, but has done very little to enlarge
our understanding of the deeper causes of violence, how it
arises from, and is an inseparable part of, the material basis
of our society. All class society, all exploitation of man by
man is violence. *The search for peace and non-violence is
meaningless if it is not associated with and a part of the determination to overthrow capitalism and imperialism.*

* *

In spite of Vietnam, in spite of the invasion of Cuba, in
spite of dozens of military interventions elsewhere since the
end of World War II, in spite of its construction of the most

powerful military machine ever known to man, U.S. imperialism has succeeded brilliantly in creating in the minds of most Americans an image of the United States as peace-loving, reasonable, non-predatory, conciliatory, and inoffensive. Words make a stronger impact on the American people than actuality. One of the standard clichés propounded by successive presidents is that the United States is not in the least interested in securing territory—that in fighting her successive wars she is acting on purely altruistic motives. The reverse of course is the truth, as any map of the world will show. After World War II, for example, though President Truman in July 1945 repeated the old cliché with the usual emphasis ("The United States will not take one inch of additional territory as a result of the part she has played in winning the victory"), the U.S. retained all the strategic bases in the Pacific which her forces had captured.

At the very height of the Cuban crisis, Adlai Stevenson made a speech to the Security Council of the U.N. in which he said:

We have sought loyally to support the United Nations, to be faithful to the world of the Charter, and to build an operating system that acts, and does not talk, for peace.

We have never refused to negotiate. We have sat at conference after conference seeking peaceful solutions to menacing conflicts.

Every phrase in this statement is a downright lie, but by words such as these, repeated often in different ways and on different occasions, the national self-image of a nonviolent and peaceful nation has been very firmly established. The huge hiatus that exists between the American self-image and historical reality is one of the principal reasons why the American people have been inhibited from taking direct action to secure control of their own destiny.

The public in capitalist countries have been conditioned against the language of violence. The Western liberal particularly prefers violence to be unseen and unheard. When the Chinese government, for example, uses violent language to denounce the United States, even some friends of China in the West become embarrassed and wish the Chinese would tone down their voice, would talk in more temperate, more "reasonable" terms; would, in other words, talk *more like us*. But the extremism of the Chinese is not exaggerated, for it relates to extreme actions. There is something revolting about a description of Hitler's gas ovens couched in "reasonable" words. When the Chinese denounce the barbarities of the United States as being the actions of a bully, and when they state with all the emphasis they can that U.S. imperialism is the greatest enemy of mankind—they are demonstrating their recognition of the extreme forms of violence that the United States is engaged in. Western "statesmen" attempt to obscure and justify acts of the utmost inhumanity by describing them in terms that are calm and unimpassioned and by using words that appear judiciously detached. They use euphemisms such as "overkill," "bodycount," "defensive measures," "retaliatory action"—the Pentagon has developed a whole vocabulary of obfuscation—in the same way that Hitler characterized his massacre of the Jews as "the final solution."

* *

To understand nonviolence we must understand the nature of violence.

The violence in bourgeois society arose, just as the violence of slavery and feudalism arose, out of the characteristic economy of the system. Bourgeois productivity was crippled and held down by the social structure of the feudal system until it was able to break the chains of feudalism. To the bourgeoisie "freedom" consisted of the freedom for every man to run his own affairs with the minimum of interference from the state. The bourgeois revolution was to secure the right of every man to do with his property exactly as he chose. "Property" in the feudal economy primarily involved ownership of *land* and the exploitation of the people who worked on it. Ownership of land involved unavoidable restraints, if only to prevent others from seizing it. Indeed, there were a whole series of restraints imposed by custom and law on those who owned land. The new bourgeoisie on the other hand were principally interested in *things*, in products, and especially in capital. Restraints on the use of their money was what the new bourgeoisie most fiercely resisted.

The relationship between master and slave, between feudal lord and serf, was a relationship between *people;* and this involved the restraint on the liberty of one for the benefit of the other. But the relationship between a man and his money is a relationship between a man and a "thing," and the capitalist calling for a total freedom to do with his money exactly what he wants uses the argument that this is an innocent relationship, for how can a "thing" be exploited?

This is, of course, a false argument, for the capital which the owner wants to use without any restraint was created by the work of people and capital represents that part of the value which he produced which was withheld from the worker. So the relationship between man and his capital is also a relationship between people, but in a disguised form. In slave and feudal societies the domination of one class of men by another was conscious, visible and clear; in bourgeois capitalism the domination of one class by another is obscured because the domination is exercised through what at first appears to be a "neutral" agency, namely capital. The whole structure of bourgeois economy is built on the violent domination of one class of men by another class through the possession in private hands of what should be social capital.

As long as a bourgeois economy is able to develop and expand its latent force, the violence of this domination remains hidden, but when the contradictions inherent in this system become apparent, when poverty and unemployment grow at a time when the economy if freed could produce plenty for all; when, in other words, private profit is seen to be a public harm, then the violence latent in the system comes out into the open. The bourgeois state is an apparatus for the coercive protection of private property. There are no lengths to which the bourgeoisie would not go to protect their property "rights," which are no rights at all. Just like the slave state, today the bourgeois state depends on violence, and it could no more last without violence than a slave state could last without restraint on the slaves. Violence lies at the very heart of the bourgeois illusion of "freedom."

Nonviolence within a violent society cannot provide a program of action; it is, indeed, a form of complicity with it. No one, not even the most dedicated, most devout, most sincere pacifist can "contract out" and establish for himself a neutral position. Either a man participates in the bourgeois economy of violence or he revolts against it and attempts as best he can, in association with others, to establish an alternative.

As bourgeois society will never submit quietly to its own overthrow and will use every means at its disposal to defend itself, the establishment of an alternative society can only come through the agency of those who are prepared to use force. To believe that "non-resistance," "pacifism," "nonviolence" is a middle course in which one can steer clear of both the violence of bourgeois society and the violence of revolution is an illusion which only serves the interests of those who want the present exploitive society to continue. Within the context of capitalism, complicity in one form of violence or the other is inescapable. The only choice is— violence for what end? To maintain the violence of the *status quo* or to overthrow it?

* *

The "haves" will always and everywhere resist disruption of the social order by the "have nots." The bourgeoisie, having achieved their ends through revolution, now deplore the very idea of rebellion. The United States that began its existence as an independent country through armed bourgeois revolution and having become the greatest "have" nation is now the greatest defender of the *status quo,* and its official spokesmen have publicly announced that the country is prepared to suppress rebellion in whatever part of the world it might appear. The bourgeoisie are fastidious, having achieved their ends, and deprecate with refined aversion any signs of violence in others. They shudder at the very mention of "revolution," as if this was a method used only by the uncouth and uncivilized.

That is the public stance. Imperialism is quite ready, as we have said, to do what it can to suppress a revolutionary movement or, if a revolutionary government is established, to bring it down. For years it was the publicly pronounced policy of the United States to destroy the revolutionary government of China. And the same with Cuba. The United States imposed a 100 per cent embargo on trade with these countries; she employs great pressure to prevent her allies from trading with them; she arms and finances their enemies; she harasses their shipping; she threatens them with atomic missiles which she announces are pre-targeted and pre-programmed to destroy their major cities; her spy ships prowl just beyond these countries' legal territorial waters; her reconnaissance planes fly constantly over their territory. And having done all in their power to disrupt these countries' efforts to rebuild their societies and by means of blockades to prevent essential goods from reaching them, any temporary difficulties and setbacks these countries may encounter are magnified and exaggerated and presented as proof that a socialist revolutionary government is "unworkable."

The "have" nations deplore the violence, the disruption,

that is involved in any revolution. They are meticulous in their calculations of the "human cost" of revolution. Their newspapers make up the wildest estimates of the supposed numbers of people who are slain in the course of the revolution, and when the bourgeoisie who have been dispossessed and who have never from the start been in favor of the revolution but instead fought against it, "escape," this is "proof" of the hideous "tyranny" that the revolution is imposing on the citizenry. There is always a human cost involved in revolution, sometimes a frightful cost, but what Western nations, even some Western liberals, very rarely calculate is the far greater human cost of *not* having a revolution.

Before China's revolution at least a million people, on an average, died every year of starvation. The International Red Cross reported that every year in Shanghai alone over 20 thousand bodies were picked up off the streets—people who had just gone under. Millions of Chinese lived so little above the biological level of survival that their bodies were permanently stunted and there was no hope for them of anything but a lifetime of sheer toil and pain. This was the "human cost" that endless generations suffered for not having a revolution. Today, no one starves in China, no bodies are picked up off the streets; there are no beggars, everyone has work, bodies are healthy, the expectancy of life is extended; opportunities for exercising skills and talents are open to everyone; the dark days of illiteracy are over forever. And in Cuba the same. How many children who are now vigorous and healthy would have died of starvation or lived stunted lives if the United States had succeeded in its efforts to overthrow the Cuban revolutionary government? Around every large city in Latin America I have seen for myself the visible human cost of *not* having a revolution— the malformed children, the sickness, the thousands of families who can exist only by scavenging the stinking refuse of the city dumps.

When on one occasion I asked Mr. Nehru why he did not

mobilize for socially productive purposes the prodigious wealth which is still owned by the upper classes of India, he replied that this would mean struggle, violence even, and he wanted to bring about necessary reforms in a "democratic" and "nonviolent" way. A classic bourgeois answer! But what about the violence, the unseen violence, of *not* being ready to meet struggle and violence? What about the huge human misery within India? What about the 500 thousand Indian children who it is estimated die every year through lack of food? This, in the bourgeois mind, is not considered "violence," but what is mass starvation if it is not bloodless genocide? But the bourgeoisie do not calculate the mathematics of suffering in this way.

Some in the West, of course, have seen beyond the immediate disruption of revolution to the goal beyond. A century-and-a-half ago Lord Macaulay wrote:

> We deplore the outrages that accompany revolutions. But . . . the final and permanent fruits of liberty are wisdom, moderation and mercy. Its immediate effects are often atrocious crimes, conflicting errors, skepticism on points the most clear, dogmatism on points the most mysterious. It is just at this crisis that its enemies love to exhibit it. They pull down the scaffolding from the half-finished edifice: they point to the flying dust, the falling bricks, the comfortless rooms, the frightful irregularity of the whole appearance; and then ask in scorn where the promised splendor and comfort are to be found. If such miserable sophisms were to prevail, there would never be a good house or a good government in the world.

* *

We must say again: there is no middle way in which violence can be avoided. We are either accomplices in the violence of the *status quo* or we join the ranks of those who are ready to use violence to overthrow it. But though the word in each case is the same word, there is a whole world of difference between them. Violence to what end? To perpetuate a system based on violence or to end it? The whole purpose of revolutionary violence is to destroy at its very roots the institutionalized system of greed which is also the institutionalized system of violence.

Human beings are very complex creatures. Within us there are many conflicting drives and, until examined, all kinds of unconscious motivations. The would-be revolutionary, before he commits himself to the revolutionary role, as we shall examine at greater length in another chapter, has an obligation to search into himself, to become as aware as he can of precisely why and under what conditions he is ready to use violence if it becomes necessary. Violence for its own sake is counterrevolutionary. Violence to gratify a deeply felt hostility towards people, or to release a long pent-up sense of personal failure or resentment, or to prove to oneself that one is "manly," all these are reflections of immaturity and have no place in revolution.

The violence of the *status quo* is at the service of greed, acquisition, the continuation of a "me first" society. Revolutionary violence is of a totally different order. If he could, the revolutionary would change society not with guns but with words, with discussion, with persuasion. But the revolutionary is also a realist and he knows that history cannot demonstrate a single instance where those who hold positions of power and privilege have given up their position peacefully. The revolutionary uses violence only when there is no other way, and never to protect his own interests, his wealth, his status, his privileges or his sense of personal virtue. He uses it only to destroy a social order which does not any longer allow men to be human to each other.

Today, with the phoney cry of "law and order" the rulers of the imperialist nations attempt to throw the onus of violence on those who are protesting the system under which they live. But the onus is not on them, for violence is the near-monopoly of the state apparatus. Compared to the machinery of violence that the ruling class deploys, the violence of the protesters is like the pop of a toy gun beside the explosion of a one-thousand-ton bomb.

Today we have reached the very limits of imperialist violence. From now on imperialist violence can only be a form of human suicide. To any thoughtful and humane man, even though it be against his own deep inclinations, there is really no choice left—he can only join with others to bring the present system to an end.

NOTES

1. This is an extract from a chapter in Christopher Caudwell's well-known work *Studies in a Dying Culture* (London: The Bodley Head, 1938), which in an abridged form appeared with the permission of T. Stanhope Sprigg, executor of the author's estate, in the *Monthly Review*, April 1969. The abridgment was done by Tom Christoffel.

   Christopher Caudwell (Christopher St. John Sprigg) died on February 12, 1937 while fighting for the Republicans in the Spanish Civil War. He was twenty-nine years old. He fought in Spain because "what I feel about the importance of democratic freedom," had to be matched with action.

   I am greatly indebted to Christopher Caudwell for my own understanding of pacifism and violence, and I have drawn freely on his ideas as expressed in the chapter published by the *Monthly Review*.

4

The "Democracy" Hang-Up

The use of the word "democracy" is about as powerful an agent of confusion, double-talk and sheer fakery as the rhetoric used by the spokesmen for religion. We have seen how they, the "religious," appropriate words such as kindliness, gentleness, love—words that call to something very deep in us all—and then use them to justify actions that altogether contradict their meaning. "Love thy enemy," they say, and then demonstrate their love by supporting and blessing the use of high explosives on him. In the same way, and causing much the same emotional and intellectual confusion, those who control our political destinies use words that carry an immensely powerful positive appeal but which have no relation at all to the real intentions of those who use them. Words such as equality, brotherhood, government of the people, by the people, representative government, the sovereignty of the people, and so on, have a profoundly moving effect on us, for they correspond to the deep longing which is in all of us for a life in which we can cooperate with each other rather than compete; a society in which we feel we belong as participating members of a true community. With these words, in combination with the ritual that accompanies them, those who possess the real power confuse and bamboozle us. The great democratic swindle—the passing off of fake democracy as genuine—has succeeded so well precisely because of this very hunger for a genuine democracy. One cannot sell a fake unless there is a demand for the genuine article.

So the first necessary step, if we are to clear our own confusions, is to sort out the reality from the idiom, to learn what kind of "democracy" we now have and to see how far it not only falls short of what a true democracy might be, but how in many essential ways it represents the very opposite.

Fake democracy really goes back to the original Greek use of the word, for their "democracy" represented a participation in government of the minority of free men in a slave society. Even then it was a tactic, a device, to help the really rich and powerful in a small city-state to manipulate the middle strata of society. Fake democracy found a new lease of life nearer to our times with the development of bourgeois society. Its essential function was (and still is) to consolidate the power of the few by creating in the minds of the many the illusion that they control their own destiny, that they have a real place in the decision-making process of government.

In Britain, the institution of Parliament was a powerful weapon of the new capitalist class against feudalism, and as such had a progressive character. Parliament later developed as a direct reflection of capitalism: it served, and still serves, the needs of capitalism; and maintaining the outward forms of Parliamentary procedures is one of the ways in which the essentially exploitative character of capitalism is concealed from the people.

In the United States "democracy"—as in Greece—began within the context of a slave society and thus it, too, was from the start a tool of the propertied class. The French Revolution also was a bourgeois revolution directed against the feudal aristocracy and, under the enormously appealing slogan of "Liberty, Equality, Fraternity," it ultimately gave "freedom" an unbridled license to the newly emerging commercial and financial oligarchies. The "Marseillaise" was a hymn of triumph of the bourgeoisie.

Democracy in Britain, France, and the United States *did* at first provide a means of participation and equality in the governing process *but only for the bourgeoisie and within the bourgeois class.* The glowing descriptions of the "democratic process" which sound so splendid are descriptions written (as are our history books) *by* the bourgeoisie.

During the nineteenth century, with the growing centralization of capital and monopoly, British Parliament lost its function as the decision-maker for the bourgeois class. From then on the focus of political power shifted from Parliament until today Parliament has lost almost all its power and its meaning. Its members ("our" representatives!) troop obediently through the division lobbies voting as they are instructed to, often not even knowing what they are voting about. Parliament's main function is now largely ceremonial; it provides the means (like a seal on a legal document) of formally validating decisions that are made elsewhere. The constitutional *theory* is that the House of Commons, representing the electorate, acts as a watchdog over the Executive. That function has long been abandoned. It is not Parliament (as Lloyd George was one of the first to say publicly) that today controls the Cabinet; it is the Cabinet that controls Parliament.

Lord Justice Denning endorsed this view:

> Over one hundred years ago Parliament was, no doubt, the supreme power in the land both in law and in fact. . . . In practice sovereignty no longer rests with Parliament. It rests with the Executive and in particular with the Cabinet

. . . Once elected, the leaders of the party are the sovereign power in the land.

And what is the Cabinet? It has no place in law. It is essentially "the Executive Committee" of the ruling class, *whichever* political party happens to be in power. Who knows how the Cabinet functions? As the British constitutional lawyer Sir Ivor Jennings pointed out in his book "Cabinet Government",

> The most important parts of the Cabinet system function in secret. Information is rarely made available until the persons concerned in particular events are dead.

Yet this extra-legal committee acting in secret and controlling the Parliamentary processes is not elected by the people and is under no legal or public control.

How far the Cabinet itself is under the control of the big industrial and financial centers of power is indicated by the *continuity* of basic national policies in spite of professed differences of political philosophy. Wilson, as the leader of the British Labour Party, spoke out bitterly against the Vietnam war *until* his party took over the Government; whereupon he announced that the war had, in some miraculous manner, undergone a "qualitative change" and it was therefore now right to support America's involvement. There is nothing more sadly revealing than to see the Labour Party (which claims to be a *socialist* party!) obey the bankers and prop up the capitalist system.

The shift of power from the Legislative to the Executive branch is also a noticeable feature of the American political scene. So independent and powerful has the Executive become that today the President can with impunity, as in the case of the war in Vietnam, defy all the supposedly foolproof constitutional restraints and commit the people of the United States to a long, enormously costly and bloody war without the sanction of Congress.

In both countries the *apparatus* and ritual of representation has been scrupulously maintained. As a result millions of people in the United States and Britain remain, as of course they are intended to, under the illusion that they can change the course of events by sending this man or that to Parliament or Congress, electing this man or that to the Presidency. But in both countries the "choice" the electorate is given is hardly a choice at all. In neither country do candidates represent significantly different political philosophies whatever they may *say*, for they are all supporters of capitalism and the major capitalist interests. There are marginal differences: minor differences in the order of national priorities, differences of "style," differences as to which of the capitalist interests they will primarily favor. But those at the real centers of power lie far beyond the people's influence, and they remain constant whoever the electorate happens to choose as the temporary managers.

The first essential step in the understanding of so-called democracy in capitalist nations is to grasp the fact that "our" representatives in no way represent *us*. After the violent and squalid happenings during the Chicago Convention in 1968 an increasing number of Americans are beginning to have second thoughts about their so-called democratic procedures. They sense that something has gone wrong. They are beginning to see through the fakery. Even many of those who are still working actively for this party or that are having to resist as best they can an overwhelming sense of futility. And not only in the United States. The people in Britain, France, Italy feel equally disfranchised. It isn't that "our man" has been defeated; it is rather that our man almost never turns up to be elected. And when on a rare occasion some candidate talks sense instead of nonsense, who instead of speaking to us in terms of cliché and banalities directs our attention to the real questions that concern us and asks the questions that we think should be asked, such a man hardly ever gets elected, and if he *does* his voice is smothered. What is more, many citizens feel they have something to say and have some contribution to make to the political life of their country *outside* of the ranks of the large party organizations, but there seems to be no way in which they can actively participate. If some issue arouses them sufficiently they can, it is true, organize public meetings, but when they do no one in the decision-making circles of government bothers to listen. Hundreds of thousands of aroused citizens come to Washingon to let their feelings be known—and the President instead of meeting with them watches a game on television. Several thousand of the country's most eminent scientists can write a letter to the Government, but it makes not the slightest impact. The reason is that the Government isn't listening to *us* at all—or only to that minimum extent necessary to know how best to quiet us if we become too troublesome. "Representative government," in other words, is a smokescreen and not a functional reality. There is nothing easier than to let the people vote every few years and convince them that they are "free." *This single act of balloting is supposed to be the sum total of what is required to ensure that we are a "democracy."*

* *

It is the fashion today, even among some circles which consider themselves progressive, to denigrate the concept of a "power elite." We are told that in the United States today decision-making is now so dispersed throughout the society and takes place on so many levels even in governmental activity, that there is no longer any single focus of power. That is essentially what is meant by a "pluralistic" society.

The evidence, however, is overwhelming that real power still resides within a relatively small circle of the rich. This small group of men, socially closely related through family, school and business, carries a determining influence on national policies. It is a nation-wide group in its operations. This tightly knit class, with its fabulous inherited and corporate wealth, controls the most important agencies and departments of the U.S. Government—especially the Departments of State, Defense and the Treasury.

Here we must notice an interesting difference between the United States and the European "democracies." In Britain and France those who really control the important decisions usually work through the professional politicians. The upper business and financial circles find it more convenient to work through the Wilsons, Heaths and Pompidous—to allow them to be their spokesmen while they operate with less public scrutiny in the background. In the United States it is otherwise. There the representatives of big business and big finance expect to have a more direct involvement in decision-making. Mr. Nixon's cabinet, for example, is composed largely of successful businessmen; many of whom are millionaires. For firms such as Standard Oil with their vast international ramifications it is important to have a say in the making of foreign policy. For many years the Rockefellers (closely associated with Standard Oil) have supplied the man for U.S. Secretary of State, regardless of which party was in office. Dean Rusk was head of the Rockefeller Foundation when he was appointed Secretary of State; Christian Herter, a former Secretary of State, had close family connections with the Rockefellers; John Foster Dulles was from the law firm of Sullivan and Cromwell, one of the Rockefellers' legal advisers, and so on. Big business and big finance almost always are represented in the highest positions of defense—Thomas S. Gates, former Secretary of Defense, was President of the Morgan Guaranty Trust; James Forrestal, who was the first Secretary of Defense after World War II, was President of the Wall Street banking firm of Dillon, Read and Company. With Charles Wilson and Robert McNamara, General Motors and Ford have both supplied the top defense position. The list of powerful business and financial interests that have through their representatives taken over the highest decision-making positions in the United States Government is endless.

Nearly all the people, in fact, in these higher levels of this supposedly "democratic" government are appointed, not elected. In 1966, Lyndon Johnson appointed 66,289 officeholders to the government. The little jobs, of course, were given to the party faithfuls—the political hacks and hangers-on; the big jobs were given to representatives of big business and big finance.

When a serious national crisis occurs (such as the confrontation with the Soviet Union during the Cuban missile crisis) it is not the elected representatives of the people whom the President calls together; it is representatives of big business. The Foreign Relations Committees and the Congressional leaders are told what the decisions are only *after* they are made. The following, for example, are the members of that inner circle of Kennedy advisers who for a period of two weeks during the missile crisis sat in almost continuous session and on whose decisions depended the future not only of the United States but of humanity itself.*

Lyndon Johnson, representative of Texas oil interests.
Dean Rusk, former president of the Rockefeller Foundation.
Robert McNamara, former president of Ford Motors.
Robert F. Kennedy, a multi-millionaire from Boston.
Douglas Dillon, a former president of Dillon Read.
Roswell Gilpatrick, a corporation lawyer from New York.
John McCone, a multi-millionaire industrialist.
Dean Acheson, a corporation lawyer and former Secretary of State.

* This group of men were prepared to plunge the world into a nuclear conflict. President Kennedy at this time announced: "We will not . . . unnecessarily risk the costs of world-wide nuclear war . . . but neither will we shrink from that risk at any time it must be faced." This is a frightening example (far too quickly forgotten) of how imperialism when put to it will risk everything rather than abandon any of its "rights." In actual fact these men had abandoned the initiative to the U.S.S.R. Editorial after editorial across the country repeated that "Our hope must be that Khrushchev will be reasonable." The people were never consulted, only told. Have the lives of so many millions around the world ever before been at the disposal of so few men as in the case of the Cuban missile crisis?

Robert Lovett, an investment banker with Brown Brothers, Harriman.

General Maxwell Taylor, former chairman of the Mexican Light and Power Company.

George Ball, a Washington corporation lawyer, later to become a partner in Lehman Brothers.

And some people still discount the influence of big business in government!

At Presidential election time the people are told that they are taking a "responsible part" in their nation's democratic process. For a few weeks there is great stir and excitement as candidates make endless speeches, but the people even then *are told almost nothing*. The political dialogue between candidates and the citizenry is kept on the least informative level. No national discussion of the issues confronting the nation; no thoughtful presentation of alternatives; only banalities, clichés, tricks and deceptions. Enormous sums of money are spent by the opposing candidates to say almost nothing. The Presidential election in 1968 was no exception. Perhaps it was even worse than most. This is what the editors of *The Sunday Times* thought about it:

> The election campaign has been the most futile for a long time. It began by demonstrating the ugly irrelevance of one element in the traditional electoral process, the party conventions. It continued by exhibiting another, the candidates platform, in all its cluttering emptiness. It will end by yielding as President one of two men who are viewed with almost equal disillusionment. Great issues divide America, yet the greater the issue the more evasive the major candidates have become. Very little of clarity was said, except by Governor Wallace, and no promise was made without a hedge. With the 1968 campaign, a *reductio ad absurdum* has been reached whereby the only fatal move a candidate can make is to spend any of his million dollars on disclosing what actions he proposes to take.[1]

Hurray for democracy!

* *

One way in which the public is kept in a state of confusion about the present democratic fakery is by placing enormous emphasis on the forms, the outward mechanism of democracy, and ignoring the essence. The general assumption is created that if only the procedures of elections, of voting, Robert's rules of debate and so on are followed, "democracy" will automatically result. Indeed we are told that the substance of democracy lies in these procedures— that they *are* democracy. The reality is that the spirit of democracy has very little to do with these political processes, but *it has everything to do with how people feel towards each other*. The United States is an example of a society that scrupulously maintains the outer arrangements while the people are becoming increasingly mistrustful and hateful to each other.

Democracy above all implies a faith in people. A real democratic society is one in which people have a sense of community, of relatedness, and in which a mutual liking and trust flows between them like a thousand invisible threads, so that people feel they belong together with no need to be watchful, competitive or tough. In the United States, more than in any other capitalist country, this physical, sympathetic flow has collapsed, and with it the real spirit of democracy has collapsed too. Democracy and exploitation are mutually exclusive; the one destroys the other, and they cannot exist together.

The democratic instinct knows that people are people, that the differences of color, of political opinion, of religious belief, are very small and irrelevant differences compared to the vast similarities we all share as human beings. This democratic instinct which sees people as people knows nothing about national boundaries. It is wholly unconcerned with them. It pays no more attention to which side of an arbitrary line a man happens to be born on than it cares about the color of hair or skin he happens to have inherited; for wherever a man is born, under whatever conditions, he shares with us our common humanity.

The fake democracy of imperialism does not at all understand this *universal* quality of true democracy. Imperialism is concerned only with its "rights" and monetary interests. The sense of human relatedness is extended only to those who, for the time being, happen to be on "our side." The rest are "enemies" and expendable. If tomorrow's newspapers should report that five million Chinese are starving to death, probably the majority of the people of the United States would be delighted—so degraded has their concept of democracy become under conditions imposed by capitalism. They can, night after night, watch on their television sets their military forces slaughtering "the enemy" without turning a hair and will applaud the dropping of napalm bombs on to defenseless villagers even though they know that the napalm will burn to a hideously painful death every living human being within reach. And why? Because—and this justifies every unspeakable barbarity—it is done to "defend democracy."

*   *

We can now understand why so many peoples around the world remain quite unimpressed when they are told of our marvelous "democracy." We chatter endlessly to them about Western values, Western culture, how all men are created equal and what a stupendous human advance Western democracy represents. Such horrors have been committed in the name of democracy that we should by now understand why, whenever we talk to a "native" about democracy he reaches for a knife. We taunt the governments of countries like China, Cuba and North Vietnam, we challenge them to demonstrate their legitimacy by holding elections—and we wonder why their people laugh! So successfully have we been brainwashed into believing that marking a ballot paper every few years is the only civilized way a nation can order its affairs, that we simply cannot believe that there might be other, more direct, more honest ways in which people can participate in their country's political life. It is almost impossible for us to accept that there can be more real democracy, say, in a village assembly in China than we ever experience for all our vaunted municipal "elections"; or that the central Governments of these countries are far more closely identified with and far more *trusted* by the people than the so-called "representatives of the people" we elect to office.

We are told that a government that is not elected by the same processes as we elect ours must be a tyrannical government. If there is one lesson which history teaches, it surely is that tyrants never arm the populace. But the people of China, of Cuba, of North Vietnam *are* armed, and in each of these countries I have seen the leaders walking unarmed and quite unprotected among their people. It is the President of the United States, the leader "elected by the people" who needs a huge bodyguard to protect him.

These contrasts do not go unnoticed by the peoples of the world. They understand very well the fake nature of imperialist "democracy." To a huge and applauding crowd in Havana, this is what Fidel Castro had to say about the question:

> Our enemies, our detractors and those who would like to see us fail, keep asking questions about general elections . . . as if the only democratic procedure to attain power were those often corrupted electoral processes devised to adulterate and falsify the will and interests of the people and to place in power the least qualified, the most incompetent, the most cunning, and the grafters . . .
>
> As if after so many fraudulent elections, as if after so many unscrupulous political deals and combines and so much corruption, it could be possible to make the people believe that

the only way to profess democracy, to live democratically, is to stage one of those old-fashioned electoral farces . . .²

The fake democracy of imperialism has discredited itself by its own actions, and by its own evasions. It rewrites its own history and creates its own heroes. Even the man who coined the briefest and truest description of democracy ("Government of the people, for the people, by the people") and who is so often held up as an example of the true democrat, is not held in such a great esteem by those who still suffer United States oppression. They do not forget these words which Abraham Lincoln spoke, but which we can be certain are never found in the school books of America:

> I am not in favor of bringing about in any way the social and political equality of the white and black races . . . [nor] of making voters or jurors of negroes, nor of qualifying them to hold office, nor to intermarry with white people . . . there must be the position of superior and inferior, and I as much as any other man am in favor of having the superior position assigned to the white race.³

But, so goes the argument, democracy in capitalist countries, for all its imperfections, does give a voice to the dissenter; it does allow protest against government, and argument and a freedom to voice unpopular ideas. This is true—*within limits*. Provided that protest never poses a threat to the established order, freedom of speech is a useful safety valve. When seriously threatened the ruling class changes the rules, and there is not a "democratic" country in existence today that would not use the most violent repressive measures at its disposal if any movement threatened the continued existence of the capitalist system.

And, looking back, when have the liberals of the United States, who both deplore the present state of their country and at the same time extoll the "democratic freedom" which they enjoy, *ever* posed a real and immediate danger to the existing order? What have they *done* with their freedom? By decades of silence, the liberal-minded people in the United States have condemned themselves. They did not make it their business (as they should have done) to know what was going on in Batista's Cuba; they did not undertake an inquiry into why the U.S. Government overthrew a legitimately elected government in Guatemala; they never insisted on knowing the real reasons for the Korean War; nor, when it might still have averted a colossal tragedy, why the United States supported French colonialism in Vietnam. (And how many liberals who now oppose the Vietnam War would have done so if it had been a *successful* war instead of a long-drawn-out national disgrace?) It was only after the Blacks began to strike back that the conscience of the liberals began to stir. The liberals at home (and this is true of every imperialism) are only mildly embarrassed at the repressions and horrors perpetrated by dictatorships that can exist only because of the money and weapons supplied by the United States.

What they will *not* see, or if they do, refuse to do anything about, is that their own comfort, their own standard of living, their stacked grocery shelves, their new cars are only possible because millions of human beings in the poorer countries are kept in conditions of virtual slavery. The liberal has made his accommodation with imperialism and that is why the Afro-American within the United States and the African, Asian and Latin American working classes don't give a damn for their support. The only support they want and will accept is revolutionary support.

The people of the Western "democracies" cannot have it both ways. They cannot claim that their government is a "democratic" government representative of the people *and* at the same time repudiate responsibility for the actions of their government. Democracy has repudiated itself. As Carlos Fuentes expressed it:

You killed women and children in Playa Giron [Bay of Pigs]. You bombed the first decent houses, the first schools, the first hospitals of Cubans who never before, during the long American protectorate over Cuba, had a roof, an alphabet or their health. And you did it in the name of liberty, democracy and free enterprise. What do you want us to think of these nice sounding words when in their names a population is murdered and the first proofs of concrete welfare are destroyed? We think the same as Simon Bolivar did 150 years ago: "The U.S.A. seems destined by Providence to plague us with all kinds of evils in the name of liberty." [4]

Belief in the fake democracy of capitalism is, I believe, one of the greatest blocks that prevents a fundamental reordering of society. As we said earlier in this chapter, we all have a profound longing to be participants in a truly democratic community. We want to belong, *to feel at home*. And because of this we are loath to give up a hope, however faint it may have become, that even a distorted democracy may somehow be made to work. There is still hope in many people that if only enough "good" men could be elected genuine democracy would result. But the fake democracy of capitalism can *never* by its very nature bring about the fundamental changes that are now needed, for what is called democracy is merely the way in which greed and exploitation have been institutionalized; it is, in other words, designed precisely to *prevent* fundamental change. The "democracy" we know presents us with the problem of *un*representative and therefore illegitimate power.

A number of years ago, Walter Lippmann expressed the feelings of the ordinary citizen regarding his role in present day "democracy."

In the cold light of experience he knows that his sovereignty is a fiction. He reigns in theory but in fact he does not govern. Contemplating himself and his actual accomplishments in public affairs, contrasting the influence he exerts with the influence he is supposed according to democratic theory to exert, he must say of his sovereignty what Bismarck said of Napoleon III: "At a distance it is something, but close it is nothing at all."

As long as those who at present have the power continue to bamboozle or shame us into participating in the great democracy swindle by marking a ballot paper every few years with an "X" for Tweedledum or Tweedledee, just so long will the swindle continue.

The first step is to refuse complicity by refusing to vote. This is much more than a negative act—it is a positive assertion that you at least have seen through the sham and will participate in this mockery no longer. Voting within the context of capitalist ideology, whatever the candidate himself might stand for, is a vote for the continuation of an exploitative society. The system will not overthrow itself. To refuse to participate is an affirmation that you refuse any longer to be shackled to a lie.

NOTES

1. *The Sunday Times* (London), 3 November 1968.
2. Speech delivered by Fidel Castro in Havana, 1 May 1960.
3. Speech by Abraham Lincoln delivered in Charleston in 1858, quoted in the *New Statesman*, 2 May 1969.
4. Carlos Fuentes, quoted by David Horowitz, *The Free World Colossus* (London: McGibbon & Kee), p. 198.

SECTION FIVE

Revolution

We have examined the nature of imperialism; now, in the last section of this book, we face a more difficult task—to attempt to understand the nature of the struggle against it.

What do we, who oppose imperialism, who want to destroy it utterly, who want to weld together a wholly new society, have to do to succeed in our aims? What is required of us? Given the political circumstances of our day and the immense strength of the system we wish to bring down, what historically relevant action can we take? And, perhaps the most immediate and most important question, where do I, as an individual, fit in? How can I, whoever I happen to be and with whatever skills I happen to possess, make my contribution in this immense encounter?

The answers to these questions, I must admit at once, are not clear to me. I can only set down, for what they may be worth, some tentative ideas and the questions which, at the present stage of my understanding, seem to me to be important. I believe it may be more valuable for us today to begin by clarifying the questions confronting us than by attempting to formulate a set of blueprints for action, for we will never find the right answers until we ask ourselves the right questions.

I

The Birth and Death
of Class Society

Seven thousand years have passed, we are told, since the beginning of recorded history. Seventy centuries since man began to give permanence to his ideas by scratching picture-letters onto clay.

Seven thousand years seems an incomprehensible, an unimaginable stretch of time. Our mind accepts it as a fact —just as we must accept the equally incomprehensible fact that "space" may have a limited dimension—but we have no inner mechanism, no time clock within our consciousness, which allows us to grasp the meaning of such a span of years. But *seventy* years—that we *can* comprehend. A life span. We can "feel" that kind of time, for it has become the normal lifetime of our bodies. Now a very simple arithmetical operation tells us something very startling—that the beginning of recorded history is not so far back after all—it is just one hundred of our lifetimes away. The whole extraordinary story of human achievement, from the first crudely scratched symbols to men walking on the moon, accomplished within just a hundred of our lifetimes. The history of civilized man was not a long-drawn-out affair at all. It could better be described as an explosion.

What is more, the really big burst of this explosion came at the very end, like an explosion that then explodes some more; and we today are in the very midst of it.

The time scale of all this is easier to grasp if we translate it into distance.

Imagine that the distance that lies between New York and the entrance to the Golden Gate Park in San Francisco (roughly 3,000 miles) represents the length of time that life has existed on this planet. Imagine, too, that you are setting out from New York to walk to San Francisco to recapitulate, as it were, man's long evolutionary journey from life's earliest beginnings to the present day.

You will walk a long, long way—over 2,600 miles—before you reach the point where the first mammals appear, and you will be less than 125 miles from San Francisco before you see the first anthropoid apes, from which man branched off. With less than nine miles to go, the first man-like creature leaves the security of the forests. In the next four miles, he discovers that a stone held in his fist gives him greater striking power, and then a long time later he learns how to shape and sharpen it.

You will be within eighty-eight *yards* of the Golden Gate before you reach the point on this time scale of man's first great cultural achievement—the cultivation of crops—which allowed him to make his first primitive settlements. This point is where civilization began, the start of the first revolutionary explosion.

The long, almost featureless miles lie behind you. Now, with your destination already within hailing distance, changes follow each other in ever quickening succession. Sixty yards to go and man learns to write. Fifty yards, and he is building his great pyramids in Egypt. Twenty-one yards, and you are at the Golden Age of Greece. Walk on another four yards, and you are at the beginning of the Christian era. When you are only three yards from the en-

trance of the Golden Gate you will have reached the time
when the first European settlers arrived in North America.
Finally, with not much more than a yard to go, there comes
the greatest step of all, the second explosion, the moment of
man's greatest technological breakthrough, the *harnessing
of power* which came with the industrial revolution. You
have arrived at your journey's end, which is today.

* *

What does this mean? How does it relate to the subject
matter of this book?

It means, notwithstanding the sudden and extraordinary
enlargement of his knowledge of the physical world around
him, that man is still a relatively rudimentary creature, with
his maturity still far ahead, in the millions of years during
which he will (unless he commits suicide) continue to in-
habit our planet. "Civilization" represents in time only one
two-hundredth part of man's existence as a separate species.
Though we have learned to peer into the outermost dis-
tances of space and have mastered some of the secrets of the
tiniest particles of what we call matter, we have not severed
ourselves from our past. The essential lessons learned during these eons of time, lessons that enabled man to survive
against all kinds of dangers, may momentarily be forgotten
in the bewilderment and arrogance that came with this burst
of knowledge—but in our deepest being the ancient survival
lessons are still with us, latent, waiting to be reawakened.

* *

"There have always been rich and poor," say the rich and
comfortable, "and there always will be." This, to them, is a
self-evident truth; it has all the force of an immutable law of
nature. But they are wrong. The division into rich and poor
did not exist until very recently in man's history—only a
few yards back on our three-thousand-mile evolutionary

walk—nor does it exist among other animals either. It is not, therefore, a law of nature; it is a "law" that man has made himself.

Indeed, if we take note of what enabled man to survive against every conceivable hardship and danger, and what allowed him to adjust to the most drastic changes in his environment which finished many species less adaptable than himself, we will see that it was his instinct for *cooperation*.

With all the more advanced animals it is the same. Nature's law does not call for *divisions within the species*. Variations of many kinds—yes; one species preying on another —yes; but never do we see animals preying on their own kind. Evolution has taught them many lessons of survival, and one of the most important is for a species at all costs to hold together. The higher the development of a species, the more marked is the degree of social organization and cooperation.* War, as distinct from individual struggle for food or for a sexual partner or for leadership of the pack, is unknown in the animal world, and was unknown to man until the most recent moments of his history. In the organized slaughter of his own species, the human animal is unique.

Man's struggle against his environment was a hard one and required the audacity of improvisation. Driven, perhaps by drought, from the security of the trees, he found himself ill-equipped to meet the alien and dangerous world of the creatures who lived on the ground. His diet of vegetation had given him no teeth or claws for killing prey; his limbs were not adapted for speed along the ground. To survive he had to rely on his wits and on his strength *in combination with* his fellow men. His upright stance freed his hands for

---

* Other species which cannot be said to be highly evolved (ants, for example, or bees) also have a high degree of cooperation and social organization. This is, however, on a rudimentary, instinctual basis, very far removed from the consciousness of mammalian social activity, and consequently does not carry with it the ability to adapt and advance. The ants, for example, have been "frozen" at their present level without any progress for millions of years.

the manipulation of objects; this ability to grasp and handle the material world around him was the first and vital foundation for the advance of his conceptual capacity. That advance in turn led to the development of primitive speech, an achievement which again accelerated man's advance by intensifying his capacity for cooperation—for organization and direction of the activities of the group. With each factor of advance multiplying the value of the others, the pace of progress began to quicken—still unimaginably slow by the standards of today, yet rapid by those of evolution.

Then, after the tens and the hundreds of thousands of years of preparation had passed, man made a further great cultural leap, when he learned not to eat the seeds of the wild grasses, but to *plant* them. An enormous step, implying self-restraint (to resist temptation now for something better later), implying a sense of time, and a trust that the good earth would reward today's sacrifice by repaying it later many-fold. And at about the same time men had the idea of taking control of animals, herding them as a source of stored-up food, instead of hunting them.

With these achievements men were now for the first time able to settle in one place, with a surplus of food over their immediate subsistence requirements.

The significance of this capacity for each family to produce more food than was immediately required for biological survival was far-reaching. It allowed for the development of specialized labor, for work other than merely for food, clothing and shelter. More important still, if ninety families could produce enough food for 100 families, then ten families could live without working. The possession of cultivable land and livestock—in short, the *possession of property*—gave a family or tribe a definite advantage over those who did not possess such property.

It was at this point that man abandoned the age-old law of survival, the law of intra-species cooperation. It was at this point that "rich" and "poor" came into being, and with this new class division came new social tensions. The few who had property had to fight to retain their privileged position, they became *warriors*. The role of the privileged ten families as warriors had a dual significance, for not only had they to retain their domination over the ninety families working for them, but they had also (in their own interests) to protect the whole social unit of 100 families from attack by other social units.

With ownership of land was born *the class society,* exploitation of man by man, and *war*. But with it also came the opportunity to accumulate *capital,* to transform the slow process of work for immediate needs into the compounding process of work which would yield greater production in the future. Not only could tools now be made, but tools to make more tools. These advantages were gained by a class division within society, by an abandonment of the principle of equality which had for so long served man so well. This was the inevitable price which had to be paid, for the ten families who could be fed and grow wealthy by the work of others were the repositories of the capital created by society. They became also the symbols of the crude material incentives of greed and fear which were (and still are, in capitalist society) the inner dynamic of technical advance.

The creation of a slave society, the most primitive form of class society, may seem to us not an advance but a retrograde step compared to the "natural freedom" which primitive man enjoyed before slavery.

But what appears as a delightful "natural freedom" in primitive man, could just as well be described as another form of slavery. It was not a human master but nature herself who enslaved him, for his life was closely circumscribed by the imperatives of sheer survival. The incessant demands of hunger on the one hand and the constant fear of attack by other species on the other held him in an inexorable grip. The life of primitive man was anything but free.

* *

The forms of society that followed slavery (feudalism and capitalism) reflected essentially the changing technical capacities of society. They were different methods by which the few could benefit from the work of the many, methods which changed, not by chance, but because new techniques of production and the discovery of new territories and new resources constantly demanded new social forms for these developments. All these forms had one thing in common— the deprivation of the many to consolidate capital accumulation, with all its privileges and power, into the hands of the ruling minority.

This whole process of exploitation, whatever form it took and however much suffering it caused, was unavoidable if mankind was to advance. Throughout the ages, individuals have dreamed of utopias which could be created in their own time to eliminate the injustices of class society. Some even tried to make their dreams real, by establishing model communities based on their ideas. But such efforts, laudable as adventures of the human spirit, were bound to fail. Man's dreams are a part of the necessary preparation for the future, but the lesson of these failures was that man cannot go beyond his social conditions. The conditions in which justice and social equality were possible had not yet come. The laws of social change, which we have only recently begun to understand, prevented the elimination of exploitation until the productive forces of society were sufficiently advanced.

Is it perhaps just another utopian dream to suppose that the time is *now* ripe for this decisive change, the change which will end the seven thousand years of class society? I believe not. I think that most of us who want this change, and work as best we can for it, have moments when we lose heart and wonder whether the revolution is not after all an illusion.

Yet what brings us back to our conviction is not mere wishful thinking or a despairing act of faith, but the hard facts of the real world around us. It is not possible, except for those who have altogether closed their eyes, to avoid seeing that our society is tearing itself apart with its intense contradictions. We cannot escape from the fact that these contradictions are insoluble within the context of class society. It is those who hope for reforms which will somehow "humanize" imperialism and force it to serve the needs and aspirations of the majority, who are in the grip of utopian fantasy, not those who aim at revolution.

"Production Is Social, But Appropriation Remains Private"

This is the crux of the matter. The industrial revolution which began two centuries ago has increasingly, and ever more rapidly, socialized production, the economic base of society. The social apparatus, the superstructure, is a *class* apparatus essentially the same as before, and is therefore hopelessly out of gear with its base. It is not dreams, but hard facts and hard logic which force us to recognize that the wealth society can now produce must also become social. Such *social* control over production and its surplus means the elimination of the class in which that control is now vested. There *is* no other way out. Man can *and must* once more become what he was for so long a time in the past, a cooperative and not an individualistic, aggressive animal.

So much of what appears as irrationality in human behavior today can be traced to this conflict between the habits of exploitation acquired in our very recent past and the deeply embedded wisdom that tells us that it is only through cooperation that we will survive and move forward. The ruthless, competitive, and individually acquisitive society that man has developed in his latter years is in truth a complex network of internecine struggle which is the very reverse of cooperation. The "free enterprise" system is essentially a "me first" system, a fearful race for "my" place in the economic sunlight, and to hell with everybody else. In the past, whether or not it meant untold suffering for the majority, this system produced results. It created modern technology. Yet the irony of today is that the "me first" system is coming to mean more and more an "all last" system. The exploitative system is now tearing apart the whole fabric of civilization. The will to "success," the will to outsell, outwit, outdo and if necessary outgun others kills the intuitive, instinctive sympathy and relatedness which we would otherwise feel towards each other, and it is these that form the invisible, essential bonds which hold societies together. As individuals, a "me first" system makes us hard, calculating and lonely. It makes the policies of nations implacable.

We are today dazzled by our own extraordinary achievements. Yet modern industrial society, if we could only see it, is only the modern form of slavery. Workers are not tied to individual employers as in the slave or feudal societies of the past. They are usually free to choose their employer and can bargain collectively for the improvement (within narrow limits) of their conditions. Modern industrial society under these conditions forces millions of men and women to devote their life's energies to work that is routine, individually meaningless and soul destroying. The system, it is true, produces commodities in immense quantities, but for the vast majority of people it suffocates every vestige of their creativity.

And how, underneath it all, we *hate* it, hate the pressures that are applied by endless commercial demands! How we hate a system which makes the buying and selling of *everything*—our products, our labor and time, even our thoughts —central to our lives! For we know that we have within us capacities for a wholly different kind of life—much warmer, much closer to our real nature, much nearer to our fundamental human needs.

There are today millions in the United States (and I'm not referring only to the poor) *who know that how they live is not the way they want to live;* but they can see no way out, and all their pent-up frustrations are bursting out in mutual recrimination and violence.

We sense with inner certainty that the era of man's exploitation of man is moving towards its end. We know, we feel it in our bones, that class society, with its massive inequalities and injustices, has today become a dangerous anachronism. It is coming to an end not because a few "left-wing agitators" or "starry-eyed idealists" demand it, but because it no longer meets our survival needs and because, having served its evolutionary purpose, it now stands in the way of further advance. In fact, its continuance will endanger the very survival of the human race. It must end because our present technical capacity to produce plenty on a world scale has to be matched by a social structure appropriate to it.

It is not only those of us who are calling for a revolutionary change that sense the urgency of our times. No other than the General Editor of *Newsweek* could write in the issue of April 27, 1970:

> We know . . . that things can't go on much longer as they're going, and the prospect of a climax to the whole human drama has its own deadly fascination . . . My own private twentieth-century fantasies center on population engulfment, DDT and oil spill spoiling all seven seas, and Melvin Laird, on the morning of Armageddon, still insisting that the ABM will strengthen our hand at the bargaining table . . .

The editor is right. Some fundamental change in our social order is required if we are to survive.

It does not matter what we *call* the new social order, and

we can't predict with certainty the exact forms that it will take. What we *can* predict is that it will be based not on the antagonisms and rivalries of a class society, of rich and poor, but on social cooperation. Man's future development now depends on how rapidly we can shed the habits of thought so recently acquired and make contact again with our own true nature.

What is the nature of this coming change? What do we want from it? What is it that people are hungering for? *A social order which will allow us to be human again.* It is as simple as that—and yet within that simplicity there is much that is difficult to comprehend, and still more difficult to put into practice. We can no longer behave humanly to each other in a capitalist society. When we try to, that society and our own unconscious involvements with it block our thinking and our actions.

Compared with the time scale of our past as well as of our future, the period of class society is but a fleeting moment. With the ending of class society—of the "rich" and the "poor"—a vast new era of advance will be possible. It is only then that the history of true civilization will begin.

That is why revolution is now in every country the first item on the agenda.

2

Revolution in Advanced Industrial Countries

There has been a good deal of speculation in recent years as to whether revolution is possible in advanced industrial countries. Even some of those who see the necessity of destroying a system that inflicts such widespread harm are haunted by a doubt as to whether a revolution can ever be carried through successfully against institutions of state that today wield such enormous power. Those who are supporters of the present system never cease to claim that Marx's analysis of the inevitability of revolution simply does not hold up in the conditions of today, and they point to the fact that no socialist revolution has yet taken place in a modern industrial state.

I believe, however, that the revolutionary process is as relevant in an advanced industrial state as anywhere else. In this chapter I wish to mention only a few of the factors which, taken together, lead one to realize that imperialism is strong in appearance only, and that there are pressures already emerging which are beginning to undermine the economic equilibrium even of the United States, the most affluent of the imperialist powers.

Without a mass force behind it, radical change is impossible, and the creation of such a force seems at the present time to be outside the realm of possibilities. In the United States and Britain, the revolutionary movement is at every turn confronted with the stark fact that the majority of the workers and certainly the labor leadership are *integrated* into the system, and have no interest in overthrowing it.

Every present-day radical movement has arrived at this dead end. The necessity to mobilize the wage earners into the revolutionary movement is recognized clearly—but how?

Collusion between sections of the workers and capitalism is not a new phenomenon in imperialist countries. Engels, writing in 1882, when asked what the English workers thought about colonial policy, said that they thought "exactly the same way as they think about politics in general; the same as the bourgeois think . . . the workers share the feast of England's monopoly of the world market and colonies."

Lenin writing on colonialism referred to the same question:

> Obviously out of such enormous *super-profits* (since they are obtained over and above the profits which capitalists squeeze out of their "own" country) it is possible to *bribe* the labor leaders and the upper stratum of the labor aristocracy. And the capitalists of the "advanced" countries are bribing them in a thousand different ways, direct and indirect, overt and covert.

That was written in 1916. The bribery still continues today, but on a much larger scale. Imperialism has now accumulated vastly greater resources from its colonial ventures than it had in Lenin's day. It is now not only "the upper stratum of the labor aristocracy" who have been bribed, but the *majority* of the workers.

Essentially the bribery consists in giving workers a "percentage" of the superprofits of imperialism, in exchange for acquiescence in colonial robbery with violence. Far from having a sense of brotherhood with workers in Cuba, for example, American workers at one point refused to load or unload any ship that had touched at a Cuban port. Until there was a general public criticism of the Vietnam war the trade union leaders gave full support to it. "Nobody likes this war," said George Meany, head of the AFL-CIO, ". . . but we are there to protect the interests and security of the American people . . . Labor's interests are closely tied to . . . the Johnson Administration."

The process of bribery in Britain is blatant. It goes so far as to give the labor aristocracy titles and honors; they are made members of the Cabinet; they are included as "labor advisers" on important government committees and in a hundred different ways are absorbed and integrated into the higher levels of the capitalist establishment.

This collusion with imperialism is why the radical movements in advanced industrial countries of today cannot reach the wage earners, and why labor is tied to reformism. The majority of people want to improve the conditions of labor under imperialism, but are far from wanting to overthrow it. As long as the superprofits continue, so long will it pay the large corporations to divert a few cents in the dollar to keeping the workers quiet.

But what if the superprofits were to dwindle? What if the terms of trade for the United States were to move against her? What if the real wages of the workers were to begin to move downward and keep moving downward instead of ever upward?

It is certain that a deep change would take place in the internal political situation in the United States. As their wages declined, who would the workers blame? Against whom would their anger be directed?

A politically conscious working class would know that imperialism was to blame, and direct its challenge there. But

American labor is not likely to turn against the very institutions with whom it has for so long been in collusion. The strong possibility is that a downward spiral of the economy will drive American labor towards fascism, as it did the German working class forty years ago. The anti-war movement, "communism," the Negroes, perhaps once again the Jews— these will be the scapegoats against whom U.S. imperialism will internally direct the anger and frustration of the American workers. Externally there will probably be *more* Vietnams.

But can fascism, even in the sophisticated and outwardly "smooth" (and therefore much more sinister) form it might take in the United States, solve the essential contradictions which are built into the very structure of imperialism? It cannot. Fascism can never provide a social climate that is humanly tolerable and can therefore never prove permanently viable. Nor can it reverse those *external* elements which are challenging the industrial supremacy of the United States. The decline in America's economic supremacy, which we will see in a moment is already taking place, is a symptom of a crisis within the world capitalist community. Tensions within and between all capitalist countries will intensify. Imperialism under challenge will drop the mask of "liberalism," of "democracy" and will openly identify itself with violence and the repressive forces on which its power rests.

When its power of bribery of the workers is lost, and when the true nature of imperialism is revealed, then the conditions will exist for a political radicalization of the masses.

* *

Is such a shrinkage of the American economy probable? There are several factors which make it more and more certain. Capitalist economies never march "in step" with each other. There is constant change in their relative positions as changing conditions favor one or another. We saw how Britain's apparently unassailable predominance a century ago was challenged, first by Germany, and then by the U.S. Today the relative *growth* of the U.S. economy is considerably slower than that of a number of other advanced industrial countries—significantly the "have not" nations of the two world wars, such as Japan and Germany, are among them; to say nothing of the even more rapid rates of growth in the socialist countries. This is the writing on the wall for U.S. imperialism.

Moreover, the very success of U.S. imperialism in penetrating the economies of the lesser imperialisms that we drew attention to in "Satellization of the Rich" creates a problem for U.S. imperialism—the more world-wide its investments, the more it stands or falls by the fate of *world* imperialism. Economic crisis for one imperialist country spells danger for all—including, and perhaps above all, for the U.S.

* *

There are several factors that make it almost inevitable that the terms of trade will shift against the United States.

For years—indeed ever since America became an industrialized country—the higher wage level of her workers was more than offset by their higher productivity. The United States was able to compete with European and Japanese industry in spite of the much higher wages she was paying her workers because of her greater industrial efficiency and her greater per capita output. Today, foreign industrial units are growing in size. As a result European and Japanese productivity is steadily advancing while their industrial wage level is still significantly lower than that in the U.S. When the time comes, as it will in the not distant future, when the United States is unable to meet the competition of foreign firms either abroad or within the United States itself, the country will be faced with a continuing crisis of major proportions. With the equalization of the present productivity differential, the United States will find herself in a wholly new world situation and her industrial supremacy will begin to be seriously challenged. Already a high proportion of steel that America (the very land of steel!) uses comes from abroad. Unable to compete in foreign trade and with growing foreign competition within America itself, an attack on the wage level of American workers is inescapable. Indeed, the *real* wages of American workers *are already declining*. Though as yet it is only marginal (about 1 per cent in the course of a year) this nevertheless represents a most significant reversal of a long-established trend.

There is another internal factor that is emerging which will put increasing strain on the *social* equilibrium in the United States—its inability to provide work for the unskilled section of the population. There has been a spectacular and still continuing decline in the number of jobs open to the unskilled manual worker. Within less than ten years the number of jobs open for the unskilled worker has dropped from 13 million to somewhere between 3 and 4 million. There may soon be almost *no* jobs open to the unskilled. What aggravates this situation is that cutbacks on expenditure for education and the consequent lowering of educational facilities is producing a large number of school dropouts at precisely the moment when jobs for them are fast disappearing. The statistical and human result of this is that while the national unemployment appears to be manageable (manageable in the sense that it will not give rise to widespread political unrest) the unemployment in certain sections of the society is unsupportably high. Among young Negro workers, for example, unemployment is around 15–20 per cent (which is what it was approximately for the whole nation during the Great Depression). How long will these sections of the population be content to have their depression go on and on indefinitely?

*   *

The revolutionary process in an advanced industrial society cannot any longer be described in terms of the forces at work in only one country. Capitalism has become global in its thinking; and *revolutionism* must be considered in its global aspect also. Under imperialism, the industrial strength of one country has as its counterpart *under*-industrialism in the same way that within a single capitalist economy the accumulation of wealth by a few requires the impoverishment of many.

If we begin to think of capitalism as an international phenomenon, one that has outgrown national boundaries, then perhaps we shall see that the revolutionary forms in the poorer countries are bound to have a decisive collective impact on even the most firmly entrenched imperialism.

The greatest threat to imperialism—even in the most affluent and most powerful nations—is the rising political awareness of the oppressed people throughout the world. More and more of them are beginning to recognize that the ruling class of the United States and the officials who implement its policies are the most dangerous group of men in the world. The anti-imperialist tide is rising—not only against United States imperialism but all imperialisms everywhere. Imperialism will have to rely increasingly on its armed network of might to protect its interests, but Vietnam has shown clearly the limits of what can be accomplished by military power against a united and politically conscious people. And how many Vietnams can the United States afford?

The world-wide tide against imperialism is rising.

One Senator at least attempted to warn the people of America of what was in store. Speaking in the Senate in May, 1965, Senator Wayne Morse had this to say:

. . . today my Government stands before the world drunk
with power . . .

. . . We shall win one military victory after another; we
shall destroy cities, industrial installations . . . we shall kill
by the million. But in my judgment, that course of action will
lay a foundation of hatred on the part of the colored races of
the world against the American people. In due course those
installations will be rebuilt, not only on material foundations,
but on the foundations of intense hatred by Asians for the
people of the United States. That hatred will be inherited by
generations of American boys and girls fifty, seventy-five,
one hundred—yes, two hundred years from now. It will be
the foundation of intense Asiatic hatred that will eventually
vent its vengeance upon future generations of American boys
and girls.

The Senator's opposition to the destructive actions of
American imperialism is salutary; but the Asian people are
politically more sophisticated than he gives them credit for.
It is in a quite literal sense that the victims of imperialism do
not "hate" the Americans or British or Japanese *people;*
they hate *imperialism.* They do not for example (and this is
peculiarly difficult for us to understand) identify the actions
of the American Government in Vietnam with the American people. Senator Morse could walk through the streets of
any village in North Vietnam after it was bombed and he
would find no hatred directed at *him,* though the people
would tell him bitterly what they feel about the policies of
his Government. And not only in Vietnam. He could stroll
through the streets of Peking or Havana with absolute assurance (much more assurance than he could in his own
country) that no one would molest him.

As the Chinese once put it to me (and I included this in
my book *Awakened China*):

We in China look across the oceans and see people in different
stages of development. We see some still in feudal conditions,
or as colonial subjects. We see some societies suffering (as

America is suffering) from the contradictions of advanced capitalism. But with the people of these countries we feel a sense of common humanity. When we shout our defiance at American imperialist policies in Asia, it is not the people of America we shout at. We cannot any more "reject" the people of America than we could "reject" ourselves—though we reject with all that is in us the corrupting influence of their public philosophies.

This has led some of your writers to suggest that we are trying to "divide" the American people from their government. We are not as naive as they suppose. What seems to us clear is that American imperialist policies abroad and the inner decay of American life at home are part of a single process. They are problems related to this specific period of American history . . . but they are not rooted in the particular "character" of the American people. Historic processes can be retarded or hastened. We shall continue to shout our defiance at America's imperialist policies, and we shall continue to feel a democratic relatedness to the people of America. And in this we see no contradiction at all.

The people living within the imperialist countries can continue to support the international imperialist structure with which their ruling class is a part or they can join with those vast numbers around the world who are ready to throw off the economic stranglehold under which they have suffered for so long. The question that faces the people in capitalist countries is really a profoundly simple one: whose side do they wish to be on?

3

The Present-Day Struggle in the United States—I.

The New Militants

The reemergence of American radicalism in the past decade revitalized the entire political scene in the United States. "The Movement," as it is loosely named, to its credit refused to align itself with either of the two major established parties. The positive contributions of the Movement, especially of the younger members and the students, have been considerable.

Their moral concern for the condition of their country was first shown in their support of the Civil Rights movement in the South, and the concern soon spread to other aspects of American society. As the war in Vietnam developed in scope and cruelty an increasing number of people used the war as a rallying point. The issue of Vietnam united an enormous number of people representing the widest possible diversity often of contradictory political views. As the war escalated and the Government continued to ignore all public protest, an increasing number of the young people began to examine more carefully the roots of American foreign policy and the causes of the many American foreign military interventions. Today they recognize that the Vietnam war is not an isolated incident, a war that has arisen through some unfortunate "miscalculation," but was a deliberate act of an imperialist nation bent on securing its areas of domination.

A large number of Americans, black, white, brown and red, are now in open rebellion against the society of which they are part. They reject the kind of life that it offers them; they are wholly opposed to the supremacy of a business ideology which has depersonalized and degraded social relationships; students are growing increasingly disenchanted with educational procedures, the main purposes of which appear to be to train them to take their part in the system they have come to despise. The old appeals of wealth and status leave them quite unmoved, for they are looking for satisfactions of quite a different order. Politically they are sickened by the rank hypocrisy of those who claim to be their political leaders and the banality of the political dialogue which they engage in. The system of political representation, they have come to realize, is a huge sham. Many of these younger members of the Movement see themselves as the new revolutionary vanguard. The time is past, they feel, for small reforms. The changes they demand are radical and revolutionary.

Towards governmental authority these young Americans are fearless and impudent. In the face of extreme police brutality they have shown extraordinary courage, a moral earnestness coupled with an endearing humor. To quite an extraordinary extent the events in Berkeley, San Francisco State College, Columbia University and other centers of American student protest became an example for students from one end of the world to the other.

One feature of the American Movement that appealed to many was its high degree of selflessness. The students' struggle was almost never for their own personal advantage but for some principle larger than themselves. Within the Movement there were two streams of endeavor which correspond closely to all our aspirations—an awakening of political consciousness and personal liberation and the juncture of these which adds to the Movement's universal appeal.

These courageous youngsters confronting the terrifying powers of the state and making fools of presidents carried an enormous appeal. Permeated with a deep distrust for all ideology they represented political, sexual, moral rebellion all in one. As Herbert Marcuse said in an interview, the opposition of American youth is

> total, directed against the system as a whole: it is disgust at the "affluent society," it is the vital need to break the rules of a deceitful and bloody game—to stop cooperating any more. . . . These young people no longer share the repressive need for the blessings and security of domination—in them a new consciousness is appearing, a new type of person with another instinct for reality, life and happiness; they have a feeling for freedom that has nothing to do with, and wants nothing to do with, the freedom practiced in senile society.[1]

Marcuse was captivated as many of us were, but he also issued a warning—that this "determinate negation" of the prevailing system was without effective organization, and it could only be in alliance with the forces who are resisting the system "from without" that their opposition could become a new avant-garde.

Marcuse's interview took place in 1967. By that time the American militant left had become an important political force among the student section of American society, and its vitality and verve gave rise to all kinds of premature hopes. Within the Movement itself there were many who believed that the new American Revolution had become a practical possibility within the foreseeable future.

Today, as I write (in early 1970), the Movement is in

disarray. It is deeply fragmented. Some of its members are disheartened. The sit-ins and teach-ins, the huge marches, the protests, the Pentagon confrontations, the draft-card burnings, the stopping of troop trains and the trucks carrying napalm, the arrests and imprisonments—what, they wonder, have all these huge and exciting efforts accomplished?

Perhaps (so those who are discouraged feel) they helped to get rid of Johnson, but now there is Nixon. The Vietnam war not only continues but was actually expanded to Cambodia and the nation's rulers appear to be as impervious as ever to the people's sense of outrage. Their efforts did perhaps awaken the eyes of Americans to the situation of the Negroes in the South, but the promises that the ruling class made for their alleviation have been implemented, if at all, at a snail's pace. The militant Negro movements are being hounded by the police, their leaders have been shot, put in prison or driven into exile, and all this with the apparent approval of the majority of Americans. Almost daily from Washington come reports of repressive measures being taken against militant movements. A new and more vicious Joe McCarthy period seems in the making. Nixon and the wealthy businessmen who form his cabinet appear to have made up their minds that "this protest nonsense" has to stop. The Movement, many of its members feel, has lost its way.

In December 1969, in *Liberation* magazine—one of the Movement's publications—there appeared three articles each with the same title. They read like a cry from the heart: "Where to? Where to? Where to?"

* *

Members of the new militant left should not feel discouraged, and most do not. No revolutionary movement has ever begun without faction. Within the ranks of militancy there are always those who are working out some personal problems of aggression or grievance and it is they who cannot stay the course when periods of setback come. But the Movement as a whole is fully aware that their activities have not been useless. Never before in the United States have so many become politicized. Millions have been made to look for the first time behind the façade and question long-held assumptions. The courage and determination of the young militants has achieved a very great deal.

But perhaps the stage has now been reached at which another, quieter, less exciting but deeper form of revolutionary activity is called for: an examination into the *meaning* of revolution and a thoughtful assessment of what is needed to bring it about.

A weakness of the American radical movement (and many of its members are the first to acknowledge this) is that the initial motive of the majority was basically not the overthrow of the existing order but an appeal to the liberal conscience of the nation. By showing up the injustices of the society, by dramatizing them, by being ready to go to jail, they hoped that some alterations of national policy would result; and this implied that they still had faith in liberal reformism as an agent for social change. (I do not speak here, or indeed, in this chapter generally, of the militant Blacks, that bitter and mobilized minority, who have long since given up *that* kind of hope.) Thus the new Movement developed a militant stance with no militant theory to support it. (There was, of course, another side to this coin. An ever growing number of young Americans became militants precisely because their appeal to the liberal conscience met with so little response. Liberalism was seen to have no answer to the nation's inhumanity.)

One San Francisco activist put it this way: "What's wrong is that Movement rhetoric has become revolutionary but its strategy is still liberal. That's a killing combination. What we need is a reformist language and a revolutionary plan."

But plan and theory are what the new militants do not yet have (though even in this there are exceptions—there *are* some smaller activist groups that have both and are operating as revolutionaries, and it is against these that police repression is chiefly directed). The Movement as a whole, until perhaps quite recently, was to a large extent anti-theory and anti-program. When challenged for some rational explanation of their philosophy, they would even give the excuse of being anti-words.

> Words, words, words—man, who listens any more? Everybody's ears are bombarded with what passes for information; people tune out for the sake of survival. Words are nothing new; everybody's heard it all before. Got to shock people into new consciousness. New media, underground press, wall-posters . . . But as Engels said, in the beginning was the deed. Define new contexts, break the deathgrip of polite and repressively tolerated wordmongering by making a new language—a language of direct action . . . Beat ideas over the head if they're not to be mistaken for another commercial. Show that the police are everybody's enemy. Teach with your body. Show by example what you cannot credibly explain in words . . . Besides, we're tired as hell of the sound of our own voices.[2]

(One encouraging feature of the Movement is the rapidity with which many of its members have matured politically. Todd Gitlin, who in 1969 wrote the article from which this quotation was taken, by 1970 was writing a long and thoughtful paper dealing with the ideological problems facing the Movement.)

As the student revolt spread across Europe in the summer of 1968, we heard from there, as we had been hearing from some of the campuses of the United States, that this was a wholly new *kind* of revolution and that all the lessons of the past could be ignored. At the heart of the Movement—it followed in this respect much the same course everywhere—was a reliance on *spontaneity*. Daniel Cohn-Bendit, one of the leaders of the French March 22 movement, described the general tenor of this new theory of revolution in an interview with Sartre:

> It is necessary to abandon the theory of the "leading avant-garde," to adopt another—much more simple, much more decent and honest—of the active minority which plays the role of the permanent fermenting agent, encouraging action without claiming to lead . . . In certain objective situations —with the help of an active minority—spontaneity finds its place in social movement. It is spontaneity that permits the thrust forward, and not the slogans and directive of a leading group.[3]

Only a few in the United States would today support such a crude kind of anarchistic position. But there is no question that within the Movement there are large numbers who take a highly personalistic position and who reject what they consider the "doctrinaire" Marxist analysis of society. There is among these young people a great deal of loose talk about the need for a new "life style"; their aim is to condemn past and present America and to build a new society in which everyone can "re-make themselves." The radicalism of these students is real enough, but in some respects it remains largely private, a path to their own liberation; it is cut off from any historical perspective, and as a consequence it disables them from effective revolutionary activity.

Revolutionary activity is a war against a strongly entrenched class which has available for its defense the massive armed forces of the state. It is an enemy that has centuries of experience behind it and which could, if it were hard pressed, call on whatever assistance it needed from allies overseas. The goal of any serious revolutionary movement is the *control of the state*. How this can be successfully carried out against such an array of state power by a revolutionary movement with no strong centralized leadership, without strategy, without planning and without discipline, relying only on an "active minority" which declines to lead, assisted by such "spontaneous" help as its supporters feel inclined to give, is impossible to imagine.

In the United States, at least, this is becoming clearer to an increasing number of the new militants. The failure of the new militants to find a political analysis of the contemporary situation on which a united program of action can be based, if it continues, will have the most damaging consequences. Some of the great gains (and they were great gains) made by the Movement in arousing the people of the United States to look behind the façade and take note of the true condition of their society will not be lost; but enormous political energies are likely to be dissipated and the final success of the American revolutionary movement will be greatly delayed. The rejection of all theory, or the belief that theory will naturally "develop out of action," has become a kind of anti-intellectualism; and contempt for historical experience can become a form of political arrogance. Unless based on rational thought, actions and words can be anti-system without being revolutionary.

If the new militants have so far found it difficult to articulate what kind of world they are fighting for, it does not necessarily mean that they have no such vision. They are 100 per cent correct in challenging the false values, the injustices and the hypocrisy of the present system. But where do we go from there? Many of them appear to be uninterested in the traditional economic aims of a socialist revolution. Socialism itself appears to many of them merely a change in the organization of government leaving the false values of society untouched. They do not ask for power to bring about the changes they want, for power itself is distrusted; it can, they fear, only express itself through just another set of rigid formulas and impersonal bureaucracies. The new revolution, these militants say, has nothing to do with the old trappings of government—it has to do only with the liberating of the human potentials that lie unlived in each of us.

There are good reasons why the young radicals look with suspicion on past experience. They have seen formerly revolutionary societies succumb to control by a soulless bureaucracy. The young refuse to sanction the suppression of civil rights and the infringement of intellectual independence which they see in some countries which claim to be socialist, and they reject a rigid, moralistic view of society which does not, as they see it, correspond to the realities of human nature. In all this the young radicals are right. It is wholly understandable why Mao Tse-tung—with his liberating doctrine that it is right to rebel against government authority if one believes it to be making wrong demands—has become the political leader of an increasing number of young people all over the world. What other leader of a great nation has been so wholeheartedly on the side of the young revolutionaries?

But I do not believe that Mao Tse-tung intended his words to sanction the repudiation of discipline and order, respect for leadership, or sustained organizational effort. Nor would he encourage the present contempt for theoretical work, the sheer hard thought that useful political analysis and the understanding of the prevailing social forces demands. Far too many young radicals have thrown all these away to preserve what they conceive to be their individuality and freedom of spontaneous action.

"Freedom" in this sense derives largely from the bourgeois ideal of being "free to do what I like" with my property and exerting my "individuality" in any way I please with the minimum of legal restraints. Genuine freedom, however, brings its own disciplines. We are free just so far as we relate to things and people and ideas in terms of reality; and we are unfree to the extent to which we deal with them in terms of acquisitiveness or fear or wishful thinking.

It is not at all surprising that ideas of freedom and individuality have become so distorted. It was dinned into us from childhood that we must "express ourselves," exert our individuality, push and strive to do what *we* want, to get *our* way and "not be influenced." Especially in the United States a child who is nonaggressive, who does not stand up for his "rights," is often considered to be in some way weak in character, psychologically crippled even, while the "healthy" child is the one who has a "strong ego" and exerts it.

All this certainly has a survival value in the capitalist jungle. But why should revolutionaries accept standards set up by an ideology they intend to overthrow? Today we are attempting to promote revolutionary organization while holding on to bourgeois concepts of "freedom" and "individuality" that make such organization impossible. As long as these mistaken concepts remain general, all attempts on the part of the movements of the left to find unity and forward thrust will fail.

Westerners find it almost inconceivable that there can be another more spontaneous, more fruitful and less aggressive form of individuality that is possible only in collaborating, instead of competing, with others. At present in the United States, whenever a number of revolutionary groups meet in an attempt to find some means of working together, each group tries to push its views and ideas, each strives to out-shout, out-argue, out-revolutionize the other, totally unaware that they are acting towards each other precisely as capitalists act and perhaps with even greater acrimony.

They have not yet begun to ask themselves *why* they act in this way, nor have they asked themselves the crucial question: "Who are my enemies and who are my friends?" They have not understood the distinction that Mao Tse-tung drew between the contradictions that arise between revolutionaries, and those that arise between revolutionaries and their enemies, and why these two kinds of contradictions demand quite different resolutions. Thus even in their behavior towards each other, many revolutionaries of today are handi-capped by their refusal to study. Unaware of historical experience, or brushing it aside as being "irrelevant" to to-day's conditions, and still more unaware that an essential element of revolutionary activity is the change that must take place in them as *people,* the young revolutionaries strike at each other blindly with their slogans and opinions. And then are puzzled why no unifying revolutionary move-ment seems possible.

With so many of the aspirations of the new militants one has sympathy. But government must go on, and it is surely part of the duty of a revolutionary movement to define—even in broad terms—the alternative structure of govern-ment and economy it is striving for. Meanwhile the enemy is around us everywhere—and how are we to deal with him? That is the question.

What has come so far—the savage police beatings, the imprisonments on false charges, the occasional assassina-tions by the police, the killings by the National Guard—present only a prelude to what lies in store.

We have never faced real repression (writes Julius Lester, one of the most perceptive and articulate of cultural workers, in the *Guardian*). Of course, people have been beaten, jailed and harassed. That is the power structure's way of trying to discourage people, not destroy them or the movement. In most of the countries of the world where liberation forces are operating, the power structure is as intent upon destroying them as they are upon destroying the power structure. After Fidel Castro led the attack on the Moncado in Santiago in 1953 and was defeated, Batista instituted a reign of terror. Thousands were murdered without "due process." Thousands more were jailed, without "due process." Today in Spain, a strong liberation movement is operating under fantastic re-pression. There a known student activist is not sent to jail for thirty days on a disorderly conduct charge. He is sent for thirty years and the charge may be no more than "suspicion." That is what is ahead of us . . . How will we deal with it?

The difference between the liberal and the revolutionary is that the liberal doesn't really believe, in his heart of hearts, that it could happen—not *here,* not in the U.S.A.! Not in Britain! The revolutionary knows without any doubt at all that when the present structure is really threatened it *will* happen.

*   *

The decadence and immorality brought on by a "me first" economy of prosperity—a decadence which is seen in its most extreme form in the United States—is a vast human tragedy; but in so far as it breaks down the structure of exploitative society it can also be seen as a revolutionary asset, provided always that the revolutionary does not himself become degraded.

We have seen in the first chapter of this book the extent to which drug addiction has now gripped the young people of America. Almost everyone is agreed that some drugs, such as marijuana, are not-addictive and no more harmful than alcohol. It is not on physiological or moralistic grounds that one would question the advocacy of these drugs by some of the leaders of the "left." Drink and marijuana are escapes from oppression and the sheer dullness of life under bourgeois conditions. Their purpose is to blur reality—which is precisely what the revolutionary would wish to avoid. He must see and cope with realities and not shield himself from them. And how certain are we that marijuana does not diminish a man's sense of responsibility (just as alcohol does)? How will a man respond when he is "high" to police questioning? Or torture? Can he be trusted any further than a man under the influence of alcohol can be trusted with secret information? Revolution is a deadly serious business and if it is difficult to imagine a revolutionary movement composed of those (they need not be drunkards) who cannot get along too well without their evening shot of scotch, it is equally impossible to conceive of a successful revolution being organized by a group who cannot get along happily without their drugs.

If one studies the history of the Russian and Chinese revolutions, one striking fact emerges clearly—that the selflessness and the exemplary behavior of those making up the revolutionary vanguard carried an enormous appeal and was one of the essential elements that led to the final success of these revolutions. Their self-discipline, their meticulous honesty, their incorruptibility stood out in sharp contrast to the normal, rather self-indulgent and self-centered life of ordinary people. It was through their behavior that doubters were convinced that here were a group of men and women who were concerned not with personal comfort, personal gain, personal security, but with something larger than themselves. As for the great revolutionary leaders—Lenin, Mao, Ho—it is impossible to imagine that these men would suggest to their followers that the correct "life style" of the revolutionary involves the sort of sloppy, self-indulgent, personally ill-disciplined behaviour that one sees among too many of the so-called "revolutionaries" of the U.S. and Britain. Nor would they for a moment condone the stealing, personal dishonesty and begging (justified on the grounds that it is "against bourgeois standards") which so many of the new militants indulge in.

In the last war, the men dropped by parachute into enemy territory underwent the most rigorous physical and mental training. Their inner discipline was such that they could stand up to anything. No scotch, no marijuana, no casual sexual encounters for them. The revolutionary in the West today does not need to be dropped by parachute; he is already within the territory of the enemy.

*   *

Revolution, we must say again, is a process, not an event. It may take decades to fulfill. Revolutionary theory does not arise spontaneously from crowds marching down Fifth

Avenue or gathering in Trafalgar Square or at the Odéon. Nor does it come from the mindless repetition of slogans, however revolutionary. The generation which finally seizes power may appear to have started the revolution, but they are only completing what was done over years and years of much less dramatic work. Revolution is not a shout of anger nor the sniping at policemen from the housetops; it is not a game; it is not romantic. Rather it is like the planning of a war against a shrewd and implacable enemy. It involves years of careful work and thought and organization. It involves the patience to await the right moment, and to work for the hastening of that right moment. It is only when a whole complex of contradictory historical forces have ripened and created a state of supreme crisis that those who have prepared themselves can seize the opportunity and act decisively. Only at such moments and with such preparation can the course of history be changed.

It is very easy to waste revolutionary material, and to fight the culminating battle prematurely is one of the quickest ways to waste it. It will take five times, ten times the effort to persuade the disillusioned that the war is still on and that they mustn't give up, than it took to mobilize their efforts in the first place.

But having said all this, and given this warning, it must also—paradoxically perhaps—be said that mass protests against actions by the ruling class must be carried on. They must mount higher and higher in strength, no longer with any false and exuberant hope that *this* is the revolution, but rather with a very clear-headed appraisal of the real purposes of mass protest. The purposes? Many. Among them— to put the power structure of capitalism on the defensive and to show up its true repressive and exploitative character; to politicize and arouse those who have not previously examined the false claims of imperialism; to show solidarity with the world anti-imperialist movement; to make people less afraid to challenge "authority" and to destroy the mystique with which the established order has clothed itself; to change the attitude of people from one of helplessness and futility to one of revolutionary optimism. These are some of the achievements of the new militants. And the optimism is fully justified. It is not pretense. For however far off it may yet be, the eventual overthrow of imperialism is an absolute and unquestionable certainty.

NOTES

1. From Günther Busch's interview with Herbert Marcuse, *New Left Review*, September–October, 1967. Originally published in *Kursbuch 9 (Suhrkamp Verlag)*.
2. From an article by Todd Gitlin in the *Guardian*, 18 January 1969.
3. Reprinted in the *Guardian*, 29 June 1968.

4

The Present-Day Struggle in the United States—II.

Race and Revolution

"Divide and rule" is the ancient imperative of oppression. Wherever there has been a minority subjecting a majority to exploitation, there you will find this rule in operation. Without it no tyranny could last.

The Roman emperors made a policy of it. The British Empire perfected it, fanning every conceivable religious, ethnic and other distinction among its subject peoples into hatreds in order to make easy its mastery over all. Every one of the modern imperialisms has practised this pitiless and evil trick.

The results can be seen all over the world. Muslims against Hindus in India; Greeks against Turks in Cyprus; Malays against Chinese in Malaya; Africans against Indians in Guiana; in Biafra, in Northern Ireland, in the Middle East—the list is endless.

Racial discrimination is a form of this "divide and rule" policy which is particularly valued by exploiting minorities. For over a thousand years, the ruling classes of Europe used antisemitism against the Jews to divert attention from themselves as the cause of the people's poverty. German fascism completed the murderous logic of the pogroms by massacring over 5 million Jews in the gas chambers. And in the United States, the slavery of the Negroes provided a ready-made target group for the racialist division of the people.

* *

With these thoughts in mind, I think there are two aspects of the Black question that we must keep clear. The first is that racial discrimination against the Negroes and other minority groups is a permanent and deliberate policy of the United States governing class.

There is no question that if the ruling circles of the United States really wanted to end the discrimination which their predecessors fostered, they could do so, and far more rapidly than most people suppose. As propagandists they are immensely skilled, and with the full weight of their resources and the use of all manner of coercive measures, they could "sell" the ideal of a "unified America" to all but the most rigidly bigoted. If they really wished to do so, they could see that the laws against educational segregation and political discrimination were enforced. When they find it in their interests to do so it can be done. President Truman ended formal racial discrimination in the armed services, which had existed since the country's birth, by a stroke of the pen, without any of the dread consequences that were predicted. In short, the racialism which the U.S. ruling class created could, if they wished, be eliminated by them; but they do not wish to do so.

Discrimination against the Negroes, Mexicans, Puerto Ricans, Indians and others is consequently not just a "legacy of history" about which the Government is helpless. It is a *state policy,* intended to keep the workers of America deeply divided and to ensure that they will never unite in a struggle against the existing order.

It has to be admitted that this policy has, from imperialism's viewpoint, been brilliantly successful. Racialism represents U.S. imperialism's greatest victory over the American people.

And it follows from this that racial discrimination in one form or another will continue to be the policy of the American bourgeoisie to the very last hour of their existence. It is too useful, too powerful a weapon for them to forego.

So deeply and for so long have the American people been inculcated with this poison of race, so profoundly have the passions penetrated into the very heart of American society that even the members of the anti-imperialist movement have been confused on this issue. They have fallen into the trap of thinking of the Blacks as if their problem was in some way separate and apart from that of the rest of American society, rather than thinking of the Blacks as the most oppressed single section of the *American working class.*＊

The Blacks have taken the heaviest brunt of the injustices inflicted by the ruling class. The economic surplus that has been wrung from their labor has been greater and their economic grievances have thus been more acute. They have been subjected socially and educationally to the cruellest victimization.

Little wonder, therefore, that when in the sixties Blacks began to voice their demands for justice with determination, many of them rejected all identification with non-Negroes, whoever they might be and to whatever class they belonged. They saw the solution to their predicament, as did many progressive whites, in terms of struggle as "Blacks," as a distinct racial and even national entity. Some even had the idea

＊ Seeing the world struggle against imperialism in terms of race leads to all manner of confusions. Even the concept of the "Third World," the "Tri-Continental Congress" and so on, shows how deeply this confusion has gone even among those who in other areas are so aware of imperialist exploitation. There are not three worlds but two—the exploiting class and those who are exploited; and these cannot be crudely divided by geography. "Ninety per cent of the peoples of the world," said Mao Tse-tung, "are oppressed." And he is right.

that the aim of their struggle should be a "Black State," situated perhaps in some undefined part of the southern states.

But this was always an illusion, and a dangerous and divisive one. For it constituted an affirmation of the essentially racist idea that the Negroes *were* "different," "not like the rest"—in short, not Americans. It therefore played right into the hands of racism. Beneath it could even be discerned an unconscious form of discrimination on the part of some of the non-Blacks who supported this separatism: the desire to "export" the problem of the Blacks.

But the deep realities of nationhood cannot be so arbitrarily set aside. For the Blacks are a part, and indeed a vital and central part, of the American nation. If they are not Americans, then one must ask who the hell *are* Americans? Americans are a people entirely composed (apart from the now small number of American Indians) of immigrants from every quarter of the globe, and hardly a single one is more American by ancestry within the American territory than a Black. And politically speaking, this deep Americanism of the Blacks, together with the special oppression they have endured, makes them a key section of the proletarian forces of the United States.

This is why the Black leadership, as well as those who are serious about the ending of racism in the U.S., are realizing that the Black question cannot be solved except in the context of the American revolution itself, and that the Blacks have a natural relationship with *all* oppressed people in the United States. The Black workers have common interests with the white workers; they have none with the Negro bourgeoisie, which will try to use Black discontents for their own benefits as a "junior partner" of the white bourgeoisie.

No one can ignore the grave difficulties in achieving this unity of the majority of the American people, black and white, in the context of the deep infection of the population with the antagonisms of the "divide and rule" policy. No one can ignore the fact that some of the most deeply infected elements are to be found among the poorest of the whites. But no one can ignore, either, the inescapable logic of revolution, that the system of oppression which utilizes racism can be overthrown only by the united force of the oppressed, regardless of the color of their skin. Whether that unity is going to be hard to achieve is one thing, but that it *has* to be achieved if victory is to be won, there can be no question.

The second aspect of the Black question that we must keep clear is that the struggle against racial discrimination is not one which belongs only to the Blacks. It is not in one sense a Black problem at all—for it is white, not Black racism that is the root cause of it all. The Blacks are 100 per cent right in calling on whites to fight against racism in their own white communities. They are 100 per cent right to point out that even among their supposed white friends there still exists a large component of white chauvinism. (As an example, the general sense of outrage in the left movement when four students were killed by the National Guard at Kent State was far more violent than when eight Blacks were killed in Georgia at about the same time.)

But in a larger sense it is neither a Black struggle nor a white struggle, but an *American* struggle, an extremely important part of the American socialist revolution. Racial discrimination is a policy aimed against the whole American people, and can only be fought by them as a people. It cannot be fought by accepting the very division of forces which the policy of "divide and rule" has created.

It is an illusion to think that imperialism practices discrimination because of some supposed "hatred" it has for a particular target group—whether it is the Jews in Germany or the Blacks in the United States. U.S. imperialism does not hate Blacks as such; what it hates and fears is the whole of the American people, as every exploiting minority hates and fears the masses whom it exploits.

We can perhaps understand this better if we work out

what is the real mechanism of racial discrimination in the U.S. The most important economic aspect of Black oppression is that the Black population represents a reservoir of cheap labor which is used against the non-Black workers. The bargaining strength of the white wage earner in America is constantly threatened by the presence of this large pool of cut-rate labor. This serves not only to deflate the *general* level of wages, but enables the ruling class to incite the white workers to *blame the Blacks* for this threat. The more intense the exploitation of the Black and the more the wages of the white workers can be deflated, the more bitterness will be generated between the Black and white workers. This is the paradoxical and vicious spiral of division which the American workers are invited by imperialism to tread.

To increase the national average wage level of the Black worker to bring it into line with that of the white worker would not trouble U.S. imperialism *economically* very much. What would cause them far greater anxiety both economically and still more politically, would be the end of the good old game of playing off the Black workers against the whites and vice versa. The coming into existence of a working class freed from the disruptions of racist divisions, and consequently able, because of its unity and powerful bargaining position, to demand a much greater share of the national surplus value—*this* the ruling class will do all in their power to prevent.

Today, non-Black labor is in a self-destructive collusion with American capitalism. It has allowed itself to be deluded into thinking that it is sharing with the employers the fruits of discrimination of the Blacks. If once the American working class—all wage earners, of whatever occupation and color—begin to see that their basic economic interests are identical, and that by standing together *both* would gain enormously, the antagonisms between white and Black workers will disappear. Ironically, the white worker would gain far more under those conditions than he gains by his collusion with his employers to secure what he considers a privileged position over the Blacks.

That is to look at the matter from the narrow angle of the existing society. The most important *political* result of the success of imperialist division of the workers is the certain guarantee that, while that division lasts, imperialism is safe. Nothing significant can be achieved towards overthrowing imperialist society while this division endures, and the imperialists know it.

Every American outside the ranks of the ruling class is the *victim,* in one form or another, of racial discrimination as a policy. The end of racial discrimination cannot be won by the Blacks alone; the attempt to do so involves playing right into the hands of those who are the creators of racism in America. The problem as we have said is not a Black problem, but an American problem. The victory cannot be a Black victory; it must be an American victory. The unity of the Black and white workers which is necessary for that victory must be forged in the course of *revolution,* the fight for the destruction of the imperialist state. The *state policy* of discrimination will not be ended until the revolution succeeds; but the revolution cannot succeed until the American workers have eliminated all traces of racism *within their own ranks.*

Thus the fight against racism cannot be fought as a separate issue; it is a part, a most vital part, of the American revolution.

5

Some Thoughts on the Nature of Revolution

Revolution begins within the consciousness of men.
MAO TSE-TUNG.

We are now nearing the end of our enquiry, these brief and all-too-inadequate notes on the nature of imperialism.

We have attempted to outline how the system of property and class arose and how it developed over the centuries into the present monstrous system of human exploitation and military violence which, if allowed to continue, will destroy all that is human in us—if it does not end the story of mankind itself.

What is the nature of the revolution—and revolutionary man—which will bring imperialism to an end?

If you were to ask a dozen or a hundred people at random to express what they consider revolution to be, almost all of them would describe it in terms of street barricades, guillotines, wild demagogues, crowds storming the Winter Palace, mobs on the rampage. We have very firmly fixed mental images of the scenes that have nearly always accompanied the overthrow of an existing order. But these violent and dramatic events are only the last moments, the final culmination, of a revolutionary movement which in each case began long before.

A world revolutionary movement is already under way. Exploitative society is now an anachronism. Revolutions do not occur because of the activities of a few agitators, but because existing institutions are no longer appropriate either to deal with expanding productive forces or to provide a means by which men's widening human aspirations can be satisfied. Today, the fantastic production made possible by modern technology is far too powerful a force to be held back, to be restricted, by the limitations of an economy which is essentially serving the needs of only a small section of the world's population. However strenuously the ruling classes attempt to resist change, their efforts will prove as futile as were the attempts of the feudal aristocracy to hold back the new productive forces of the eighteenth and nineteenth centuries.

Today, other forces are also at work. It is not only the pressures of modern technology that are straining the system of modern competitive capitalism to the breaking point, but the insistent demands of millions for a more just and more humane ordering of life. These millions have recognized that life cannot be measured merely in economic terms, and they are voicing the world-wide hunger for a system that allows men to be trusting and cooperative with each other instead of competitive and violent.

When the revolutionary process which is already taking place will reach its culmination no one can say, nor can we foresee exactly what form it will take, what kind of struggle and violence it will involve or how fiercely the ruling classes will attempt to retain their positions of power and privilege. Today's revolutionary process will reach its culmination in a way very different from the giant upheaveals that took place in Russia and China. The consequences of revolution in a capitalist country will be very different, too, for it will come not to an industrially backward country whose new government from the moment that it takes over must spend most of the nation's productive energies and resources merely to keep the people alive. A socialist revolution in an advanced industrial country is a much more complex proposition politically, but it will have the benefits of the huge existing technical and industrial apparatus that can at once be made to serve the public good. The most remarkable advances would be seen immediately. The present immense expenditures for the military, for unrewarding flights to the moon, the creative energies now wasted on absurd commercial rivalries could be channeled to where the human needs are greatest—to rebuilding the cities, to providing health facilities for all, to cleaning the air and purifying the lakes and rivers and making our lives livable again.

The industrial resources of the advanced countries, when once this revolutionary change comes about, would not benefit themselves alone but could be applied to help the poorer countries develop their own resources, and—much sooner than we think possible—want and misery and illness and ignorance would finally become part of man's nightmare past.

It was physical hunger and despair that provided the impetus and momentous thrust of the revolutions in France, Russia and China, the huge collective fury of millions whose conditions were such that they had nothing to lose. There are, of course, hungry and despairing people in the United States today, but dispersed over the country as a whole they cannot form the nucleus of a general revolutionary uprising.

It will be quite another kind of hunger that will drive the masses in advanced capitalist countries to revolt. We eat more in a day than those in poorer countries eat in a week, but we are on a psychological starvation diet. Capitalist society has failed (in spite of all its luxuries and physical comforts) to provide the majority of its citizens with adequate emotional satisfactions. The meaning has gone out of our lives. We are today alienated from ourselves, from our work and from each other. We are so distrustful of each other that we no longer even come to each other's help for fear of "being involved": thirty or more people in New York can watch from their windows a murder taking place in a court-yard while not a single one so much as telephones the po-lice. The sense of interrelatedness has so diminished in our societies that vast numbers of people are left lonely and deeply deprived of emotional satisfactions which are essen-tial for health and sanity. This deprivation will lead eventu-ally to a despair as great and action as violent as any that arises from an empty belly.

* *

Revolution is only possible if the mass of the people sup-port it, and traditionally it has been the "proletariat" that has been relied on to provide this mass support. Along with the many other assumptions about revolution we have brought along with us from the past is the notion that the "proletariat" consists chiefly of industrial workers. Modern technological advances, however, and especially the intro-duction of partial or full automation, have drastically re-duced the numbers of workers involved in production, while the numbers employed in the distribution and servicing sec-tors of the economy have vastly increased. Modern technol-ogy has had the effect of multiplying many times the pro-ductivity of the industrial worker engaged in production, and this in turn has reduced the numbers that are employed in this way.

This reduction in the number of factory workers has led many to doubt whether revolution in a technically advanced society is possible.

The question, I believe, arises from an erroneous idea of what the proletariat really is. The proletariat does not con-sist only of the industrial workers; the term includes all who have essentially *nothing to sell but their labor*. In this sense

—though they may not recognize it yet themselves—a huge proportion of employees in an advanced industrial society are members of the "proletariat," and they will indeed still form the mass revolutionary base when they have understood the realities of their position. And far from diminishing, the proletariat in its real meaning is vastly increasing its relative strength.

Today the bourgeoisie have skillfully blurred and confused this issue. By introducing, in all kinds of subtle ways, a *consciousness of status,* they have succeeded in submerging the *consciousness of class.* Titles and labels, how wages are paid, the varying lengths of holidays that are granted, bonus shares in the business, the size of offices, even the kind of rug on an office floor are all inducements to persuade certain employees that they are *not* members of the working class, but something better, that they are rather "above" the workers on the factory floor. Companies have devoted an enormous amount of care to the cultivation of snobbery in their employees, so that when, for example, industrial disputes arise, the office workers and management staff will identify with "their corporation" rather than with the production workers.

But all this is *appearance* only. The *reality* is that the man in the white shirt in a front office and the girl stenographer and the accountant and nearly all the others who are made to feel superior, *are as much members of the working class* as the man on the assembly line. Sooner or later, when the economic squeeze is on, they will realize that in the eyes of the company that has flattered and bamboozled them while the going was good, they are just as expendable.

Already among many of those in these supposedly "superior" positions there is a growing realization that to obtain their economic rights they must use the weapon that the industrial workers have used for years, namely, the strike. A year or two ago no schoolteacher would have dreamed of going out on strike. It would have injured his self-esteem and lowered his status in his own eyes. Today tens of thousands of teachers in the larger American cities don't hesitate to strike; neither do aircraft pilots, police officers, nurses, firemen, civil servants. The aims today may still be economic, not political, but the implications are clear: these workers on so-called "higher status" levels are beginning to realize (though most of them would still shun the word) that they are indeed members of the proletariat.

When the era of everlasting "prosperity" comes to an end (as it is bound to do, for all the basic contradictions of capitalism are still present) and when the economic pressures are beginning to be applied and wages are steadily reduced, as they already have begun to be, I find it very easy to imagine the white-collar workers of a country such as the United States refusing to be fooled any longer by all the tricks and deceptions of the bourgeoisie and coming to realize that they are members of the working class. How many in America today are their own masters working for themselves? The United States more than any other is a nation of *employees*. And when this enlarged proletariat becomes politically as well as economically engaged, it will join with radical students and the Black and other minority militants and demand a change, a fundamental change in the ordering of their society—and when that happens, who could oppose such a united force?

That confrontation I find it easy to imagine.

What I cannot foresee, and what is visionary and unreal to think is possible, is that such a confrontation can succeed *without widespread and prolonged political preparation.* How can an alternative system be offered to the people if no alternative system has been planned?

If no revolution can succeed without a mass base, then to build such a base is the first task—and this means the political radicalization of the masses. Every revolutionary movement has recognized the need to create such a base, to create a unified political organization that draws its vitality from below. Yet so far all efforts to integrate existing revolutionary movements in the capitalist countries with the working masses have failed.

But even though these efforts have failed, the *need* for a revolutionary party still exists. Until such a party is created it will be impossible to develop an adequate and contemporary critique of present society and a program of action which will integrate at a higher level the numerous sectional demands and grievances which today constitute the main impetus of the radical movements in capitalist countries. The absence of a revolutionary party results in a multiplicity of demands for *partial* objectives: the ending of the Vietnam war, civil rights, better housing, higher wages, students' rights, worker representation in factory management, Black Power, G.I. unions, an end to the draft, better schools, women's liberation, socialized medicine, fairer tax laws . . . the list is endless. These all represent potential anti-imperialist movements but they lose their force by continuing to fight their battles separately and by their inability to look beyond their immediate discontents to the root cause of them all, namely, the capitalist relations of production.

The need for revolutionary organizations in Western countries which can evolve a unifying critique of the existing order and a program of political education and action *which is immediately relevant to the daily-life needs of the masses and will therefore draw the masses to it* has been voiced over and over again. Some attempts at organizing such a party have of course been made, but they have all failed and their failure has resulted in the non-connection between those who have most clearly seen the need for revolutionary action and the workers who would most benefit from it and who alone can give it power.

Why has there been this failure?

I believe the answer lies in our profoundly mistaken ideas of the meaning of "freedom" and "individualism." We do not realize the extent to which our present ideas of freedom and individualism are *bourgeois* ideas carried over from the past. This misunderstanding has led the radical movements of today to reject all theory, to sweep away all revolutionary discipline however legitimate and however much proven by the past to be necessary—all in the name of personal freedom and the sacred inviolability of their "individuality."

But, as Lenin pointed out, "Without a revolutionary theory there can be no revolutionary movement." This does not imply that a revolutionary program can be worked out in detail in advance and in isolation from the struggle. Socialism is not something which is hastily constructed after the revolution has triumphed; it must be constructed within the thinking and actions of the masses in and through the struggle, and in and through the revolutionary party of the masses. It requires the careful study and analysis of all the social forces that are involved.

We have, in this book, over and over again spoken of the "bourgeoisie" or the "imperialists" doing this or that to further their economic interests very much as one might describe a group of gangsters plotting the raiding of a bank. Although for convenience and brevity we have spoken this way it gives an altogether misleading impression. The human mind is extraordinarily adept at concealing and rationalizing its true motives, so that almost *every* act we perform is thought (by ourselves) to be both sensible and morally unassailable. When members of a board of directors in New York or London decide that they should, shall we say, expand their interests in Latin America or Africa, they would be astonished to be told that they were furthering the economic exploitation of the people of those countries. Among the owners of industrial plants not one in a thousand will have ever considered the question of the expropriation of surplus value from the workers. They know that without the workers' labor they would not have any profit, yet they are conditioned to believe that, by applying their capital to production, they are doing the workers and society at large a great favor. The processes of self-deception are enormously subtle and depend very largely on which aspect of "reality" we choose to pay attention to. Our views of how things operate are largely determined by our interests.

Every ruling class wears blinkers. Though highly skilled in protecting their immediate economic interests (and their cleverness in this respect should never be underestimated), the ruling classes in other respects simply do not know what kind of world they are living in. This makes them both frightening and vulnerable.

The gap between objective reality and how the ruling classes *see* reality is enormous. They have available to them the most elaborate machinery for assembling information; they have at their disposal the finest experts in every field; they have a huge army of intelligence gatherers with almost unlimited funds. Yet history abounds with elementary errors of judgment made by the ruling class when confronted with phenomena of which they have no personal experience. Take their response to the Russian Revolution— wrong on every count:

> We didn't anticipate the revolution; when it occurred, we didn't think it would succeed; when it was successful, we thought socialism was going to be abandoned; when it wasn't, we thought we wouldn't have to recognize the new Soviet State; when we did, we acted first as if it was like the Western democracies and then as if it was like the Nazis; when the Germans invaded, we thought the Russians could only last six weeks; when they survived the war, we thought they couldn't recover quickly from it; when they recovered quickly, we thought they didn't have the know-how to build missiles and so on . . .[1]

History provides numberless similar examples. The ruling classes were wrong about China, they were wrong about Cuba, they were wrong about the Dominican Republic, they were wrong about Korea, they were wrong about Vietnam. Very sophisticated and cunning when it comes to things that they know within their own experience, when confronted by a people's revolutionary movement, even though the information and expertise they can call on is of a very high order, they are misled by their class prejudices.

* *

This leads us to a question which we in turn must ask ourselves: are we who oppose the ruling class equally blinded by our prejudices? How far are any of us conscious of our deeper intentions? How far do wishful-thinking, dreams of utopia and hidden resentments determine our views? These are important questions, and we are not going to find answers for them unless we are ready to probe very deeply into ourselves and to come face-to-face with our more hidden impulses. The leaders of the ruling class, so self-assured, so certain of themselves, would not make the errors they do if ever they became aware of how profoundly their class prejudice distorts their view of things. We need not make a similar mistake. "Know yourself, know your enemy" is the two-sided recipe for revolutionary success.

We can now perhaps understand why in China (as earlier in the Soviet Union) such great emphasis is placed on "criticism and self-criticism." To our Western, bourgeois-conditioned minds, to be asked to expose our inner thoughts and motives to the scrutiny of others appears a grotesque proceeding and a horrible invasion of our privacy. The very thought of it fills us with embarrassment and scorn. Especially to an intellectual, for he may discover the extent to which he has developed his intellectual attainments in order to gain status, admiration, a comfortable job, security, authority over others, self-esteem. So protective of its individual self is the bourgeois-conditioned mind that it cannot conceive of "mutual criticism" being a form of *mutual help*. To those, however, who have once understood that the overthrow of imperialism is impossible unless they also overthrow their old conditioned manner of thinking and

acting—*and that this is as essential a part of the revolutionary process as the physical overthrow of the capitalist power-
structure*—anything that will help them overcome their past
conditioning is welcomed. Once a group of people working
together begin to see that this conditioning is common to
them all, that there is not the slightest "blame" attached to
it, that they have all been culturally deformed by their up-
bringing and the conditions of society, then they will be as
anxious to help each other as they would be to help each
other overcome a physical deformity. It is extremely difficult
to see in oneself the many subtle and still-unconscious attitudes which are hangovers from the past, while others can
often see them clearly enough. So mutual "criticism"—
which sounds to us so harsh and unfriendly a word—is seen
not at all like "criticism" in our sense, but is a very important tool with which to untie old mental bonds. And who
would not want to be released once he recognizes that he is
bound? It is this initial step—the recognition that we *are*
bound—that is the first and most difficult hurdle of all.
Through this process and the breaking down of all pretense
comes a sense of shared experience, a mutual affection that
we who remain isolated and protective behind our "individuality" can never know.

A revolutionary, therefore, is a man who has freed himself from self-defensiveness and is in consequence free to
know himself. From the moment that he understands that a
transformation is required in his own consciousness as well
as in the outer world and begins to act on this knowledge, he
is engaged in the revolutionary struggle. Once he is ready to
examine himself without defending himself or blaming himself, but to *know* himself, he will no longer be content to
play at life; he will demand clarity and unity. He will no
longer be able to live in conformity either with the hypocri-
sies of the existing order or with those in his own behavior.
The revolutionary above all wants passionately to quit the
world of pretense and enter the world of reality and action.

As Camus so eloquently said, *the revolutionary affirms life*. The very fact of being a revolutionary implies that he has not lost faith in mankind. From now on he says NO to the society around him because he says YES to a vision of what life could be.

Personal resentment against the prevailing conditions of life is not revolutionary. Resentment is embittering and not releasing. Resentment, even if shared with others, encases a man in his own isolated world. Resentment nearly always is resentment against oneself and is often impelled by envy. The revolutionary is not concerned with his own misfortunes, he is not envious, he is not embittered. He has work to do that far transcends in importance the problems and difficulties of his personal life.

* *

When we look carefully, as we have tried to do in this book, at the social conditions in the advanced capitalist countries and at the widespread human misery that the violence and exploitation of imperialism create, we see that revolution is ripe, overripe. And yet the revolutionary moment seems as far away as ever. Why do we allow the present state of affairs to continue? Why do we allow ourselves to remain under the tyranny of a very small minority? What is it that is holding back the revolutionary movement? It is almost as if people are hypnotized by the immensity and apparent inevitability of the present structure, so that the very notion of overthrowing it seems hopelessly visionary and unreal. It is somewhat analogous to the power that Britain was able to exercise over the large population of India. If ever the Indians had realized their power and had combined, the British could have been swept out of India without any difficulty. Yet so strong and so carefully nurtured was the "mystique" of British authority that a mere handful of British were able for more than a century to control and

exploit over 400 milion subject peoples. There was no Indian Mao Tse-tung to tell the Indian people that the British
—whatever their *apparent* power—were no more than
"paper tigers." The Indians did not realize where their solution lay—that is, within themselves. They never realized
their own power, were never able to unite—and the British
of course did their best to see that they never did—and
British colonial rule was able to continue until quite other
factors resulted in India's "independence."

Certainly the people in capitalist countries have the physical power to overthrow the existing order. Every major
strike proves that a comparatively small section of the industrial working class has the capacity to bring the whole
system to a halt. Yet every time, with some trivial upward
adjustment in wages, the strike is settled and the old state of
affairs continues as before.

Why?

We have been so accustomed to thinking of the enemy as
"out there"—the tangible forces of exploitation and repression which we can see with our eyes and whose bludgeons
we feel on our heads when we attempt to fight it—that we
have not yet realized the extent to which the enemy has conditioned and repressed our *minds*. We are like the people of
India, unaware that the ruling classes are very cleverly di-
viding our forces and buying our allegiance; unaware of
how successfully they have persuaded us that we are really
ruling ourselves, that we are "free," that they have our interests at heart. We don't realize how they have conditioned
us to think that the very idea of an alternative system is both
treasonable and absurd. Like the Indians, we cannot get it
into our heads that the tiny minority who exploit us are
"paper tigers."

I have thus come to believe at the present stage of my
thinking that the single greatest reason why the revolutionary movements develop so slowly in Western capitalist

countries and why they remain so weak and so fragmented is because our minds have been deformed by the social conditions imposed upon us. This means that *the initial battle needs to be fought within ourselves*. We have never paused sufficiently to reflect that our own consciousness, the way we feel and think and act, has been created by the very system we now hope to overthrow. As with the Indians, as long as our consciousness remains a "colonial" consciousness we will remain helpless. *Revolutions in other words can be made only by those who are themselves in a state of revolution.*

* *

We have shown in the course of this book how all attempts to *reform* capitalism are bound to be self-defeating. There is no part of it which does not link up with and support every other part, and if we are to change society in a fundamental way it must be by a radical, that is a revolutionary, change in which the whole apparatus of the old exploitative power structure is totally destroyed.

I have come to believe that this is equally true of our inner consciousness also. We cannot hope successfully to overthrow the capitalist order while we retain in ourselves a capitalist consciousness. Even if an external revolutionary change *is* achieved and a "socialist" economy instituted, as long as we still retain our old, acquisitive, "me first" consciousnes, the revolutionary endeavor is bound eventually to fail. The "new man" cannot come into being within the matrix of the old exploitative society, nor can the "new society" develop if our consciousness is still the old consciousness. The dialectic of revolution is that it has to be made by the "old" man who transforms himself *in the course of the struggle* into the "new" man. A viable and lasting revolution requires both the overthrow of the external social order and a continuing revolution within the mind of man himself.

NOTES

1. Fred Warner Neal, *U.S. Foreign Policy and the Soviet Union*
(Santa Barbara, Calif.: The Center for the Study of Democratic
Institutions).

6

"Where Do I Come In?"

The title of this chapter is intended to be taken literally. Where do *I*, the writer of this book, come in? I cannot speak for the reader, for he must discover for himself what relevance, if any, this book has to his own life. And in a way I am in the same position as the reader, for I have been learning as I have been writing and I am not at all sure yet what the full implications are of what I have learned. Except that if I believe (as I do) that what I have written about imperialism is true, then I cannot merely nod my assent and tuck it away in my mental file of useful facts. I have an uncomfortable intimation that what I have learned while writing this book is more like a time-bomb lying somewhere in the quiet of my mind, and that I will never again be altogether unconscious of its ticking. I must come to terms with what I have come to understand, or lead the half-life of those who have seen and cannot face the implications of what they have seen.

We all know people who have a vast fund of information about imperialism and revolution, who have studied Marx and Mao, whose minds are a veritable file index of quotations, who can see with great sophistication and clarity the urgent need to overthrow the present structure, and yet whose lives are curiously unchanged by all this knowledge. They seem, as it were, unrelated to it. I have therefore come to think that intellectual knowledge is both important and can be a trap, for "knowing about" can very easily become a substitute for action.

"Revolutionary thinking" can so easily become a kind of intellectual game. Especially in the United States, professors and other intellectuals who feel guilty, perhaps for living such secure and comfortable lives, are able by attaching themselves to some radical movement to feel a certain psychological release. It is a form of opportunism; they use revolution for their own emotional needs. And with almost no danger or even discomfort to themselves. For today in the United States opposition to the existing order, in most academic circles, is generally approved of. To be "in" you almost *need* (quite apart from the merits of the case) to be against the Vietnam war and "against imperialism." The expression of verbal opposition to the nation's policies is, in the words of Professor Hans Enzensberger,

> in danger of becoming a harmless spectator sport, licensed, well-regulated and up to a point, even encouraged by the powerful. The universities have become a favorite playground for this ambiguous game . . .

To have an understanding of imperialism so we can fight it is important. But the accumulating of more and more facts about it, or writing books about it or conducting seminars or being able to expound brilliantly to students on the history of capitalist exploitation—all this activity will have about it an odor of futility and barrenness unless at the same time it is reflected in one's behavior. It doesn't matter how many revolutionary books are on our shelves or how many protest marches we have taken part in or how many radical causes we have supported or how much we detest all that imperialism stands for; unless our "capitalist consciousness," our conditioned actions and attitudes are understood as clearly as we understand the structure of capitalism itself, our actions will be fruitless, and unconsciously we will still be in collusion with imperialism. What this means (to bring it back to myself) is that as long as there is a separation between what I think as a political person and how I think and behave in "ordinary life," I cannot claim to be on the side of revolution.

* *

So many who detest the present ordering of society and want to take no part in it are asking themselves: *What can I do? How do I act? How do I earn money and not become compromised in a society I abhor?* Many have said to me: "I have marched, I have protested, I have taken part in teach-ins and be-ins and love-ins; I was among those who picketted the Pentagon, I have stood up to the police and the tear gas, I have torn up my draft card, I have raided the napalm factories, I have written a thousand letters to the President, I have been to jail—*now* what do I do? Tactically, I'm dried up, burned out."

I have, like everyone else in the Movement, asked myself these questions; and for the first time I believe I see the outlines of an answer. While the outward political activity must go on and I must play my active part in them, I have come to believe that the initial battleground is in myself. Revolution like any war is far less dramatic than it sounds; and most of it is spent in unexciting and anonymous work. We must start by tackling the enemy who is closest home. I am beginning to understand that as long as my life is governed by "me" and "mine," *my* rights, *my* economic interests, *my* wants, as long as these remain the central focus of my life, I am not yet engaged in the real battle. It must be in association with others that I will understand myself. It will be my political task—in however simple and tentative a way it may begin—to start exploring the real nature of our society and the extent to which it has distorted our thoughts and feelings. This is less exciting than fighting the cops, but it is revolutionary work nonetheless and in the end may be more effective. For the political climate of a nation will become a revolutionary climate only when there exist a myriad of such small and dedicated groups which individually may appear insignificant, but which when linked up will form an effective and militant revolutionary movement.

It is not a comfortable conclusion that the first adversary to tackle is my "old self." This, as I have indicated, does not mean that I will cease to do with all my energies whatever I can "out there." I shall continue to protest when that seems necessary and march and make speeches; I will go on writing books and making films which might—who knows?—have some political use. But if, as I said earlier, revolution can be made only by those who are themselves in a state of revolution then I know that at this stage my primary revolutionary activity must be with myself. Not, I must add, to seek a kind of personal salvation by becoming a "good revolutionary" in the way religious people hope to achieve salvation by becoming good Christians, but that I can finally get rid of the distortions that capitalist conditioning has implanted in me, that I can see political realities more clearly, and that my political work can become more effective.

* *

One of the remarkable features of the revolutionary struggle is the astonishing rapidity with which very deeply embedded cultural habits can be shed by those engaged in revolutionary struggle. In China, to take one example, the centuries-old attitude to women as inferior beings was changed within a few years. Anyone who has been to China, North Vietnam or Cuba will have seen the enormous energies and individual initiative that are released—like a veritable explosion—when a new society provides conditions which meet deeply felt human needs. In each of these countries there are millions who would under capitalist conditions have been very much "me first" people who are today working with enormous zest in cooperative endeavors. This is by no means just a passing phenomenon. Years after the initial excitement and elan of the revolution have worn off, most of the people in these countries are working with far greater enjoyment than they ever did when working merely for personal gain. They feel in touch again with themselves, and are linked affectionately with each other in a way that we can hardly understand.

Those of us in capitalist countries who are beginning to be politically aware often envy those who are working in socialist countries—especially those of us who are writers or artists. From our side of the fence it appears that our counterparts in the countries which have had a genuine socialist revolution no longer have to battle our most insidious enemy—the underlying cynicism that today pervades all capitalist countries. There is a weary assumption that men can never really transform their society. They can patch it up, modify it, make it a little more bearable; they can do something here and there to even out the worst injustices. But a *fundamental* change? Oh, no! That is considered naïveté appropriate only for the very young. Our fellow workers in socialist countries no doubt have their struggles too, but at least they don't have to fight *that* battle. They know by all that they see around them, by their own living experience, that this capitalist assumption is simply not true. Human relationships *can* be changed, societies *can* be transformed, the initiatives open to individuals *can* be dramatically and immeasurably widened.

To a writer and occasional filmmaker like myself, the West offers many privileges, many comforts. Especially today when a certain "leftism" is fashionable, to write about the need for revolutionary change is quite acceptable—it sells well! Much of my work, I must admit, is rather like an enjoyable game. I mean the discussions with lecture agents and publishers, the frequent travels to remote places, the royalties that come in unexpectedly from time to time, the easy access to libraries, the occasional sudden look of recognition by a stranger in the street. And there is nothing like a balance at the bank to reduce the general level of anxiety.

All this I am beginning to question. I don't mean that the work I do should not be enjoyable and exciting; but it is the trappings that go with it that represent the strings that tie me to my old self and which make me feel enveloped in an insidious form of corruption. I am beginning to be very much on my guard when I meet the "nice guys" who occupy important positions. I have met them in the Pentagon (senior generals, even the men at the very top who actually run the show), and one meets them in the Foreign Office in London or in the State Department in Washington or at dinner with an editor. They seem such quiet and intelligent people, these who have reached near the top, until I remind myself what they are actually helping to *do*—like burning up children and peasants in Vietnam or sending arms to Nigeria to defend their oil interests.

We must be on guard against these nice reasonable men. They have learned that a quiet and passionless manner carries an extraordinary credibility, and this is especially true in Britain where the tone in which something is said is more important than what is said. But with a creeping sense of horror one realizes that it is these reasonable men, for all their plausibility, who have made the world what it is. The reasonable men cannot understand the ferment that is in the streets. They cannot understand the passionate determination of the oppressed to gain their freedom. They are at a total loss to understand what the young everywhere are rebelling about. As an editorial in *Ramparts* Magazine once expressed it,

Vietnam will no doubt be recorded as the reasonable man's war. Every decision, every intervention was made reasonably and was justified with careful liberal rhetoric—until the slow accretion of reasonableness built a bloody pyramid of madness. . . .

They have fooled us too long, these reasonable men. They don't deliver the goods they promise. These men who sound so knowledgeable, so informed, are certainly not providing the answers we are looking for, and for us to expect them to do so and to get angry because they don't, is as foolish as to get angry with water when it refuses to flow uphill. They believe in money and power; and we believe in people. And as long as we remain in awe of them we will always be led in the wrong direction. They will go on telling us that of course they are taking us south towards the sun and we will continue to find ourselves further and further towards the cold north. We must get rid of these false navigators; we must begin to distrust utterly everything they say. The history of imperialism is chock full of statements made by apparently wise and rational men in support of totally illegitimate policies. Just listen to the politicians of any capitalist country carefully attempting to justify humanly unjustifiable actions! Never before has so much precision been attached to so spurious a rationality!

* *

"Pig! Pig!" cry the young militants at the policemen in America, and if I were being clubbed and beaten by them I would call them pigs too, no doubt, or epithets much worse. Yet, in spite of our outrage, I feel it is important for us to remember that those who are using the clubs against us are the victims of imperialism as well as its agents, and that under other conditions they would be on our side. Julius Lester once wrote (and he expresses my thoughts better than I can myself):

We look at them, their fat, sagging bellies, hard faces, tight lips, and we despair. It is logical that they should support Wallace, for they are ugly and Wallace is ugly and we are beautiful and gentle and want to do nothing more than love everyone in the rising of each sun. We look at them and the conclusion is quickly reached that they will never change. They will always be filled with resentments, fears and hates. And having so concluded, we end our examination and analysis of them and prepare to wait for more propitious times.

It is difficult to be a revolutionary, for to be a revolutionary means to believe in the innate goodness of man and it is to know that man in this environment has been programmed into non-man. Our job is to change the environment so that man can be man . . .

None of us were born revolutionaries. Therefore, if we have found within ourselves the capacity to change, we must acknowledge that everyone has the capacity to change. Once we acknowledge this, we must begin to live and act as if we believe it . . .

Yes, they are ugly. Their faces are filled with hate. But did they deliberately sit in front of the mirror and create these faces? Or were they forced to live lives which tightened the flesh of their faces into a perverted contortion of humanity?

"One must have faith in the best of men," Jose Marti wrote, "and distrust the worst. If not, the worst prevails." [1]

*   *

This book, as readers will have seen, is largely about the United States. This is partly because I have lived there for over thirty years, more than half my life, and partly because that country represents imperialism in its most violent form. The BIG LIE of our time is that each man (and each nation) must strive for himself, and that only in wealth, possessions and power can human beings find happiness. All imperialisms accept this lie but its greatest perpetrator is the United States. There is violence and inhumanity in every country, but in official America it has become institutionalized. It is built into the very substance of government to such an extent that it can now only lead to the country's self-destruction. The official policies of the United States today reek of death. Wherever official America goes it brings destruction to the human spirit. Wherever America sends her imperial legions they bring misery, corruption and death, and they destroy all that is most tender and trusting. "We are the most frightening people in the world," said Governor Rockefeller and for once he was right.

Yet, having said this, I must also voice my belief that of all the advanced capitalist countries the people of the United States will be the first to break the chains of their system and establish a wholly new and beneficent society. It is not for further material riches that the young people in America are battling the old order, but to bring to birth a nation whose people can find their humanity again. The very extremity of their present predicament, the very extent of the deprivations the present system is imposing, will force the people of America to break the system and start anew. When once Americans really grasp what their imperialism is doing to them and to the world, they will be far readier to revolt against their system than the people of Europe, for at heart they are less cynical and by nature more optimistic. When that day comes we shall see astonishing and magnificent results! Americans, it seems, are destined to be pioneers, and it is my belief that they will be the first to show the world how an advanced industrial country can revolutionize itself and use its vast resources and skills, not to exploit the people of the world, but to benefit them. That is my hope for America. That will be the day to see!

But until it comes, the fight must go on.

* *

Those of us who are engaged in the struggle against imperialism are members of a much wider community than we realize. Looking, parochially, only at the numbers within our Western countries, we seem pitifully weak. We are a tiny minority, very easy to ridicule. But linked with the others on our side throughout the world we are in fact members of a huge majority, members of a fraternity that stretches from one end of the world to the other—indeed, wherever men are still poor and exploited.

Unless those of us in the rich and comfortable countries become aware of the great process of revolt and struggle that is stirring in the world and become a part of it and participate in it, unless we share with the vast masses of the world the exhilaration they feel as they fight off their oppressors and emerge at last from their squalor and impoverishment to a new life and new consciousness, unless we share in this and stop being frightened of it, we will indeed find ourselves alone, and the great chance missed.

NOTES

1. Julius Lester, "From the Other Side of the Tracks," *Guardian*, 2 November 1968.

Index

ABOUT THE AUTHOR

FELIX GREENE, who recently returned to Britain after thirty years' residence in the United States, has traveled extensively in China. He is the author of two internationally acclaimed books about China, *Awakened China* and *A Curtain of Ignorance*. His film *China!*, which had a record run in New York and was shown in theaters throughout the United States, won a first prize at the Melbourne International Film Festival and was given the Award of Merit at the Edinburgh Film Festival. He also obtained exclusive filmed interviews with both Chou En-lai and Ho Chi Minh for Western television. *Vietnam! Vietnam!*, published in 1967, combined the author's commentary on the war and its origins with more than a hundred pictures by some of the world's leading news photographers. In the same year he made a full-length color film on North Vietnam showing the life of the people under intensive bombing attacks. This film, which has now been shown in theaters or on television in over thirty countries, won a British Film Academy nomination as one of the four best feature-length documentaries distributed in 1968.

Felix Greene has lectured extensively throughout the United States. He was at one time a Senior official of the British Broadcasting Corporation and has been closely associated with the movement opposing United States policies in Vietnam.